THE BRICS SUPERPOWER CHALLENGE

T0347258

The BRICs Superpower Challenge
Foreign and Security Policy Analysis

KWANG HO CHUN
Chonbuk National University, Korea

Routledge
Taylor & Francis Group

LONDON AND NEW YORK

First published 2013 by Ashgate Publishing

2 Park Square, Milton Park, Abingdon, Oxon OX14 4RN
711 Third Avenue, New York, NY 10017, USA

Routledge is an imprint of the Taylor & Francis Group, an informa business

First issued in paperback 2016

British Library Cataloguing in Publication Data
A catalogue record for this book is available from the British Library

The Library of Congress has cataloged the printed edition as follows:
Chun, Kwang Ho.
The BRICs superpower challenge : foreign and security policy analysis / by Kwang Ho Chun.
  pages cm
ISBN 978-1-4094-6869-1 (hardback : alk. paper) — ISBN 978-1-4094-6870-7 (ebook) — ISBN 978-1-4094-6871-4 (epub) 1. World politics—21st century. 2. Security, International. 3. Brazil—Foreign relations—21st century. 4. Russia (Federation)—Foreign relations—21st century. 5. India—Foreign relations—21st century. 6. China—Foreign relations—21st century. I. Title.
JZ1310.C495 2013
327—dc23

2013021069

ISBN 978-1-4094-6869-1 (hbk)
ISBN 978-1-138-24635-5 (pbk)

Contents

PART IV   CONCLUSIONS

Acknowledgements

I would like to thank all those who helped me to complete this research. My thanks go to Dr Chungwon Choue, who first inspired me on this topic and in starting my research, Prof. Dr Luc Reychler of Katholieke Universiteit Leuven, Prof. Dr André-Paul Frognier of Université Catholique de Louvain, Prof. Christoph Bluth of the University of Leeds and Prof. Hazel Smith of the Woodrow Wilson Center. They all helped me develop and polish my ideas regarding this research topic through valuable comments and constructive criticism. I would particularly like to express my whole-hearted gratitude to my lifetime adviser, Dr Chungwon Choue. I am equally grateful to Dr Guh Suk Seo, the President of Chonbuk National University, Korea for his financial and undoubted support and trust in me as a researcher. They ceaselessly encouraged and stimulated my work with a great deal of kindness and endurance during my research.

I also wish to acknowledge the assistance of those who offered me valuable comments on the text, including my editor, Brian Austerfield of the University of Central Lancashire.

This research required an enormous amount of material and a number of occasions for practical observation of the BRICs countries. The Royal United Service Institute, the International Institute for Strategic Studies and University of Central Lancashire helped me greatly in this matter. I would like to extend my warm gratitude to members of all these research centres and many others.

Finally, I also would like to take this opportunity to express my deepest love to my family, Dr Sung Eun Kim and Hyung Mo. The completion of this work in England was possible only thanks to my family's full-time support, endurance and sacrifice.

List of Abbreviations

APEC	Asia-Pacific Economic Cooperation
ARF	ASEAN Regional Forum
ASCM	anti-ship cruise missile
ASEAN	Association of South East Asian Nations
ASEM	Asia–Europe Meeting
ASF	African Support Force
AU	African Union
BNDES	Brazilian Development Bank
BRICs	Brazil, Russia, India and China
C4ISR	command, control, communications, computers, intelligence, surveillance and reconnaissance
CIS	Commonwealth of Independent States
CNO	computer network operation
CTR	Cooperative Threat Reduction
DDG	guided-missile destroyer
EAS	East Asia Summit
EU	European Union
FDI	foreign direct investment
FOCAC	Forum on China–Africa Cooperation
FOCALAE	Forum for East Asia–Latin America Cooperation
GATT	General Agreement on Tariffs and Trade
GDP	gross domestic product
GICNT	Global Initiative to Combat Nuclear Terrorism
ICBM	inter-continental ballistic missile
IMF	International Monetary Fund
IR	international relations
IRC	International Relations Center
ISS	International Institute for Strategic Studies
ISTC	International Science and Technology Center
LACM	land attack cruise missile
MIC	military-industrial complex
MPC&A	Materials Protection, Control and Accounting
MTCR	Missile Technology Control Regime
NCO	non-commissioned officer
NGO	non-governmental organization
NPT	Nuclear Non-Proliferation Treaty
NRF	NATO Response Force
NSG	Nuclear Suppliers Group

OAS	Organization of American States
OPCW	Organisation for the Prohibition of Chemical Weapons
OSCE	Organization for Security and Co-operation in Europe
PLA	People's Liberation Army
PLAAF	People's Liberation Army Air Force
PLAN	People's Liberation Army Navy
PRC	People's Republic of China
RATS	Regional Anti-Terrorist Structure
SAM	surface-to-air missile
SCO	Shanghai Cooperation Organization
SLBM	sea-launched ballistic missile
SRBM	short-range ballistic missile
UAV	unmanned aerial vehicle
UNASUR	Union of South American Nations
UNSC	United Nations Security Council
WTO	World Trade Organization

PART I
Background

Chapter 1

Introduction

Introduction

Since the collapse of the USSR in the early 1990s, the United States has been enjoying a dominant position in the global power system as the sole superpower nation. However, there have been arguments by some international relations (IR) and political science academics and commentators to the effect that the US may not continue as the world's sole superpower in the near future; rather, a power shift is likely to be witnessed as some of the contemporary major powers step up their resources and power games to become major forces in the global arena. At the dawn of the twenty-first century, some economic analysts, led by Goldman Sachs, noted the rapid pace with which the economies of the BRICs countries (an acronym for Brazil, Russia, India and China) were growing and noted that in the near future, their economies will have overtaken most of the current major world powers.[1] In particular, Goldman Sachs extrapolated figures predicting that China's economy would be the largest globally, having far overtaken that of the US, and that India's economy would be almost on a par with that of the US.[2] According to Goldman Sachs, the combined economies of the BRICs will also catch up with or overtake those of the six major economies combined (see Figure 1.1).[3] In a 2003 paper, Dominic Wilson and Roopa Purushothaman predicted that within about half a century, the BRICs would be the world's 'engine of new demand growth and spending power', which would be better placed to 'offset the impact of graying populations and slower growth in the advanced economies'.[4] This revelation heightened the debate that had been under way among IR academics and analysts about the future of the BRICs in the global power system, and in particular what the future might hold for them. It is a debate that remains highly controversial to date.

---

1 Goldman Sachs, *Building Better Global Economic BRICs*, Global Economics Paper, 30 November 2001. See also Deutsche Bank, 'Globale Wachstumszentren 2020. Formel-G für 34 Volkswirtschaften', *Aktuelle Themen* 313 (2005).

2 Ibid.

3 The six major economies referred to are: the US, Japan, Germany, the UK, France and Italy. See Goldman Sachs, *BRICs and Beyond* (2007). See also Dominic Wilson and Roopa Purushothaman, 'Dreaming With BRICs: The Path to 2050', Goldman Sachs Global Economics Paper no. 99 (2003).

4 Ibid., p. 2.

This book critically examines the BRICs countries' potential, with a view to drawing conclusions about whether they have prospects of attaining world superpower status in the future, either individually or as a bloc.[5] In exploring the research question, the author adopts June Dreyer's concept of superpower: 'a superpower must be able to project its power, soft and hard, globally'.[6] Since superpower status hinges on global projection of power beyond the nation's borders, the BRICs' foreign policies and military power will be central points of focus, as these are the core tools for advancing a country's power externally. While military power is a significant source of hard power, foreign policy may be used to exercise both the soft and hard power.[7] A clear understanding of the concept of superpower and why some nations are or were once categorized as superpowers is also essential in developing some of the checklists used to assess whether or not the BRICs may assume superpower status. Finally, it is vital to assess the BRICs' relationships with each other and with other major global power determinants and entities in order to understand their possible impact on the BRICs' current and future global power status. Synchronizing and consolidating this analysis enables us to arrive at conclusions about the prospects of the BRICs becoming future superpowers.

Background of the Study

On the BRICs' potential to become superpowers, Subhash Jain comments: 'After the collapse of the Soviet Union, the United States became the lone superpower of the world. But it may not be able to hold this dominant position for long. … US companies must train their current and future managers to compete with firms in the BRICs.'[8] An earlier article by Samuel Huntington accepted the dominance of the US in the world politics and IR, but argued that such dominance as a

---

5   The research for this book commenced in 2009. During that year, South Africa began to lobby to be included in the BRICs group, and on 24 December 2010 it gained formal membership, and the BRICs became the BRICS. Although it has the largest economy in Africa, South Africa has a population of under 50 million and its GDP is far lower than the other countries in the new BRICS group. For these reasons, it does not have the same potential to become a major power as Brazil, Russia, India and China, therefore it has not been included in the analysis in this study.

6   June T. Dreyer, 'Chinese Foreign Policy', *The Newsletter of FPRI's Wachman Center* 12:5 (February 2007): http://www.fpri.org/footnotes/125.200702.dreyer.chinese foreignpolicy.html (accessed 19 January 2012).

7   See the detailed discussion of the concepts of hard and soft power in Chapter 2, under analysis of Dreyer's definition of 'superpower'.

8   Subhash C. Jain (ed.), *Emerging Economies and the Transformation of International Business* (2006), p. xv.

superpower state would be short-lived.[9] He argued that the world was actually in a transitional stage, and there would soon be a power shift in the twenty-first century, with the US becoming an ordinary major power. He contended that the current global power system was a hybrid (uni-multipolar) system, with global power vested in the US as a lone superpower on one hand, and many other major powers acting jointly on the other. But according to Huntington, global politics would only support this hybrid system for one or two decades (from 1999, when he wrote his article) before the world became a fully fledged multipolar system. Although Huntington did not focus on the BRICs, the group's relatively strong political-economic influence and its steady rise in global politics give it head start in future global governance.

However, in the IR literature, countries' (including the BRICs') potential global power is not essentially a result of their rapid growth rate, projected economic might and size; rather, it stems from the fact that economic power is a powerful tool that can be used to advance other aspects of power (politics, military, foreign policy and diplomacy, and cultural factors). As will be shown in Chapter 2, a strong economy and economic power have always played a principal role in attaining and maintaining superpower status. Thus, there is more to being a superpower that merely being an economically mighty nation. A country also needs to be able to command dominant influence in IR and diplomatic relations, and attain overwhelming hard and soft power on a global scale.[10] Thus, it is essential to look beyond the speculated economic dynamism and the countries' economic size in answering the question of whether the BRICs will become future world superpowers.

The ongoing debates about the possibility of the BRICs attaining superpower status attract significant academic interest. On the one hand, the BRICs countries' prospects appear promising, particularly in terms of their economic performance. Economic power is a useful tool in advancing other forms of power, like boosting the military capacity to promote dominance in international military operations and other conventional wars, implementing foreign policies and establishing empowered and well-equipped diplomatic relations. On the other hand, massive economic development alone does not necessarily lead to proportional influence on the global order and international relations, otherwise a country like Japan,

---

9 Samuel P. Huntington, 'The Lonely Superpower', *Foreign Affairs* 78:2 (March/April 1999), pp. 35–49.

10 The terms 'soft power' and 'hard power' are used extensively used in this book. 'Soft power' refers to the an entity's ability to advance its interests or obtain what it wants not merely by means of influence, but by means of co-option and attraction. 'Hard power' refers to an entity's ability to advance its interests through coercion or by means of payment. See Joseph S. Nye, *Soft Power: The Means to Success in World Politics* (2004), pp. 9 and 26, and Douglas Lemke, 'Dimensions of Hard Power: Regional Leadership and Material Capabilities', in Daniel Flemes (ed.), *Regional Leadership in the Global System: Ideas, Interests and Strategies of Regional Powers* (2010), pp. 31–50.

owing to its economic strength,[11] would now be dominant in world politics – which is not the case. A deeper, more qualitative study of the BRICs countries is therefore essential, with a major focus on those factors which would significantly boost their image and project their influence globally, especially the impact of their foreign policies and military power on their foreign relations.

Overview of the Concept of Power and Superpower

Although power is a central concept in IR academic discourse, there is no uncontested or straightforward definition of it, which in turn makes it difficult to define the concept of 'superpower'. Some IR scholars view power in terms of relationships between or among actors (essentially states), and as entailing the extent of influence wielded by one actor over the other.[12] Thus, whenever one talks of a powerful nation, a great power, a major power or a superpower, it will always involve a relationship where one state is more influential (powerful) relative to the other(s). The more powerful entity is able to utilize its influence to advance its interests over the less powerful entity or entities, or even to manipulate their behaviour.[13] An alternative view is that power has to do with control of resources, and in particular military resources. In this view, states that have strong military forces or which have the greatest say in the control of global resources would be the most powerful.[14] However, other IR scholars assert that power is determined by productive ability[15] – what an entity or a state is able to or deliver – while some believe that it basically connotes authority.[16] This book will use the term 'power' in an integrated sense, incorporating all these perspectives, but with a bias towards the first perspective – viewing power as a relationship between two or more entities where one entity exerts influence over the other(s). This view is preferred as it seems to implicitly incorporate the other perspectives, or their eventual outcomes. Since this research essentially analyses diplomatic relationships and the relations between countries in global politics, it is interesting to focus on how the states analysed have performed in terms of their diplomatic and IR influence.

---

11   Japan is listed as the second leading economy globally, after the US; see Goldman Sachs, *BRICs and Beyond*.

12   David A. Baldwin, 'Power and International Relations', in Walter Carlsnaes, Thomas Risse and Beth A. Simmons (eds), *Handbook of International Relations* (2002), pp. 177–91.

13   Joseph S. Nye, *The Paradox of American Power* (2002), p. 4. See the detailed discussion on Nye's conception of soft and hard power in Chapter 2 of the current volume.

14   Baldwin, 'Power and International Relations', pp. 177–91.

15   David A. Lake, 'Escape from the State of Nature: Authority and Hierarchy in World Politics', *International Security* 32:1 (2007), pp. 47–79.

16   Michael Barnett and Raymond Duvall, 'Power in International Politics', *International Organization* 59:1 (2005), pp. 39–75.

IR academics have categorized countries into a power hierarchy depending on their influence and political-economic, diplomatic and military might. Again, there is no consensus on the architecture of global power, which leads to controversy over the analytical dimensions. One popular classification is to group the states deemed as powerful (world powers)[17] in the following order, on a descending scale: superpowers, great powers/major powers and middle powers.[18] According to this analytical framework, a superpower is leading nation in the international power system that is able to project its soft and hard power globally. 'Power system' in this sense encompasses power in economic, military, political, cultural and diplomatic terms. Great or major powers, on the other hand, are countries which, though they command significant hard and soft power in international relations, rank second to superpowers in the global power system. They wield massive diplomatic, military, economic and political influence on the global stage, but not as much as the superpowers.

Other scholars refute the concept of 'superpower', arguing that since the contemporary literature identifies the US as the only world superpower and the term is a legacy of the huge gap between the US and the former USSR and other major powers, 'superpower' is not best term to portray the gap between the US and other major world powers over the past decade.[19] To these analysts, the term 'superpower' is a misnomer, and they prefer the term 'hyperpower' to refer to the US. This analysis would entail an extra rank above superpower status, and imply that there is a vacuum in the global power architecture with regard to superpower status. However, this book will assume that 'superpower' denotes the highest global power rank. Much of the debate over the term 'superpower' will be covered in Chapter 2.

Other analysts have also considered regional power relations, arguing that an analysis of power in geo-global politics cannot ignore power exerted by states at the regional level, especially in the past two decades when regional organizations have become very influential in the global arena.[20] This analysis adds to the power architecture another category, 'regional powers', referring to states that may be regarded as powerful in their regions even if they do not qualify as superpowers or great powers. However, it should be understood that this categorization first groups countries into regions, then examines power

---

17 The term 'world power' will be used in this book to refer to those countries or international organizations which generally command significant influence, solely or jointly, in international political relations and global affairs. A world power may be a superpower, great power or middle power.

18 See Dreyer, 'Chinese Foreign Policy', and Evelyn Goh, 'Great Powers and Hierarchical Order in Southeast Asia', *International Security* 32 (2007/2008), pp. 113–57.

19 Huntington, 'The Lonely Superpower'.

20 Amitav Acharya, 'The Emerging Regional Architecture of World Politics', *World Politics* 59:4 (July 2007), pp. 629–52.

relations within those regions and not essentially at the global level, and is therefore not germane to the analysis employed in this book.

The BRICs

To avoid confusion, 'BRICs' in this book refers to four countries – Brazil, Russia, India and China – and will be used interchangeable with 'BRICs countries'. This section of the chapter will only offer a general overview of the BRICs, both individually and as a bloc. A more detailed analysis of the BRICs is presented in Parts II and III.

The BRICs, both individually and collectively, have a noteworthy demographic advantage. For instance, about 20 per cent of the world population is believed to be residing in China, while India accounts for about 17.5 per cent, making the two among the most populous countries in the world. The other two BRICs countries, though not as large in terms of percentage of the global population, are equally highly populated: Russia's population accounts for about 2.2 per cent of the global population, while Brazil accounts for about 2.9 per cent. They are geographically extensive: Russia occupies 17 million square kilometres, China 9.3 million square kilometres, Brazil 8.5 million square kilometres and India 3.2 million square kilometres.[21]

The diversity among the BRICs also extends to their economic, cultural and political backgrounds (past and present), which presents technical problems in conducting an empirical and systematic study of the BRICs as a group. China has a rich cultural background, and is arguably among the most ancient nations in the world. It is a country that has undergone severe economic and political turmoil, attaining its current booming status only in the past decade or so. Some of the most regrettable historical events that have afflicted China include: the Chinese civil war which left so many dead and so much property damaged or lost; general political instability and the eventual secession of Taiwan from the Republic of China; the Japanese invasion that again led to many Chinese deaths and much damage to property, and political and economic decadence during the Maoist era that attached little value to positive economic and political reforms.[22] These events led to economic and political deterioration of China, from which it took a long time to recover. A meaningful recovery was only achieved in the late 1990s and over the past decade.

Russia, as the legal successor to the former USSR, has also suffered significant challenges, some of which it is still enduring. The disintegration of the USSR superpower left Russia as the remnant of the formerly powerful Soviet Union, and Russia is still grappling with the challenge of rising to the high status of its

---

21   Paulo Roberto de Almeida, 'The BRICs' Role in the Global Economy', in Cebri-Icone-British Embassy in Brasília, *Trade and International Negotiations for Journalists* (2009), pp. 146–54.

22   Ibid.

predecessor. This is no easy task, and continually subjects the nation to a lot of power pressure and high public expectations. Having officially and legally taken over from the USSR, Russia had to meet all the obligations of the former Soviet Union even if they were not of Russia's making (as the successor to the USSR, Russia had to take over all its predecessor's rights and liabilities – including its debts). It also suffered a huge loss of technological, material and human resources as each of the component states sought to form their own sovereign territories and systems of government, thus withdrawing their people and input from the federal pool of resources, most of which were concentrated in Russia. It is a country renowned for its ancient traditions, from the Middle Ages through to the Soviet Empire, and has historically been known for its strong appetite for power, conquest and internal security.

Like China and Russia, India's history can be traced to the Middle Ages and beyond, and remains another epitome of an ancient civilization. It is a country marked by a diverse ethnic and cultural make-up – a factor that makes India as a nation culturally unique, yet at the same time forms one of its core weaknesses (especially against the backdrop of some past ethnic clashes, incidences of ethnic hatred and tribalism, nepotism and related incidences of corruption). In fact, India as a nation was only united as a result of foreign invasion, by the Mughal Empire and subsequently the British colonialists, who then drew the boundaries of India. Thus, strictly speaking, India as a country is a colonial invention.[23]

Like India, Brazil is another colonial invention whose boundaries were principally determined by its former colonialists, the Portuguese. Compared to the other BRICs countries, Brazil seems to feature less socio-ethnic and economic diversity. It has a flourishing economy, well-established and strong democratic ideals, and peaceful relations with neighbouring states. The lack of external and internal threats is one reason why Brazil has made better economic, political and social progress than most other countries in the region, and is what also gives it a competitive advantage over the other BRICs countries. It has been regarded as a stimulant of industrial and economic growth and an epitome of desired global peace – factors that have earned it widespread diplomatic admiration and inclusion in most international and regional organizations and initiatives.[24]

Although these countries each have their own unique political and economic systems, they have often been grouped together as they are regarded to be at similar phases of economic development, rapidly advancing, and to some extent becoming increasingly powerful in their global political-economic relations. The BRICs acronym was first coined by Goldman Sachs, after noting the exponential rate at which these four countries' economies were growing and how advanced they were projected to be over the next fifty years or so. Of late, there have been good political and diplomatic ties among these nations, and they have been exploring prospects for further co-operation. The four BRICs countries'

---

23   Ibid.
24   Ibid.

leaders[25] held their first official summit on 16 June 2009.[26] Significant items on the agenda of this first summit were how the BRICs countries could become more vocal and involved in global affairs, along with the need for a more stable, diversified and predictable global reserve currency.[27] The coming together of the BRICs countries is therefore seen as a potential challenge to US dominance, in terms of global affairs in general and the US dollar's status as a major global reserve currency.

Politically, all the BRICs countries have federal systems of government. However, the political ideologies of the four countries are quite dissimilar. India has a well-institutionalized democracy with a parliamentary system. Brazil, like India, has a well-developed democracy, but with a presidential system. Russia, on the other hand, is inclined towards authoritarianism, although it declares itself a democracy. At the extreme, China remains essentially a Marxist republic, and thus has a system of government that is largely at odds with the other BRICs countries'.[28] The four nations have all embraced economies that are essentially capitalistic, and gradually becoming more strongly so, and are highly industrialized.

China and Russia are significantly integrated into the global economy, and in 2005 had high gross domestic products (GDPs) of 64 and 48 per cent respectively.[29] Brazil and India are not as highly globalized, as evidenced by their relatively lower GDPs – in 2005, 25 and 29 per cent respectively. The BRICs enjoy fairly healthy trade surpluses, except for India, which has continually run into foreign debt. The nations have diversified exports profiles, with Russia being a major world supplier of high-quality petroleum and other energy products. China is as well endowed with natural resources as the other BRICs, but it relies more on exporting secondary and tertiary goods (basically manufactured, industrial and technological goods).

The BRICs as Potential Superpowers

The Goldman Sachs team called the BRICs countries the four prospective 'engines of growth', thus suggesting that there were excellent investment

---

25   The leaders referred to here are Luiz Inácio Lula da Silva of Brazil, Dmitry Medvedev of Russia, Manmohan Singh of India and Hu Jintao of China.

26   See 'First Summit for Emerging Giants', BBC News, 16 June 2009: http://news. bbc.co.uk/1/hi/business/8102216.stm (accessed 21 January 2012), and Gleb Bryanski and Guy Faulconbridge, 'BRIC Demands More Clout, Steers Clear of Dollar Talk', Reuters, 26 June 2009: http://www.reuters.com/article/marketsNews/idUSLG67435120090616 (accessed 21 January 2012).

27   Ibid.

28   Nazneen Barma, Ely Ratner and Steven Weber, 'A World Without the West,' *The National Interest* 90 (July–August 2007), pp. 23–30.

29   World Bank, *The Little Data Book* (2007).

opportunities within the four economies. The assumption is that since their large domestic markets are expected to expand rapidly as the growth of the middle class creates new consumers, there will be a rapid increase in demand for such things as automobiles, electricity and local capital markets. Risks to investors should also be lower in larger emerging-market economies compared to smaller emerging-market economies due to the fact that larger economies are generally less dependent on trade and global pressures than smaller economies, and hence are less exposed to exogenous economic shocks. However, as noted above, both China and Russia are heavily dependent on trade.

The four countries are also seen as future competitors of the US and other advanced industrial countries. Subhash C. Jain observes:

> After the collapse of the Soviet Union, the United States became the lone superpower of the world. But it may not be able to hold this dominant position for long .... US companies must train their current and future managers to compete with firms in the BRICs.[30]

In the end, the core argument in the business and financial literature as to why the BRICs countries are significant rests upon the relative economic size of the four countries, both at present and in the near future, and the implicit (and possibly dubious) assumption that large size implies economic dynamism. The central organizing principle for the BRICs group is not growth rate, nor opportunities for investor profit, but rather sheer economic size.

Statement of the Problem

Economic analysts have projected that in the next four decades, the economies of the BRICs countries will have developed and overtaken most of the currently more advanced economies, which will give them an upper hand in influencing global affairs and politics. Some scholars have also predicted that in the future, other superpowers will rival the US, giving rise to a multipolar world of many superpowers. In recent times, the four BRICs countries have increased their political and diplomatic ties, holding their first summit in 2009. However, these countries have not attained the highly coveted status of superpowers, and are still far from doing so.

This has given rise to an academic interest among political scientists and IR scholars as to whether the BRICs countries, either individually or as a bloc, would really meet the demanding challenges of being the next superpower, and if so, what this power transition would portend for the future global power architecture. This academic interest is motivated by current and past observations

---

30 Subhash C. Jain (ed.), *Emerging Economies and the Transformation of International Business* (2006).

of the key roles that the world superpowers play in terms of security and diplomatic relations in the global arena.

Although the prospect of the BRICs, as individual countries or a bloc, becoming the next superpower is a topic of significant debate in global politics, it has barely been explored systematically in the existing literature. The few works that have analysed the BRICs have tended to adopt behavioural science or economic approaches rather than an IR approach to global order, with a greater focus on economic power[31] rather than the military and political power wielded by these countries. The few works that have adopted an IR perspective on the question of the BRICs' superpower potential have often examined these nations in isolation from each other, not as a group. Hence the focus of this book is on conducting a deep, systematic investigation of the BRICs – individually and as a bloc – from the IR perspective of superpower.

Research Questions

The primary question that this research seeks to answer is:
- Do the BRICs nations have prospects of becoming future superpowers, either individually or as a bloc, and to what extent?

This question gives rise to the following secondary research questions:

- What leads a country to be classified as a superpower?
- What current foreign policies of the BRICs countries may enhance their prospects of attaining superpower status?
- What impact do the BRICs countries' foreign policies have on issues of global concern?
- To what extent have the BRICs countries been participating in global affairs, in particular those which raise global security issues?
- To what extent have the BRICs countries asserted their military power in ensuring or contributing to global order?
- Do the BRICs countries' current and past participation in global affairs, global military involvement and equipment, and foreign policy point towards equipping them for global dominance to the extent of attaining superpower status in the future?

Research Methodology

Like most other political science literature, this research essentially relies on secondary sources, mainly the relevant IR and political science literature.

---

31   Ibid., p. xv.

Review of this literature informs the study by offering relevant theoretical and academic background, and revealing relevant qualitative and quantitative information that helps to answer the research questions. To capture some of the recent developments and observations relating to the BRICs countries' global participation which might not have been captured adequately or at all in the existing academic literature, reference will be made to some of the more reliable mass media, including global and regional newspapers, magazines, and television and radio station transcripts. Internet research will supplement the print literature and media sources.

The first step will be to analyse the theoretical literature and develop a framework of the possible theories on the research questions. This will be accomplished by analysing major academic works such as books and significant academic journal articles that have established the theoretical benchmarks or landmarks in the broad disciplines of political science. The circumstances of the BRICs countries will then be analysed, first individually, then collectively, while referring to various literature and researchers' observations. In this way, the research will adopt an inductive reasoning approach to analyse and draw conclusions aiming to answer the research questions.

Chapter Summary

Some commentators and analysts have predicted that a more multipolar world is likely to develop during the twenty-first century – a development that would neutralize the current hegemony enjoyed by the US as the world's sole superpower. In this predicted power shift, it has been speculated that the BRICs countries – Brazil, Russia, India and China – will form the four most probable poles of power, particularly in view of their vigorous, advanced and rapidly developing economies. A harmonious and well-co-ordinated bloc of these four emerging powers would definitely alter the global power balance and give the group an upper hand in influencing global affairs. The BRICs countries have recently moved towards increased diplomatic, political and economic co-operation – a development that will raise their global power profile. However, there is more to attaining superpower status than merely having an advanced economy. There is also a need to advance and bolster other spheres of power, including military strength and increased participation in global affairs. This therefore leaves political scientists and IR scholars with the academically demanding task of examining in detail how well equipped the BRICs countries are to attain overwhelming global influence on the scale of a superpower.

Although it is obviously not possible to look into the future, the answer to the question of BRICs countries' future superpower status can be sought through careful analysis of their past, present and projected performance or participation in matters of global interest and the influence they have or may be able to command in the context of diplomatic relations and IR. The prospect of these countries attaining superpower status is the key question to be addressed by this research, and the purpose of this chapter was to lay the foundations for the analysis that will follow. The following chapters will proceed with a deeper examination of the concept of superpower, the BRICs countries' performance with regard to certain specific power indicators, and an analysis of their prospects of attaining superpower status.

Chapter 2
The Concept of Superpower

Introduction

International relations and political science scholars have had different and sometimes inconsistent conceptualizations of the term 'superpower'. However, a review of the literature seems to suggest that the concept of 'superpower' in the context of international relations between states is about a country's global reach and its ability to exert overwhelming global influence using its diplomatic resources, foreign policy and military power. While acknowledging that there are many possible definitions for this concept, and varying parameters for determining superpower status in relation to a country's international relations, this chapter will review various literature on the concept of 'superpower', providing contemporary and historical illustrations, and distinguishing the concept of 'superpower' from other closely related concepts that will be of vital importance in the analytical framework of this research.

The chapter begins by evaluating the meaning, parameters and historical evolution of the concept, while providing relevant examples where necessary, and exploring the diverse academic debates surrounding the concept. It then clearly distinguishes the concept of 'superpower' from three other closely connected concepts: great/major powers, middle powers and regional powers. An analysis of the Cold War superpowers, especially the United States and the Union of Soviet Socialist Republics (USSR or Soviet Union) and the present superpower – the United States – will be conducted with a view to pointing out what it takes to be a superpower, and particularly why these nations qualified as superpowers of their time. It will explain the preferred definition of 'superpower' for the purposes of this research, and the justification for choosing this definition.

The Superpowers

It takes significantly large amounts of influence and resources for a country to attain superpower status. It is such a high standard in the global power structure that none of the world's nations except the US has been able to meet it. Since the collapse of the USSR, which rivalled the US as the only co-superpower in the Cold War era, the US has remained the largely unchallenged global superpower, prompting some analysts to refer to it as a hyperpower (much more influential than a superpower). But what does it take to be a superpower? This section seeks to answer this question, but as will become apparent, there is no straightforward answer.

The Meaning, Parameters and Historical Evolution of the Concept of 'Superpower'

The clear definition and comprehensive use of the term 'superpower' in the political science literature can be traced back to William Fox, a political science scholar and political analyst who coined the term in 1944 to refer to countries that had achieved unmatched dominance in international political relations, and which had achieved supreme global reach.[1] According to him, the US, USSR and UK were super-empowered nations that had achieved unrivalled positions in shaping international affairs, including global peace. They were therefore superpowers. Later on, in the wake of the Cold War, other dimensions of the concept of 'superpower' evolved: superpower status was determined not necessarily in terms of a country's global reach, but mainly in terms of its military might, strategic military capacity and its possession of nuclear power and nuclear deterrence which granted it unsurpassed potential destructive power in relation to other states. The doctrine of nuclear capability, which was presumed to match military capacity, was also the main parameter used to distinguish the superpowers from the great powers, whose nuclear capabilities were not as dominant as those of the superpowers. This left the USSR and US as the only nations fulfilling the criteria as world superpowers at the time.

In the post-Cold War era, with more emphasis being placed on globalization and multinational relations, political scientists gradually developed a view that the traditional parameters (nuclear capabilities and global reach) would no longer be sufficient to define world superpower status.[2] The term needed to be expanded to include the ability of a country to maintain diplomatic relations and military and economic resources that were adequate to preserve international order and influence international relations. In this scenario, the superpowers were the core actors, while other states played peripheral roles.[3] Since the disintegration of the USSR, the US is said to be the sole contemporary world superpower, according to contemporary criteria.

It has been hypothesized that it is possible that China will attain parity with the US in the near future, thus emerging as the second superpower.[4] Others have

---

1   William T.R. Fox, *The Superpowers: The United States, Britain and the Soviet Union – Their Responsibility for Peace* (1944), cited in Lawrence Freedman, 'China as a Global Strategic Actor', in Barry Buzan and Rosemary Foot (eds), *Does China Matter? A Reassessment: Essays in Memory of Gerald Segal* (2004), p. 24.

2   Ibid., pp. 23–6.

3   See Hedley Bull, *The Anarchical Society: A Study of Order in World Politics* (1977). Bull gives a classic analysis of the role of superpowers in maintaining the global order in what he refers to as a 'society of states'.

4   See James Wood, *History of International Broadcasting*, vol. 2 (2000), ch. 19.

opined that the European Union, Brazil, Russia and India could also achieve superpower status during the twenty-first century.[5]

Even though the term 'superpower' gained currency in the mid-twentieth century, some analysts have sought to apply it in retrospect to some historical state entities that commanded significant inter-state influence. Some of these states and empires which, according to historians, could be regarded as the superpowers of their time include: ancient Greece, ancient Egypt, the Roman Empire, the Persian Empire, the Portuguese Empire, ancient China, France, the Mongol Empire and the British Empire.[6] These entities are said to have possessed unmatched capabilities in military might in comparison to their contemporaries, and the ability to impose their ideologies on other states of their time, therefore qualifying as superpowers for the purposes of historical analysis.

The Parameters for Determining World Superpower Status

There is no consensus among international relations and political science scholars about the precise definition of the concept of 'superpower', nor is there clarity as to the precise parameters that are to be used in determining whether or not a state qualifies as a superpower . However, it is widely agreed that the US and the USSR were the superpowers of the Cold War era, and that at present, the US is the sole world superpower. Many superpower analyses have therefore sought to examine some of the unique factors that enabled the countries categorized as present or past superpowers to exert overwhelming dominance in the arena of international relations, and then apply these as the criteria for determining world superpower status. Since different analysts have focused on different aspects they have deemed essential, the precise parameters for establishing whether a country is or has the prospect of being a superpower have remained quite controversial, and to some extent indistinct.

Lyman Miller argues that whether or not a state is a superpower should be examined against the backdrop of four axes of power: political, military, economic and cultural ('soft power'). Thus, for a country to attain superpower status, it must achieve extreme advancement, advantage and dominance on each of these dimensions, particularly in relation to other states. Drawing from these dimensions, Miller defines a superpower as: 'a country that has the capacity to project dominating power and influence anywhere in the world, and sometimes, in more than one region of the globe at a time, and so may plausibly attain the status

---

5   See Ronald Steel, 'A Superpower is Reborn', *New York Times*, 24 August 2008: http://georgiandaily.com/index.php?option=com_content&task=view&id=6527&It emid=68&lang=ka (accessed 19 June 2013); the author of this article is a Professor of International Relations. See also Steven Rosefielde, *Russia in the 21st Century: The Prodigal Superpower* (2005); Erik Ringmar, 'The Recognition Game: Soviet Russia Against the West', *Cooperation & Conflict* 37:2 (2002), pp. 115–36.

6   Emmanuel Le Roy Ladurie and Mark Greengrass, *The Ancient Regime* (1998), p. 512.

of global hegemony'.[7] He defends his definition by contending that the UK's categorization as a superpower was essentially because it had unmatched power with regard to these dimensions, thus qualifying as the superpower of a certain period. The passage below captures his well-articulated and well-illustrated argument about the UK's superpower status:

> Using these dimensions [military, economic, political, and cultural], arguably, Britain was the prototype superpower in the nineteenth century. Britain's industrial revolution preceded other European states by several decades, giving London superior economic, military, and political power that allowed Britain to reign as the international order's hegemon from 1815 until the early twentieth century. An island country lacking in industrial resources, Britain created a worldwide empire of colonies that sustained British economic power and made the British pound the standard of exchange in the international economy. Britain's wealth was sustained by the maritime superiority of its navy and commercial fleet and by the chain of bases and strategic strong points from Gibraltar through the Suez Canal and around the Cape of Good Hope to the Straits of Malacca that it commanded. Britain was the prevailing power against which all of the late-coming industrial powers, France, Germany, and Russia, competed in the nineteenth century's rivalries for spheres of influence and colonies in Africa, the Middle East, and Asia during the great wave of imperialism after 1870. Britain sustained its hegemonic position for a nearly a century, until the rivalry of Germany under Wilhelm II and the 'long war' from 1914 to 1945 ultimately undermined its hegemony.[8]

Miller appears to be basing his argument on the premise that the four dimensions referred to in his parameters are the basic drivers of high-scale global influence and dominance of one country over others in the global arena. Nevertheless, the definition of the concept of 'superpower' he cites seems to only remotely incorporate his four dimensions, if at all. Like many other analysts, his definition suggests that at the core of determining superpower status lies the ability to exercise power, dominance and influence in the context of international relations. Since power, dominance and influence are quite abstract and difficult to measure, the parameters Miller suggests should be understood merely as broad guidelines in determining whether a state can be classed as commanding such exceptional influence or dominance.

On the other hand, Queen's University political scientist Kim Richard Nossal argues that the term 'superpower' is legacy of the Cold War era, and that it is wrong to use the term to describe the contemporary dominance of the US

---

7 Lyman Miller, 'China an Emerging Superpower?', *Stanford Journal of International Relations*: http://www.stanford.edu/group/sjir/6.1.03_miller.html (accessed 12 January 2012), para. 4.

8 Ibid., para. 5.

compared to other states. According to Nossal, a more appropriate term for the US is not 'superpower', but 'hyperpower' (which connotes a higher scale of power). He argues that that the term 'superpower' was generally:

> used to signify a political community that occupied a continental-sized landmass, had a sizable population (relative at least to other major powers); a superordinate economic capacity (again, relative to others), including ample indigenous supplies of food and natural resources; enjoyed a high degree of non-dependence on international intercourse; and, most importantly, had a well-developed nuclear capacity (eventually normally defined as second-strike capability).[9]

He then contends that the term is intricately connected with the rivalry that existed between the US and the USSR in the Cold War era, denoting the power distance between these two overwhelmingly capable countries and other major world powers (or great powers).[10] To summarize Nossal's view, he feels that the term 'superpower' referred to the dominant position of both the USSR and the US compared to other great powers. Since 'superpower' was predominantly a Cold War term that denoted power distance, it may not best describe the contemporary position of the US, considering that it has significantly widened this power distance through the post-Cold War developments it undertook and its overwhelming expenditure on the military during the Bush and Clinton administrations. For this reason, the term 'hyperpower' better captures the huge expansion that has been undertaken to date by the US and the extensive power distance that currently exists between it and other nations.

Nossal's analysis is vital in placing the superpower debate in its historical and evolutionary context. His suggested definitions offer easily identifiable parameters for determining the status of a country as a superpower (such as economic capacity, population size, a high degree of independence in international relations, and nuclear capacity or 'second strike' capabilities). These parameters serve as key guidelines in analysing international power relations, particularly with regard to the doctrine of superpower. However, he does not clearly specify the threshold for transition from a superpower to a hyperpower.

Paul Duke presents yet another closely related conception of the term 'superpower', from the perspective of military capability, economic command and ideological influence in international relations. His view is that: 'a superpower must be able to conduct a global strategy including the possibility of destroying

---

9   Kim R. Nossal, 'Lonely Superpower or Unapologetic Hyperpower? Analyzing American Power in the Post-Cold War Era', paper presented at the biennial meeting of the South African Political Studies Association, Saldanha, Western Cape, 29 June–2 July 1999: http://post.queensu.ca/~nossalk/papers/hyperpower.htm (accessed 12 January 2012), para. 10.

10   Ibid., para. 11.

the world; to command vast economic potential and influence; and to present a universal ideology'.[11] Again by referring to the popular classification of the USSR and the US as the superpowers of the Cold War period, he cites the two nations' abilities to influence the world with their ideologies.[12] For instance the US propagated liberal democratic and capitalist ideologies in a number of states in the West and Latin America, while the USSR propagated its Marxist-Leninist and communist ideologies in the Asian continent and some African states. Duke offers quite a simple and straightforward definition of this controversial concept. He expressly identifies three parameters to determine whether or not a country is a superpower, derived from three questions:

1. Can the country conduct a global strategy independently?
2. Is the country's economy large enough to support various global operations and strategies?
3. Does the country command overwhelming power in influencing many other states to adopt its ideology?

Only if the answer is 'yes' to all three questions can a state be regarded as a superpower.

Duke specifies the ability of a country to wipe out the old world as a vital component in assessing superpower status. Strictly speaking, in view of current globalization, the growth in complexity of diplomatic relations and increasing institutionalization of global governance though various multilateral legal instruments and institutions, it is unlikely that one country acting in isolation could carry out such a strategy without being deterred by the international community. The main point of Duke's definition appears to be that military strength is a fundamental parameter in determining a country's superpower status.

June Dreyer offers yet another widely cited definition of 'superpower': 'A superpower must be able to project its power, soft and hard, globally.'[13] To appreciate this definition, one needs to have a clear understanding of the terms 'hard' and 'soft' power. 'Soft power' refers to an entity's ability to advance its interests or obtain what it wants not merely by means of influence, but by means of co-option and attraction.[14] 'Hard power', on the other hand, refers to an entity's ability to advance its interests through coercion or by means of payment.[15] Contrary to the popular belief that soft power is synonymous with influence, Dreyer submits that soft power goes beyond influence, since influence can also be secured by means of hard power. There must be a willingness on part of the entity being influenced to be co-opted into and be attracted by the influencing entity's interests.

---

11 Paul Dukes, *The Superpowers: A Short History* (2000), p. 1.
12 Ibid., pp. 1–2.
13 Dreyer, 'Chinese Foreign Policy'.
14 Nye, *Soft Power*, pp. 9 and 26.
15 Ibid.

The attraction that characterizes soft power always culminates in acquiescence. In the context of international relations, both forms of power can be exercised not only by state entities, but also by non-state actors like multilateral institutions and non-governmental organizations. Some of the parameters for measuring a state's hard power include quantitative measures such as a country's gross domestic product, military assets and population size.[16] These may serve as tacit indicators of a nation's capacity to facilitate and promote its desired outcomes or ideology. Soft power, on the other hand, is often reflected in the extent of a nation's diplomatic relations with other countries, the extent to which the countries it relates with are willingly attracted to and adopt its ideology, its culture (including language and popular culture) and so on. In international relations, states normally achieve soft power through public diplomacy and foreign policy (like foreign aid).[17] Other instruments of soft power include the mass media and popular culture, strategic communications, economic development and reconstruction, and civic action.[18]

Dreyer therefore suggests that both hard and soft power must be wielded on a global level if a country is to qualify as a superpower. This brief definition makes it easier to develop the determinants of superpower status, especially in a comparative perspective. All one needs to do is to assess the country's capacity to wield soft and hard power (using the parameters above), and if the country passes the tests, then the relevant conclusion may be reached. However, it should be noted that Dreyer does not clearly specify the extent or bounds of the hard and soft power to be attained, so comparative analysis is necessary (especially of how close in terms of power the country is to contemporary or historical superpowers).

Superpowers Versus Great Powers and Middle Powers

The implication of the discussions above is that a superpower nation is one that commands the ability to have an enormous influence on global affairs and to project and exercise its soft and hard power on a global scale. The term 'great power' is used to refer to countries which, though they command significant hard and soft power in international relations, rank second to superpowers. 'Great power' is often used interchangeably with the term 'major power'. Essentially, great powers are able to exert diplomatic, military, economic and political influence owing to their massive strength. Classification of a state as a great power is therefore relative to those that rank as superpowers, so it is subject to the same parameters applied to superpowers. Countries that have been said to belong in the 'great power' category

---

16   Douglas Lemke, 'Dimensions of Hard Power: Regional Leadership and Material Capabilities', in Daniel Flemes (ed.), *Regional Leadership in the Global System: Ideas, Interests and Strategies of Regional Powers* (2010), pp. 31–50.

17   Y. Fan, 'Soft Power: The Power of Attraction or Confusion?', *Place Branding and Public Diplomacy* 4 (May 2008), p. 42.

18   Matthew Fraser, *Weapons of Mass Distraction: Soft Power and American Empire* (2005), p. 30.

include the permanent members of the UN Security Council (except the US, which is classed as a superpower), Japan and Germany.

Closely related to the concept of 'great power' is that of 'middle power'. Unlike superpowers and great powers, which that can act unilaterally to exert hard or soft power, middle powers are influential in matters of international relations, but need to form coalitions with other powers to advance their ideologies and foreign policies globally.[19] In other words, middle powers rank third in the global power order, below great powers.

In determining whether a state meets 'great power' status, due regard needs to be given to the state's capacity and ability to contribute to the global order, as this determines its ability to project its soft and hard power. Secondly, the state should exhibit a high degree of internal cohesion and lack of conflict, as this will allow it to act effectively to further its ends, including projection and implementation of its foreign policies. Thirdly, the state should be capable of competing favourably with other major powers in terms of military strength, especially in the context of conventional warfare, as this defines its hard power. Typically, it should be in a position to intervene militarily virtually anywhere. In addition, it should command sufficient economic power to facilitate global-level actions such as offering investment and foreign aid to less-developed nations to promote its international 'brand'.

Superpower Versus Regional Power

While the term 'superpower' designates the top rank in the global power relations, the term 'regional power' refers to countries that are powerful or overwhelmingly influential in their own regions (such as Africa, Europe, the Middle East and Latin America). Thus, it is possible for these nations to be concurrently categorized as major/great or middle powers in the global context. Detlef Nolte emphasizes that the ability to wield power is a prerequisite for global power status. He offers a checklist that can be used in empirical evaluation of whether or not a country qualifies as a regional power. To paraphrase his view, a regional power is a state that meets the following criteria:[20]

1. It considers itself to hold a position of leadership in its region.
2. It is geographically, economically, politically and ideologically delimited.
3. It displays the material (military, economic, demographic), organizational (political) and ideological resources for regional power projection.
4. It has great influence in regional affairs (in terms of activities and results).
5. It is a state in its own right.
6. It is economically, politically and culturally interconnected with the region.

---

19   Robert O. Keohane, 'Lilliputians' Dilemmas: Small States in International Politics', *International Organizations* 23:2 (1969), p. 296,
20   Ibid., pp. 889–90.

7. It has a significant influence on the geopolitical delimitation and the political and ideological make-up of its region.
8. It exerts this influence by means of regional governance structures.
9. It defines and articulates a common regional identity or project.
10. It provides collective benefits for the region, or participates in a significant way in the provision of such collective benefits.
11. It defines the regional security agenda in a significant way.
12. Its position of leadership in the region is recognized, or at least respected, by other states both inside and outside the region, especially by other regional powers.
13. It is integrated into inter-regional and global forums and institutions where it not only articulates its own interests, but also acts, at least in a rudimentary way, as a representative of regional interests.

Thus, it does not follow that every region will necessarily have a regional power.

The empirical parameters provided by Nolte to assess whether a country qualifies as a regional power may be adapted to assessment of a country's superpower status. Both concepts – superpower and regional power – concern power relations, the distinction being the geographical level of focus and the relatively lower standards of influence expected in the case of a regional power.

World Superpowers from the Post-Second World War Era to the Cold War Era

The UK's decline in influence due to the Suez crisis and the massive industrial destruction of the First and Second World Wars left it significantly weakened economically, to the extent that it could not pursue its foreign policy goals as sustainably as the emerging superpowers (the USSR and US). The UK had to choose whether to advance its global dominance through foreign policy tools at the expense of internal economic development and the financial strength of its currency, or to concentrate on reconstruction and strengthening its economy at the expense of entrenching its foreign policies. It chose to reduce its involvement in international political rivalries and to concentrate more on domestic affairs.

The ensuing decline of the UK on the world stage left the USSR and US as the sole global superpowers. A major advantage for US was that the Second World War had been fought quite far away from its borders, so it was spared the massive civilian casualties and industrial destruction that affected large areas of Europe and Asia. Although affected to some extent, the USSR had invested heavily in military capacity, and was able to contain a number of military threats, which mitigated some of the adverse effects. The dire need for post-war reconstruction by many European and Asian countries increased the demand for long-term credit, and infrastructural and technological goods. This worked in favour of the US: it served as the world's principal long-term creditor and the largest supplier of the highly in-demand infrastructural and technological goods, while at the same time developing its military strength by developing its high-tech and industrial infrastructure.

The USSR's position in the military, economic and political arenas rivalled that of the US (although the US appeared to be slightly more dominant). The rapid expansion of the USSR led the US to take countermeasures, leading to polarization of global politics and an intensification of the Cold War. The two superpowers battled for supremacy, as reflected in their conflicting political and economic ideologies, and the formation of opposing military alliances. While the US advocated for liberal democracy, multi-party state systems and market liberalization (the free market) as the tenets of its ideology, the Soviet sought to advance communism, single-party state systems and planned economies. Military opposition was reflected in the formation of various military alliances across the globe aligned to one or other of the superpowers: the USSR formed the Warsaw Pact with its military allies, while the US formed NATO with its European allies, such as France and the UK. This battle for supremacy between the two superpowers led to a world that was apparently bipolar: most of the world's nations strived to create ties with one of the superpowers, or on rare occasions, both.

A number of factors have led analysts to categorize the US and USSR as the world superpowers of the Cold War era, but principally the fact that the two nations possessed both economic and military strength that far exceeded those of the other major world powers, including the UK, Germany, France and Japan. For instance, by 1990 the USSR's GDP had risen to US$2.9 trillion, making it the second largest economy globally (second only to the US).[21] It also had extensive energy and mineral resources within its borders and produced and manufactured most of the technological and industrial goods it required, leading to a high degree of self-sufficiency with minimal expenditure on imports. Owing to this favourable economic environment, the USSR could afford to grant its citizens a number of socio-economic incentives, including free or highly subsidized healthcare, formal state education and guaranteed employment. It extended a number of economic benefits to those countries with ties to it, especially its satellite states in Eastern Europe. The US, on the other hand, had the largest economy in the world. For instance, by 1990, when the USSR's economy had a GDP of US$2.9 trillion and the rest of the other major world powers' GDPs lagged far behind, the US's GDP stood at US$5.2 trillion. The US had a much larger industrial and technological base than the USSR,[22] a much more highly modernized and extensive agricultural industry (an area in which the USSR lagged behind it), extensive energy and mineral resources, and a number of renowned multilateral corporations with the US as their home country. In addition, its citizens enjoyed a higher standard of living owing to easier and cheaper access to agricultural, industrial and technological goods. After the Bretton Woods Conference, the US dollar served as the major global reserve currency. The US's strong economy was further boosted by its close ties to most of

---

21   Central Intelligence Agency, *1990 CIA World Factbook* (1990).
22   Ibid.

the major Western and G7 economies. The strong economic influence enjoyed by these two world powers enabled them to pursue their foreign policies sustainably, and thus command greater soft power among their allies. In addition, they used their strong economies to boost their military resources and activities.

The two nations were equally advanced in terms of military might and nuclear capability – far surpassing their contemporaries. By the second half of the Cold War era, the USSR was said to have the largest army globally, the second-largest air force (after the US), one of the globe's major navies, and the largest nuclear weapons stockpile. In addition, it took initiatives to boost its global military strength by forming ties through the Warsaw Pact with other states which promised loyalty and military co-operation in exchange for economic and technological support from the USSR (the 'satellite states'). The USSR also had close military ties with guerrilla and paramilitary groups that were increasingly becoming widespread in the developing countries. Coupled with massive production facilities and a well-co-ordinated intelligence system, these efforts meant that the USSR emerged as a well-armed, globally networked and superior military power in the global arena. The US, on the other hand, had an unsurpassed navy of huge size (said to have been greater than a combination of the 13 next-largest navies) and an air force and army rivalled only by those of the USSR. For the first half of the Cold War, the US is said to have had the largest nuclear arsenal globally, only overtaken by the USSR during the second half of the Cold War. At the time when the USSR was busy entering into and concluding the Warsaw Pact, the US was also courting its powerful Western European allies to form a military alliance – the North Atlantic Treaty Organization (NATO). Like its rival the USSR, the US developed military ties with guerrilla and paramilitary groups to boost its global military network. It had the largest military expenditure globally, and invested heavily in the production of armaments. The massive military power wielded by the US and the USSR gave these two countries overwhelming hard power, and therefore influence on issues of international relations, to a great extent contributing to their superpower status.[23]

Both the US and USSR wielded extensive political power and influence in the global arena. As part of their foreign policies, both strove to sell their contrasting political ideologies to other nations throughout the world. The US was – as it has been since its formation – a firm constitutional republic of democratic multi-party ideals with a strong capitalist ideology. The USSR, on the other hand, firmly practised and advocated for a communist political ideology and a single-party political system. The US's ideology was embraced by most of the Western European countries, the Commonwealth and some Latin American countries with which the US enjoyed good diplomatic ties, whereas the USSR's ideology was embraced predominantly by most of the Eastern European nations, and some South-East Asian and African nations. The struggle for political supremacy and

---

23   See Barry Buzan, *The US and the Great Powers: World Politics in the Twenty-first Century* (2004).

influence by the rival superpowers was a major driver of the Cold War, which essentially hinged on these two nations. This superpower rivalry between the US and USSR was waged fiercely until the early 1990s, when the USSR ultimately dissolved.

Superpower(s) of the Post-Cold War Era

With the disintegration of the Soviet Union, the US was left as the sole world superpower, free of the pressure of the struggle to contain the expansion of the USSR's influence. The position of the US as the current world superpower is seldom contested, unlike the questions of whether the world in the post-Cold War era has remained unipolar and whether the US's global political influence is increasing or declining. Some international relations and political science analysts feel that the US has maintained its sole superpower status because its authority and pre-eminence are being exerted across every sphere of power, including military, ideological, diplomatic, economic and cultural.[24] Therefore, they argue, the US retains an overwhelmingly unmatched global reach and capability to advance its interests throughout the world.

However, some analysts have rejected this unipolar world view, arguing that the globe remains multipolar, with the US as just one of the most influential powers. Proponents of this school of thought point to the complexity of international relations in the contemporary world, especially in view of the intricate interdependencies in global economics and diplomatic relations.[25] Another argument advanced is that there are many other major and emerging powers that also command comparable influence, which rules out the prospects of a unipolar world with the US as the sole superpower. In commenting on the unipolar–multipolar debate, international relations analyst Samuel P. Huntington argues that the present world is a unique hybrid system: on one hand there exists the US as the sole world superpower with near-unipolar influence, and on the other hand there are many other major powers that also command significant influence.[26] This results in what Huntington terms a 'uni-multipolar' system. The twenty-first-century major world powers identified include the European Union, the UK, France, Germany and the BRICs countries.[27] Therefore, in Huntington's view, it is inaccurate to claim that the world remains unipolar, as this would mean that the US is still the only superpower, with few or an insignificant number of other major powers to rival it; yet this is not the case.

---

24   David Lake, 'Regional Hierarchy: Authority and Local International Order', *Review of International Studies* 35:S1 (2009), pp. 35–58.

25   See Robert. A. Pastor (ed.), *A Century's Journey: How the Great Powers Shape the World* (1999).

26   Huntington, 'The Lonely Superpower'.

27   Ibid.

Whether or not the US will continue to enjoy the position of world superpower remains a controversial topic. There are analysts who argue that the US's soft and hard power are being eroded by its contemporary political, economic and technological challenges. Some of these include increasing economic hardship among its population and deterioration of its economy (which has seen a decline in the value of the US dollar), the rapid rise of other great or major powers in the global arena, and increasing globalization and regulation of international relations through international instruments and institutions (which to a significant extent regulate some decisions that the US would otherwise make unilaterally in its favour).[28] In view of these challenges, it is speculated that the US risks losing its superpower status in future. However, the socio-economic and political challenges that currently face the US, such as economic hardship, are not unique to the US. In fact, the emerging world powers are equally affected by most of them. It should also be remembered since the end of the Cold War, the US's ascendency led to a major power gap which will be very difficult to close. On the gap that currently exists between the US and other world powers, international relations scholar Kim Nossal comments:

> the gap in military capacity between the United States and any (or all) other countries now far exceeds any gap that existed during the Cold War. Because the administrations of both George Bush and Bill Clinton continued to spend on defence during the 1990s, particularly on research and development in new weapons systems, the United States government now has a means of projecting military force on a global basis that no other country (or group of countries) can even begin to rival. Not only does the United States retain the massive nuclear arsenal it developed during the Cold War, but it also remains the only country in the world with a truly global airlift capability. Because of quantum improvements in targeting accuracy, mainly involving GPS (global positioning system) technology, American forces have the ability to engage in highly precise bombing, as the 78-day bombing campaign against Yugoslavia in 1999 clearly showed. Moreover, the defence industrial base in the United States is unmatched by any other country in size, sophistication, and complexity. In a similar fashion, the United States dominates access to space, crucial for both civilian and military missions.[29]

Therefore, other world powers cannot be expected to close the gap between them and the US in the near future. Some political analysts have also argued by that the US remains a very smart player of the 'soft power' game, and in this respect it still

---

28   Paul C. Roberts, 'The Coming End of the American Superpower', *Counterpunch*, 1 March 2005: http://www.counterpunch.org/2005/03/01/the-coming-end-of-the-american-superpower/ (accessed 19 June 2013).

29   Nossal, 'Lonely Superpower or Unapologetic Hyperpower?', para. 13.

has a large head start over the emerging powers.[30] Nossal agrees with this analysis, and cites a number of examples showing why the US's soft power is likely to remain unbeatable, including: the technological assistance the US gives to other countries, such as the US-originated computer software being used to run virtually all the computers in the world; the dominance commanded by American English in various institutions globally; the dominance of American popular culture throughout most of the world, and the US being the most popular immigration destination in the world.[31]

Future Superpowers?

Alongside the debate over whether the US will remain the world superpower, scholars and analysts have been debating the possible emergence of the next or future superpower, particularly in the twenty-first century. In 1980s, it was speculated that the rapid economic growth of Japan and its enormous GDP would enable it to position itself as the next superpower – a theory that has not been borne out to date. The BRICs countries and the European Union are often cited as some of the potential superpowers of the future, mainly because of their rapidly growing economic and military strength, their influence on global politics and international relations and their extensive markets.[32] Others argue that although these entities are potential superpowers, attaining that status in the near future will not be easy, since it takes a long time and much effort to develop soft power, especially on a scale to rival that commanded by the present sole superpower or that enjoyed by the pre-Cold War and Cold War superpowers.

Another controversial debate concerns whether the current potential contenders would replace or merely rival the US if they were to achieve superpower status.[33] Some believe that the US is more likely to remain in its own class and unchallenged, so that even if any of the candidates do attain superpower status, they would still rank second to the US. Defending the argument that none of the contemporary major powers are likely to eclipse the US's position as sole superpower, nor render it an 'ordinary' superpower alongside others, Nossal cites a number of reasons why this scenario is highly unlikely:

> it can be argued that three factors militate against this eventuality. First, it is not altogether clear that the structural power enjoyed by the United States today

---

30   Josef Joffe, 'The Secret of US World Domination', *The Globe and Mail* (Toronto), 27 September 1997.

31   Nossal, 'Lonely Superpower or Unapologetic Hyperpower?', para. 15.

32   William H. Overholt, *Asia, America, and the Transformation of Geopolitics* (2008); G. John Ikenberry, 'The Rise of China and the Future of the West', *Foreign Affairs* 87:1 (2008), pp. 23–7.

33   John McCormick, *The European Superpower* (2007), p. 2.

will be eclipsed or matched any time soon. Huntington's analysis depends on a particular reading of the tea leaves: notably, his unit of analysis is the 'civilization' rather than the 'nation-state,' and as a consequence the empirical measures of power he reports are highly skewed. Needless to say, if one chooses to aggregate a number of different countries together to form a single 'civilization,' one will get a very different picture than if one were to disaggregate these civilizations into their component nation-states and compare the structural power of individual nation-states. Second, in order to be 'ordinary,' one must think that one is ordinary, and such a mind-set is unlikely to grip Americans – particularly American élites – any time soon, particularly given the ethnocentric lenses through which Americans view the world and their country's place in it. The third factor is the unique form of government that Americans have devised for themselves, one that gives them even more capacity to secure their interests over others in the international system.[34]

The question of whether the BRICs countries – individually or as a bloc – may emerge as the next superpower will be discussed extensively in subsequent chapters, so we will not explore it any further in this chapter.

The Concept of 'Superpower' Employed in this Research

The discussions above about the evolution of the term 'superpower' have shown that the achievement of transnational competencies is crucial to understanding the concept of 'superpower'. Thus, apart from being a superpower in the conservative sense (which emphasizes global reach and nuclear capability), a superpower of the twenty-first century needs to be: (a) diplomatically influential, an achievement mainly attained through the country's foreign policies, and (b) militarily outstanding. Diplomatic influence will be reflected in transnational competencies that facilitate interaction with and influence over other states, multilateral non-state actors and multilateral governing institutions (including the UN and other influential regional bodies like NATO and the EU), as well as other institutions and instruments of global dominance.

This book will take an international relations approach to defining 'superpower', and will focus on countries' foreign policies and military power in relation to their ability to influence current or future global relations and the world order.

The definition of the concept of 'superpower' adopted in this book therefore resonates with Dreyer's: 'A superpower must be able to project its power, soft and hard, globally.'[35] Therefore, the analytical framework adopted in this book is based on the following definition:

---

34   Nossal, 'Lonely Superpower or Unapologetic Hyperpower?', para. 31.
35   Dreyer, 'Chinese Foreign Policy'.

- A superpower is a leading nation in the international power system that is able to project its soft and hard power globally.

The power system here encompasses various aspects of power, including economic, military, political, cultural and diplomatic.

Chapter Summary: The Concept of Superpower

International relations and political science scholars have adopted diverse definitions of the concept of 'superpower', probably because of varying understandings of the concept of power. Drawing on Nye's definition of power as the ability to obtain what an entity wants and to advance the entity's interests over those of less powerful entities, this book will adopt a definition of superpower that connotes projection of influence. Of all the definitions explored in this chapter, the most appropriate for the purposes of this research is therefore June Dreyer's, which defines a superpower as one that is 'able to project its power, soft and hard, globally'.[36] Thus, attaining superpower status is not merely a matter of owning or controlling resources on a global scale, although this is a vital empowerment factor, but more about the international influence achieved by utilizing those resources.

This chapter has shown that at present, only the US among all the world's nations remains qualified as a superpower. So high is the degree of influence it commands across all spheres of power (political, economic, cultural, military and diplomatic) that some analysts feel that it should be given a higher status than it had during the Cold War, and should be regarded as a hyperpower.

The literature reviewed has indicated various parameters that have been used in the past to designate rankings to countries in the geopolitical power architecture, including superpower status. Some of these parameters include: the ability to own or control massive military, political, economic and cultural resources that can sustain global operations; the ability to exert significant influence in global affairs and issues of global concern, particularly through foreign policy tools; the ability to define or influence the global security agenda and to participate actively in global security issues, and the ability to be dominant over other global major powers. All of these parameters can be summed up as the ability to command hard and soft power. From the IR and diplomatic relations perspectives, a state's foreign policy agenda and the extent to which it reaches out to other nations will be key factors in determining that country's position in the global power order. Similarly, a state's military power will significantly determine its participation in security issues – a major issue in global affairs, and by extension, a determinant of a state's power ranking.

This chapter has also distinguished some concepts closely related to superpower and often used in discussions of international power relations, such as

---

36   Ibid.

great/major power, middle power and regional power. Since this book will focus on establishing the likely future positions of the BRICs countries – individually and as a bloc – in the global power ranking, an understanding of these aspects of the power hierarchy is essential. The theoretical and analytic framework laid out in this chapter has provided the background for the examination of the issues in the chapters that follow.

PART II
The BRICs: Political Relations, Foreign Policy and Military Power

Chapter 3

Introduction to Part II

Chapter 2 established that the concept of superpower depends on international power relations, and that the attainment of superpower status (or a related power status in the international power hierarchy – great power, middle power or regional power) is largely shaped by a nation's political relations, foreign policy and military power.

Predicting the future and whether a country is likely to achieve a particular power status is a complex undertaking. Part II will explore the BRICs countries' major global power indicators – political relations, foreign policy and military power – in both the past and present, how effectively (or otherwise) they have used them, and their impact on shaping the countries' future in the global power architecture, as well as some constraints the countries face.

It begins by giving an overview of the role of foreign policy and military power in international political relations, in particular with regard to shaping a country's power status on the international stage. Subsequent chapters will then analyse each of the BRICs countries in turn, supplying a brief background summary for each of the nations before examining their foreign policies, the impact of these policies on international political relations, their military power, their involvement in matters of global security, and their overall participation in global affairs and other matters of international concern.

The aim of Part II is to present a detailed picture of each BRICs country, and in particular the extent to which each country is globally integrated and how such integration affects, or is likely to affect, the global projection of its soft and hard power. The core factual and empirical findings presented in Part II will provide the analytical framework for Part III, which will offer more specific analysis of the prospects of the BRICs attaining superpower status.

The Role of Foreign Policy in International Political Relations

The term 'foreign policy' is used broadly in political science and international relations to refer to a set of political guidelines, goals and objectives that determine, shape or guide the relationships and activities of a state with other states or state entities (such as inter-governmental institutions and international NGOs).[1] A state's foreign policy is often premised on certain values and calculated to achieve

---

1   See Michael J. Hogan and Thomas G. Paterson, *Explaining the History of American Foreign Relations* (1991).

particular goals deemed vital to the state's interests in international political and diplomatic relationships. Also central to foreign policy are various tools or instruments that a state employs to implement, manifest or advance its foreign policies. These include diplomacy, international political alliances, international trade, war or military actions and foreign aid.

The essence of foreign policy is to protect a state's interests at the international level. Such interests are varied, and include but are not limited to the state's national security, ideology and ideological goals; its economic interests and prosperity; its global image and posterity, as well as its peaceful coexistence and interaction with other states or state entities. A state may also invest heavily in foreign policy in order to promote international peace and unity, but more particularly with a view to addressing matters of common interest with other state actors, or advancing certain geopolitical interests, ideologies or cultural aspects that the state advocates.

There are a number of foreign policy tools that a state may use to command international influence and to project its power at the global level. These tools or instruments may be broadly categorized into political tools, economic tools and military tools of foreign policy.[2] Political tools are essentially those diplomatic measures or other instruments a state employs to exert influence on other nations to adopt certain courses of action, especially those which they would have otherwise not chosen. Political tools include but are not limited to foreign aid and assistance, inter-state political alliances, foreign military aid and sales, and moves to advance or advocate for human rights beyond the state's borders.[3] Through these measures, the state seeks to maintain favourable relationships with the countries that benefit from its initiatives.

Forging a political alliance or granting foreign aid, for instance, would have the effect of fostering support or loyalty among allies, and influencing them to refrain from creating ties with other nations perceived as rivals or adversaries. The US, for instance, commands significant loyalty and support from many developing and Third World countries owing to its foreign policy of advancing foreign aid to these nations. The support that the US enjoys from countries like the UK, France and Italy, particularly in the context of recent humanitarian military interventions, is largely because these countries are traditionally its allies (an alliance that has been greatly strengthened by NATO). Virtually all the influential multilateral organizations, including the United Nations, are products of political foreign policy tools serving the aim of forming political alliances and transnational co-operation and integration. Political foreign policy tools are therefore key instruments in promoting good international political relations and projecting a state's political interests in the global arena.

Economic foreign policy tools include economic strategies that aim to shape or guide a state's economic relationships and economic activities with other states. Salient examples of economic foreign policy tools include export and import

---

2   See Norman A Graebner, *Ideas and Diplomacy* (1964).
3   Ibid.

controls, trade tariffs, sanctions and trade embargoes, and control over other barriers to trade.[4] These economic tools may be employed strategically to promote cordial relationships among countries favoured by the policies, or to curtail relationships with those countries which stand to lose from them. Measures like embargoes and trade sanctions may be employed by the major exporting nations to compel importing nations to adhere to particular interests deemed vital by the country or countries imposing sanctions.

The strength of economic foreign policy in expanding a nation's power is best exhibited by American foreign policy and its national industrialization policies of the 1890s which promoted the US's influence in developing countries around the world at the expense of other powers.[5] These policies overwhelmingly expanded American power globally, and significantly contributed to the rise of the US as a world power. Again, the US's foreign policy framework served to promote its liberal idealism globally when it led other like-minded nations in advocating for the adoption of the General Agreement on Tariffs and Trade (GATT), the forerunner to the World Trade Organization. The WTO and its predecessor GATT, through various international legal instruments, have significantly lowered barriers to trade – an ideology strongly advocated by the Western powers led by the US.[6] Economic foreign policy tools are therefore vital in promoting good international relationships, forging inter-state co-operation, enforcing a state's interests directly on indirectly at the international level and promoting its global 'brand'.

Military foreign policy instruments include the employment of a nation's military resources in support of or against other states to achieve a desired foreign policy or domestic goal. Military engagement overseas is normally an opportunity to project a nations' military might, and contributes to its influence in the geopolitical arena. Once again, the US provides a typical illustration of a country that has managed to stamp its political authority on the global arena and maintained its superpower status through military interventions overseas.[7] Military action as a foreign policy tool promotes coercive diplomacy, serving a compelling role in imposing a militarily stronger state's will abroad.

Military actions also influence public opinion about the power status of nations, enhancing the prospects of wielding soft and hard power. Another aspect of the employment of military actions to address global security issues is their use to combat terrorism and large-scale abuses of human rights. These are matters of great global concern, and any state that commits itself to pursuing them is likely to enhance its diplomatic relations with other world powers, most of which share these core values.

---

4   Richard N. Gardner, 'The Comeback of Liberal Internationalism', *Washington Quarterly* 13 (Summer 1990), pp. 23–39.

5   Jerald A. Combs, *American Diplomatic History: Two Centuries of Changing Interpretations* (1983), p. 45.

6   Ibid.

7   Hogan and Paterson, *Explaining the History of American Foreign Relations*, p. 48.

The Role of Military Power in International Political Relations

The exercise of a country's military power on the international stage should be expected to be an exceptional measure confined to nations such as the US which are notorious for foreign military intervention.

The most common situation is where a country deploys its military power to protect its territorial integrity against actual or perceived acts of aggression, or to pre-empt them as part of its defence policy. A nation may also employ military force to protect its international interests as part of its foreign policy, as in cases of humanitarian foreign military intervention or the granting of humanitarian assistance during disasters. The latter is more relevant to the discussions in this book, as it normally has an effect in international political relations, depending on how the countries targeted by the military actions are affected by or benefit from them. Michael Howard of the Royal Institute of International Affairs argues that a nation's military power plays a significant role in, among other things, enforcing and extending its authority and influence in the international arena.[8] He argues:

> The power which states exercise in international affairs is compounded of many attributes, economic, diplomatic, cultural and ideological as well as military. But military power, the capacity to use violence for the protection, enforcement or extension of authority, remains an instrument with which no state has yet found it possible completely to dispense. Indeed, it is not easy to see how international relations could be conducted, and international order maintained, if it were totally absent. The capacity of states to defend themselves, and their evident willingness to do so, provides the basic framework within which the business of international negotiation is carried on. That this framework should be as wide and as flexible as possible hardly needs arguing; but if no such limits existed, if it were known that there were no extremes of surrender and humiliation beyond which a state could not be pressed, the maintenance of international order would surely be, not easier, but incalculably more difficult. It is significant that nearly every one of the new states which has emerged since the Second World War has considered it necessary to create at least a token military force, even when the strategic need has been as negligible as the financial capacity to support it. Such a force is not purely symbolic.[9]

Military power is therefore as vital as other domains of power – economic, political and cultural – and plays a unique role in strategic global power positioning. One of the key factors that contributed to the superpower status of the US and USSR during the Cold War was the international military might they commanded, which

---

8   Michael Howard, 'Military Power and International Order', *International Affairs* 40:3 (July 1964), pp. 397–408.

9   Ibid, p. 405.

they bolstered by entering into military alliances through NATO and the Warsaw Pact respectively.

The military alliances of the First and Second World Wars and the bipolarity of the world in the Cold War era, characterized by the sharp divisions between the two superpowers and their allies, show that military power can have varied results. On the one hand, it can serve to bring nations together and boost their international power status. On the other hand, it can serve to disrupt the world order, leading to the souring of international diplomatic relations, or even wrecking them. Michael Howard, in explaining the role of military force in the international relations, acknowledges this in his argument:

> armed forces constitute a purely destabilising factor on the international scene, and that their abolition would lead to greater stability among nations. The arguments in favour of such a view are familiar and formidable, for it is true that the weapons which a nation considers necessary to its own defence will always be likely to appear to its neighbours as an actual or potential threat to themselves. The military preparations carried out by the Triple and Dual Alliances in pre-war Europe were inspired almost wholly by considerations of self-defence, but they appeared to offer reciprocally an intolerable threat, to be countered only by yet more intensive armament. It is no doubt as difficult today for the Soviet Union to believe in the purely defensive intentions of the bombers and missiles which ring her territory, and whose devastating powers our political and military leaders frequently extol, as it is for us to believe that the powerful units with which the Soviet Union could strike at Western Europe will never be used for aggressive purposes. In any case the ' Balance of Terror' is never wholly stable. It is maintained only by constant effort, heavy expense and the dedicated work of military specialists. Those specialists must constantly be thinking of the worst possible case, and it is not always easy under the circumstances to retain a sense of proportion and to realise that this may be the least probable case. It is simpler to judge the political intentions of a possible adversary according to his military capabilities; but the actions, writings and speeches stemming from such a judgment are likely to engender reciprocal alarm and bellicosity on the other side. The result is likely to be one of those arms races which inevitably, we are told, end in war.[10]

A state's military power, how it uses that power, and the states (or equivalent entities) against which it exercises that power may therefore have significant positive or negative effects on international relations and diplomatic order.

Military power is a tool that allows a nation to wield hard power. The US's ability to combat the threats of global terrorism and large-scale human rights abuses has been greatly boosted by its military power. The recent killing of Osama Bin Laden as part of a strategy to disrupt and destroy Al-Qaeda, the capture of Saddam

---

10   Ibid., p. 406.

Hussein in Iraqi military operations in a bid to ensure reparations for the massive human rights abuses he committed while serving as president and the recent killing of Muammar Gaddafi in an effort to contain the mass killings perpetrated by pro-Gaddafi forces and overcome the refusal to honour the democratic will of the Libyan people are a few examples of how military power can further a state's ideological interests at the global level. The success of these operations is essentially attributed to the military command of the US armed forces.

However, military power also has a place in promoting a state's soft power. The granting of military and security assistance by militarily powerful states to developing or under-developed states – such as military training, supplying armaments, intervening in situations of instability, sending humanitarian relief, setting up rehabilitation programmes and offering support to combat transnational terrorism networks – promotes good relationships with the recipient states, and normally serves to appeal to their loyalty.[11] Military power is therefore an intrinsic component of the soft power game and projecting a state's international influence.

---

11   See Combs, *American Diplomatic History*.

Chapter 4

Brazil

Introduction

Many studies consider Brazil to be an emerging power that has the potential to be a future superpower.[1] This has been acknowledged by a number of scholars from the 1970s onwards, partly based on the country's industrialization during the 1950s and 1960s, and partly on its size, resources and its foreign policies, which seem to reveal its ambitions in this direction. The country therefore warrants consideration as a candidate for possible future superpower status.

Another outstanding factor about Brazil that supports this view is its position in the United Nations. Brazil was among the UN's founding members, and has held a rotating seat on the Security Council numerous times since then. This position has been cited by scholars such as Glazebrook[2] and Riddel[3] as a defining characteristic of an emerging power, highlighting Brazil as a potential world superpower. This chapter will examine a number of factors that may lead to Brazil attaining this status in the future.

The Relevance of Brazil's Historical Background to its Gaining Superpower Status

Historical context is very important, not only in understanding Brazil's current position and influence in the international political economy, but also in understanding the country's international identity. For instance, Brazil's historical background offers evidence that the Brazilian elites and policy makers have for a long time believed that the country deserves a superior position on the global

---

1 Ryerson Christie and David Dewitt, 'Middle Powers and Regional Security', paper prepared for the conference 'Emergent Powers and Regional Security: The Experience of IBSA (India, Brazil, South Africa)', Universidad de San Andrés, Buenos Aires, May 2006, p. 245; Chris Alden and Antonio M. Vieira, 'The New Diplomacy of the South: South Africa, Brazil, India and Trilateralism', *Third World Quarterly* 26:7 (2005), p. 1,087; Gilberto Dupas, 'South Africa, Brazil and India: Divergence, Convergence and Alliance Perspectives,' in Fabio Villares (ed.), *India, Brazil and South Africa: Perspectives and Alliances* (2006), pp. 311–39.

2 G. Glazebrook, 'The Middle Powers in the United Nations System', *International Organization* 1:2 (1947), pp. 307–15.

3 R.G. Riddell, 'The Role of Middle Powers in the United Nations', *Statements and Speeches* 48:40 (1948).

scene.[4] In fact, their opinion has been that the country has what it takes to become a world power. It is important to study how this has shaped the country's policies and led to its being a contender for future superpower status.

Rodrigues points to national unity and territorial integrity as being the most crucial conditions that determine whether a country will dominate world affairs in the future.[5] Examining the particular circumstances that led to the formation and development of Brazil is vital in understanding the dearly held belief among the country's elites that Brazil deserves a more prominent position in global affairs. This will also give an insight into the country's security over the years, as well as its territorial integrity, helping us to gauge the possibility of the country emerging as a superpower.

Brazil's Historical Background

Brazil traces its origins to a territory that was founded by the Portuguese at a mythical island whose boundary was marked by two rivers, probably the Plata and the Amazon.[6] According to Magnoli, the concept of Brazil being an island served two major functions: it symbolically asserted the importance of territorial identity tied to the naturally occurring landscape, and it allowed the colonizers to define the country's borders and to support their claim for the Plata region being part of Brazil.[7]

Strictly speaking, the founding of Brazil originally resulted from the exploration of the new land of South America by those Lafer refers to as the *bandeirantes* ('scouts') and the diplomats who took it upon themselves to negotiate the new country's boundaries.[8] However the Portuguese conception of Brazil as an island was upheld during the demarcation of borders through the signing of the Treaty of Madrid between the Spanish and the Portuguese crowns in 1750.[9] One of the most outstanding characters among the diplomats was Alexandre de Gusmão, who negotiated for two basic demarcation rules to be included in the treaty. The first rule was that occupation of territory through *uti possidetis* (the principle of acquiring territory through occupation) had to be recognized. Secondly, he negotiated for

---

4   José H. Rodrigues, 'The Foundations of Brazil's Foreign Policy', *International Affairs* 38:3 (1962), pp. 324–38.

5   Ibid., p. 325.

6   Christian Lohbauer, 'Die Beziehungen zwischen Brasilien und seinen Nachbarländern II', in Gilberto Calcagnotto and Detlef Nolte (eds), *Südamerika zwischen US-Amerikanischer Hegemonie und Brasilianischem Führungsanspruch: Konkurrenz und Kongruenz der integrationsprozesse in den Amerikas* (2002), p. 144.

7   Demétrio Magnoli, *O Corpo da Pátria: Imaginação Geográfica e política Externa no Brasil, 1808–1912* (1997), p. 111.

8   Celso Lafer, 'Brazilian International Identity and Foreign Policy: Past, Present, and Future', *Daedalus* 129:2 (2000), p. 3.

9   Lohbauer, 'Die Beziehungen zwischen Brasilien und seinen Nachbarländern II', p. 144.

natural features like mountains and rivers to mark the colonial boundaries.[10] These rules evidently had a lot of impact on the establishment of Brazil, as a colony and later a nation.

Brazil, unlike other countries in Latin America, underwent a peaceful decolonization process. In 1808, Napoleonic troops occupied the Iberian Peninsula while the Portuguese monarchy temporarily relocated to Brazil. As a result, Brazil was elevated from being a colony to being a kingdom together with the Algarve and Portugal. In 1822, Brazil attained independence, though the constitutional monarchy continued to reign under Dom Pedro, the son of Dom João VI, the King of Portugal at the time.[11] Brazil gained assistance from the UK to become a fully independent and internationally recognized empire in 1825. This left Brazil with strong links that led it to be more strongly oriented towards Europe than the Americas.[12] This gave Brazil quite a unique entry onto the international scene.[13]

The sovereign constitutional monarchy persisted in Brazil until 1889. This led to both national and territorial unity, promoting the country's unique status as a newly established empire.[14] Therefore, right from the time of its formation, Brazil stood out in various ways that distinguished it from other countries in the region, including its size, and the unique pattern of colonization and later decolonization that saw the country retain both political and territorial unity and the imperial status that it enjoyed until 1889.[15] Moreover, unlike other countries in Latin America, the racial composition of the country was quite distinct, much of the population being of African origin, with only relatively few indigenous people. In addition, the country was distinctive linguistically, being a Portuguese-speaking nation despite the fact that it was located in a region where Spanish was the language of the day. The fact that Brazil looked up to Europe and later turned to the United States rather than focusing on indigenous or Latin American traditions for political ideas also contributed to its political success.[16]

The unique origin of Brazil was complemented by the country's diplomats' peaceful negotiation of the border disputes between Brazil and its neighbours, mainly Argentina and Paraguay,[17] and its successful incorporation into the

---

10   Celso Lafer, *A Indentidade Internacional do Brasil e a Política Externa Brasileira: Passado, Presente e Futuro* (2001), pp. 30–31.

11   Lafer, 'Brazilian International Identity and Foreign Policy', p. 4.

12   Rodrigues, 'The Foundations of Brazil's Foreign Policy', p. 327.

13   Lafer, 'Brazilian International Identity and Foreign Policy', p. 4.

14   Ibid.

15   Ibid., p. 5.

16   Andrew Hurrell, 'Brazil as a Regional Great Power: A Study in Ambivalence', in Iver B. Neuman (ed.), *Regional Great Powers in International Politics* (1992); Martin T. Katzman, 'Translating Brazil's Economic Potential into International Influence', in Wayne A. Selcher (ed.), *Brazil in the International System: The Rise of a Middle Power* (1981), p. 26.

17   Lafer, 'Brazilian International Identity and Foreign Policy', p. 7; Rubens Ricupero, 'O Brasil, a América Latina e os EUA desde 1930: 60 Anos de uma Relação Triangular',

international scene. As a result of these unique factors in the country's origin and early stages of development, Brazil ended up being geopolitically stable by the time it became a republic in 1889.[18] It is also one of the very few countries whose entry into the international arena was heavily based on diplomatic means of solving conflicts.

It size means that Brazil has ten neighbouring countries, making it one of the countries with the greatest number of neighbours in the world. Among the continent-sized countries such as Russia, the US and China, only Brazil has managed to rely solely on peaceful means to demarcate its borders.[19] Although Brazil relied on Europe for political ideas, the fact that it was quite geographically distant from ongoing international tensions[20] and that it had insufficient military resources led the country to adopt a different political style from that of the European powers. This may also explain its emphasis on diplomatic conflict-resolution.

Economic Background

The Brazilian elites have long considered national economic development to be one of the fundamental ways to help the country exert a good deal of influence on the international scene. This became even more pronounced from the early part of the twentieth century.[21] Antonio Barros de Castro points out that unlike the great powers, whose international influence is guaranteed by their military and economic resources, countries like Brazil are forced to construct their influence.[22] He goes on to explain that industrial expansion and national economic development are the quickest methods to achieve such influence.

Brazil's geopolitical location and the circumstances of the country's formation may help to explain the country's emphasis on economic development. Brazil is situated in a region which is relatively free of inter-state animosities and conflicts, so it is subject to very few security threats and the only real external challenges it faces are economic. As a result, its foreign policies focus on the prevailing economic development model.[23] This emphasis on economic development and

---

in José A.G. Albuquerque (ed.), *Sessenta Anos de Política Externa Brasileira 1930–1990: Crescimento, Modernização e Política Externa* (1996), p. 38; Maria R. Soares de Lima, 'Aspiração Internacional e Política Externa', *Revista Brasileira de Comércio Exterior* 82 (2005), p. 4.

18   Ibid.
19   Lafer, *A Indentidade Internacional do Brasil e a Política Externa Brasileira*, p. 7.
20   Lafer, 'Brazilian International Identity and Foreign Policy', p. 6.
21   Pedro da Motta Veiga, 'A Política Comercial do Governo Lula: Continuidade e Inflexão', *Revista Brasileira de Comércio Exterior* 83 (2005), p. 2.
22   Lima, 'Aspiração Internacional e Política Externa', p. 6.
23   Maria R. Soares de Lima and Mônica Hirst, 'Brazil as an Intermediate State and Regional Power: Action, Choice and Responsibilities', *International Affairs* 82:1 (2006), p. 22.

its influence on Brazil's foreign policy gives a clear insight into the country's international identity.

The path taken by Brazil in its economic development, both in the colonial and post-colonial eras arose from the country's close links to the capitalist nations among the European powers.[24] Like any colonial economy, Brazil relied greatly on the export of primary goods, such as coffee to the US, and also on the UK for loans as well as foreign direct investment (FDI).[25]

In 1929, the financial crisis which developed into a global economic recession forced a number of states to resort to neo-mercantilism,[26] isolating the Latin American markets from the rest of the world economy.[27] This highlighted the disparity between Brazil's economic limitations and its expected international role. Lafer explains that the disparity between the potential of Brazil (given that it is a continent-sized country) and the reality on the ground stimulated reflection about the country's limitations, and even led to idea that Brazil was under-developed.[28]

In response to this situation, Brazil resorted to a kind of goal-oriented nationalism with the aim of integrating the country by using development to correct its deficiencies.[29] The economic and political characteristics of Brazil changed drastically from 1930, when President Getúlio Vargas assumed power. The country adopted a new model for its economic development which was more oriented towards national industrialization.[30]

The development of economic nationalism in Brazil also resulted in the remodelling of the country's foreign policy following two main guidelines. The first maintained that policies had to enable the country to exercise autonomy by finding its own solutions to its own problems.[31] The second was that policies should assist in identifying external resources that could be used to advance national development.[32] This inevitably meant that the country's national development was closely linked to its foreign policies.

---

24   Andrew Hurrell, 'Hegemony, Liberalism and Global Order: What Space for Would-be Great Powers?', *International Affairs* 82:1 (2006), p. 16.

25   Frank D. McCann, 'Brazilian Foreign Relations in the Twentieth Century', in Wayne A. Selcher (ed.), *Brazil in the International System: The Rise of a Middle Power* (1981), p. 4.

26   Robert W. Cox, *Production, Power and World Order: Social Forces in the Making of History* (1987), p. 236.

27   Paulo Roberto de Almeida, *O Estudo das Relações Internacionais do Brasil* (1999), p. 24.

28   Lafer, 'Brazilian International Identity and Foreign Policy', pp. 13–14.

29   Ibid.

30   Alexandre Q. Guimarães, 'Historical Institutionalism and Economic Policymaking: Determinants of the Pattern of Economic Policy in Brazil, 1930–1960', *Bulletin of Latin American Research* 244 (2005), p. 531.

31   Horácio Lafer (1959), cited in Lafer, 'Brazilian International Identity and Foreign Policy', p. 14.

32   Ibid.

President Vargas maintained good political and economic relations with the UK, US and Nazi Germany while ensuring that Brazil did not get involved in international tensions, thereby improving the country's bargaining position.[33] This neutrality allowed Brazil to manipulate the then great world powers to its maximum advantage.[34] For instance, President Vargas persuaded the US to make a number of investments in Brazil, such as in the steel industry as well as in the country's infrastructure. He also secured the provision of military equipment from the US, as well as a guarantee of a market for Brazil's products; in return, Brazil formed a military alliance with the US,[35] not only for economic gain, but also for military advantage. The alliance enabled the country to participate in the world economy and gave it an opportunity to take part in the Second World War as one of US's allies, giving Brazil more international recognition as well as influence.[36]

From 1950 onwards, Brazil experienced more rapid industrialization, and the country enjoyed an economic boom until the late 1970s, registering a commendable annual economic growth rate of more than 6 per cent over three decades.[37] Brazil also made significant strategic progress in the fields of agriculture, oil and energy,[38] leading the country from almost total dependence on foreign oil in the 1950s to being self-sufficient from 2006 onwards.[39] Although the Brazilian economy has been liberalized and the country has been successfully incorporated into the global economy, the country's desire for autonomy has persisted over the years. Consequently, the country advocates for autonomy by participation – that is, retaining autonomy in the global economy while doing away with authoritarianism and giving the potential for liberal globalization the recognition it deserves.

From the mid-1940s to the mid-1970s, the average annual economic growth rate of Brazil was a commendable 7.4 per cent, but from 1974 to the end of the twentieth century it was relatively low, averaging 3.7 per cent, and quite volatile. It dropped even further to slightly above 3 per cent during 2000–2006, below that of most of Brazil's immediate neighbours. However, prominent economist Antonio Barros de Castro says that comparing the economic growth rates of Brazil with those of India and China today would be inappropriate, given that Brazil concluded its transition from a primary economy to an industrialized economy much earlier than these other countries.

Currently, Brazil's is among the top ten largest economies in the world.[40] The country's economy is not only open, but also well-established in terms of

---

33   Ricupero, 'O Brasil, a América Latina e os EUA desde 1930', p. 42.
34   McCann, 'Brazilian Foreign Relations in the Twentieth Century', p. 10.
35   Ibid.
36   Lafer, 'Brazilian International Identity and Foreign Policy', p. 15.
37   Juan de Onis, 'Brazil's New Capitalism', *Foreign Affairs* 79:3 (2000), p. 108.
38   Ibid.
39   Raúl Zebichi, *Brazil and the Difficult Path to Multilateralism*, (2006), p. 3.
40   Luiz F. Lampreia, '*Brazilian Foreign Policy: Continuity and Renewal*: http://www.un.int/brazil/brasil/brazil-un.htm (accessed 16 January 2012).

international public relations. A number of factors have contributed to this. One of these is Brazil's large size, which gives it a vast range of natural resources, including two enormous hydrological basins: the River Plate basin and the Amazon basin. As pointed out above, the country is also bordered by ten different nations, some of which have highly populated borderlands, creating opportunities for commercial activities. Brazil also has a relatively high population of roughly 160 million people, providing a sizeable workforce for the development of the economy and a large domestic market for the country's products. The populations in Brazil trace their origins from different parts of the globe, including Poland, Lebanon, Germany, Japan, Portugal, Ukraine and Italy, and Brazil has established special links with these nations, enhancing its economic opportunities.

Brazil also has a very strong and diverse industrial economy, giving it an economic advantage over other countries. The country is also a major producer of beef and other agricultural products, as well as minerals. Moreover, Brazil's good foreign relations with four great trading areas mean that its international trade is well balanced. These areas include the European Union (which accounts for roughly 28 per cent of Brazil's international trade), the Pacific Rim, Latin America and the US (each of which account for 20 per cent of the country's international trade). The country has a highly complementary economy, and is very competitive in the agricultural sector as well as in industrial and cattle products, though this has exposed it to protectionist barriers in the developed markets.[41]

It has been estimated that Brazil will undergo steady growth of 3.5 per cent per annum in the next decade, as long as the country experiences stable as well as prudent governance, a fairly favourable international environment and good macroeconomic policies.[42] On that basis, it is expected that the country will emerge among the top seven largest economies in the world by the middle of this century, given that none of the already mature industrial economies is likely to expand at such a rapid rate.[43] Consequently, if a well-founded industrial base and economic size are anything to go by, then Brazil is likely to break out of its current limits as a regional power.

Foreign Policy

As Hurrell puts it, 'would-be great powers' believe that their roles should be a more influential, especially in global terms.[44] This belief is often manifested in countries' foreign policies, making it essential to take these into account in determining the possibility that they will emerge as superpowers in future. In Brazil for instance,

41   Ibid.
42   Ibid., para. 3.
43   Paulo Sotero and Elliott Armijo Leslie, 'Brazil: To Be or Not To Be a Bric?', *Asian Perspective* 31:4 (2007), p. 54.
44   Hurrell, 'Hegemony, Liberalism and Global Order', p. 2.

there is a widespread belief in the country's global influence, as expressed in the words of Brazil's former president, that the country's obsession with its potential and its belief that at some point Brazil will attain greatness is comparable to that of a child. Similarly, as mentioned above, the history of Brazilian foreign policy reveals that for a long time there has been a belief among the Brazilian elites that the country has all that it takes to achieve the status of a world power. This goal has played a very significant role in the formulation of Brazil's foreign policies ever since the country became a republic in 1889.[45]

For a long time, Brazil's was a perfect example of a 'sleepy' foreign policy.[46] Although it was and remains the largest country in Latin America, with a population of over 160 million, it concentrated solely on its internal affairs for most of the twentieth century. Although Brazil had a highly able diplomatic and professional corps, decades of tyranny, severe economic crises and its autarkic economic development policies led the country to focus on domestic concerns at the expense of foreign policy. As a result, the US easily acquired regional dominance, leaving Brazil with only a small role in the Organization of American States (OAS) despite the fact that it was the only other continent-sized country in the region, and thus best equipped to face up to the US in the fight for regional dominance. In fact, as late as the year 2000, the Brazil was quite reluctant to get involved in seeking an end to the armed conflict in neighbouring Colombia.[47]

However, Brazil has developed its foreign policies significantly in recent years, pursuing its vision of a multipolar world – a world with several regional powers rather than a single global superpower. The country has also established very cordial relationships not only with its neighbours, but also with developing countries throughout the world, with the strategic aim of improving the country's prospects of surpassing the existing global powers to become a world power in its own right.

Foreign policy in Brazil received a very significant boost from José Paranhos, Baron of Branco's term in office at the Ministry of External Relations in the very early twentieth century, which had a lasting impact on the country's foreign policy. During that period, the ministry started to establish a more professional and apolitical approach to Brazil's national affairs.[48] Its foreign policy at that time was mainly geared towards consolidating its territory, since the country's national

---

45   Albuquerque, *Sessenta Anos de Política Externa Brasileira 1930–1990*; Lafer (2004); Eugênio Vargas Garcia, *Cronologia das Relações Internacionais do Brasil*, 2nd edn (2005).

46   Adam Isacson, 'Brazil's Foreign Policy Awakens: Is the United States Ready? Is Brazil Ready?', *Foreign Policy Digest*, 1 January 2011: http://www.foreignpolicydigest. org/2011/01/01/brazil%E2%80%99s-foreign-policy-awakens-is-the-united-states-ready-is-brazil-ready/ (accessed 9 January 2011), para. 12.

47   Ibid., para. 6.

48   Burges (2004), p. 5.

boundaries had just been demarcated.[49] Foreign policy was viewed as serving to defend the state's political and territorial integrity, so it was accorded precedence over national politics.[50] Since then, the Brazilian elites have tended to regard foreign policy as an autonomous function, which accounts for the exceptionally high status of the Ministry of Foreign Relations in the country's state apparatus.[51] In fact, the status of this ministry in Brazil has been referred to as 'hegemonic'.[52]

The stability of Brazilian foreign policy can be attributed to this high status. The country has even put in place measures to ensure that in times of structural change, the ministry is able to acclimatize to the new situation while ensuring continuity, to avoid upheaval.[53] It can therefore be seen that the way Brazil was founded coupled with the resulting belief that Brazil deserves an influential role on the global stage has led to the formulation of a foreign policy that is currently famous for its linearity and stability. The characteristics of Brazil's foreign policy, including this stability and continuity, especially over the past century, have promoted the belief that the country holds the potential to be a great power.[54] Not only does Brazil have a clear view of the world order, but it has a very strong international identity.

Brazil's Current Foreign Policy as Stipulated in the Constitution

International relations in Brazil are founded upon Article 4 of the country's Federal Constitution, which stipulates that the relationship between Brazil and other nations, as well as multilateral organizations, will be guided by principles such as international co-operation, non-intervention, peaceful conflict resolution and self-determination. Under the Constitution, the ultimate authority for establishing foreign policy priorities is vested in the president, while congress is responsible for considering and reviewing all international treaties, diplomatic nominations and legislation linked to the country's foreign policies.[55]

Brazil also has a constitutionally instituted Ministry of Foreign Relations which advises the president on matters relating to foreign policy as well as being responsible for foreign relations with international bodies and other countries. The ministry, commonly referred to as Itamaraty, has a very wide scope, including political, financial, commercial, economic, cultural and consular relations.

---

49 Corrêa (1995), p. 16.
50 Lima, 'Aspiração Internacional e Política Externa', p. 4.
51 Ibid., p. 5.
52 Veiga, 'A Política Comercial do Governo Lula, p. 2.
53 Lima, 'Aspiração Internacional e Política Externa', p. 5.
54 Lafer, 'Brazilian International Identity and Foreign Policy', p. 12.
55 Article 84 of the Federal Constitution of Brazil.

Regional and Global Manifestations of Brazil's Current Foreign Policy

Brazil's current foreign policy is a result of the country's unique position as Latin America's major regional power, an emerging power on the world stage and a leader among the developing countries. The country's foreign policy discourages intervention in other countries' affairs, encourages peaceful settlement of disputes and heavily emphasizes the principle of multilateralism.[56] This multilateralist diplomacy is pursued through international organizations such as the United Nations and the Organization of American States, and Brazil has managed to increase its ties with various developing countries both in Africa and Asia. It advocates for regional integration rather than pursuing unilateral initiatives.

More recent manifestations of the country's foreign policy have enhanced its prospects of becoming a great power. For instance, Brazil receives virtually all the credit for the foundation of the Union of South American Nations (UNASUR). This is the only diplomatic union in South America, and it is expected to continue with most of the peace-building and political responsibilities that are currently performed by the OAS. UNASUR has already been actively involved in resolving disputes, though it has yet to appoint a permanent secretariat and its members have not reached consensus on some of the key decisions affecting the organization.[57]

Brazil's foreign policy is not just confined to South America; the country extended its foreign policy to strike a nuclear deal with Iran in May 2010. In defiance of Europe and America, President Lula da Silva came to the decision that the various international sanctions were not the best tools to check Iran's long-held ambition to develop nuclear weapons, and peaceful dialogue and negotiations were more likely to succeed. In collaboration with Turkey, Brazil persuaded the Iranian government to transfer part of Iran's uranium stockpile to Turkey. The US government viewed such a deal as a well-formulated plan that would enable Iran to delay the sanctions imposed on it by the UN while continuing to enhance its weapons capabilities, leading to friction with Brazil. The negotiations between Iran and Brazil have been considered Brazil's most ambitious venture into global diplomacy to date, though such diplomatic activities are expected to increase in the near future. Brazil has also shown a great deal of commitment to collaborating with other Portuguese-speaking countries.[58] It has also gained very powerful influence in East Timor, where it is heavily involved in development and peace restoration.[59]

Brazil's trade policy is still heavily dominated by the country's Ministry of Foreign Relations. As a result, commercial interests in the country are often driven

---

56   Georges D. Landau, *The Decision-making Process in Foreign Policy: The Case of Brazil* (2003), p. 79.

57   Isacson, 'Brazil's Foreign Policy Awakens'.

58   Embassy of Brazil, 'Foreign Policy Overview': http://www.brasilemb.org/foreign-policy/overview (accessed 20 January 2011).

59   Ibid.

by the desire to achieve great goals in foreign policy terms, such as enhancing the influence of the country in both Latin America and the rest of the world, for example by prioritizing the signing of trade agreements with developing countries such as those in Asia, Africa and the Middle East rather than those in the developed world such as Europe and the US.[60]

As well as enhancing its hard power through military and economic development, Brazil has also sought to increase its soft power as a way of grounding its foreign influence. Brazil mainly employs institutional strategies to enhance this soft power, including developing diplomatic coalitions to constrain the influence of the established great powers. Its strategy has been to prioritize establishing political dialogue with a number of entities, including the other BRICs countries, in order to enhance its soft power with the aim of achieving its ambition to become a global great power.

Brazil extends universal scholarships and export credits to its neighbours in Latin America on a regular basis. Moreover, the Brazilian Development Bank (BNDES) recently granted other countries in the region loans worth US$5 billion. The country has also progressively offered technical assistance and financial aid to the other countries of Latin America. Cuba, Honduras and Haiti have been the top three beneficiaries of Brazil's assistance, each receiving more than US$50 million a year during 2005–2009.[61]

As has been seen, Brazil plays a very important role in various regional organizations. Although the country is primarily motivated to participate in such organizations by the desire for integration, these organizations also give Brazil an opportunity not only to exercise leadership, but also to build a consensus which favours its stances on both global and regional concerns. The organizations have enabled the country to assert its position as a regional power.[62] The country has also attempted to expand its influence in neighbouring regions through involvement in Central America and the Caribbean.

The Impact of Brazil's Foreign Policy on Issues of Global Concern

As mentioned above, Brazil previously had a 'sleepy' foreign policy, especially during the colonial years. However, this policy changed rapidly after a democratic regime took over the country's leadership. The Brazilian elites strongly believed that the country deserved to rank among the world powers, so they formulated foreign policies that furthered this ambition, and Brazil sought to gain the attention of other countries and position itself strategically to achieve it.

---

60   J.F. Hornbeck, *Trade Policy and the United States*, CRS Report RL33258: http://www.nationalaglawcenter.org/assets/crs/RL33258.pdf (accessed 14 January 2011), p. 3.

61   Ibid., para. 5.

62   Ibid., para. 6.

One of the principles underpinning Brazil's foreign policy is the principle of international co-operation.[63] This led Brazil to set up a variety of regional groups that the country has used in two different ways. To begin with, the groups have helped in regional integration, hence helping Brazil to unite some of the developing countries against the well-established powers. The unions formed between Brazil and other developing countries have also helped Brazil to establish its regional power by assuming a leadership role and building consensus with those other countries, centred on its own foreign policies.[64] Having realized the strength of the established global powers, Brazil is now advocating for multilateralism, where there are many regional powers rather than just one or two global superpowers. If and when this comes to fruition, Brazil would have no rival as the Latin American regional power.

As discussed above, Brazil places a lot of emphasis on the diplomatic resolution of conflicts, which is an express provision of its Constitution.[65] This has led the country to attempt some solutions that other nations, especially those enjoying world power status, have seen as wrong-headed and bound to fail. For instance, after developed world powers such as the European countries and the US concluded that the only solution to the potential threat posed by Iran's ambitions to make nuclear weapons was to impose sanctions to limit its capacity to do so, Brazil came up with a different approach based on its foreign policy, maintaining that peaceful dialogue rather than the imposition of UN sanctions was more likely to succeed in preventing Iran from manufacturing such dangerous weapons.

Brazil also offers loans, aid and other forms of financial assistance to developing countries, especially those in Latin America. Through such financial aid, Brazil seeks to win the support and loyalty of such countries, hence positioning it strategically as a global power. It seeks the favour of developing countries in various ways, including representing them in international bodies such as the UN. When asked for its views on reforms in the UN Security Council, Brazil's government's responses suggest that it is serving as the voice of the developing nations.[66]

Through its foreign policies, Brazil has demonstrated its immense soft power, as evidenced by the country's success in diplomatic engagement and the signing of many treaties with other nations committing them to legally binding agreements to refrain from manufacturing, storing or selling weapons of mass destruction. Among the most outstanding treaties initiated by Brazil, which will potentially spare the world from a lot of misery and destruction, are those declaring the southern hemisphere and its environs a nuclear weapons-free zone, and those

---

63   Article 4 of the Federal Constitution of Brazil.

64   Isacson, 'Brazil's Foreign Policy Awakens', para. 5.

65   Article 4 of the Federal Constitution of Brazil.

66   Mission of Brazil to the United Nations, 'Security Council Reform, Brazil's Position': http://www.un.int/brazil/brasil/brazil-scnu-reform.htm (accessed 2 January 2012).

committing a number of countries to forgo chemical and biological weapons.[67] Brazil even managed to sign such a treaty with Iraq, which for a long time held onto the ambition to develop nuclear weapons. Brazil's successful use of diplomatic methods of dispute resolution with various nations is another illustration of its soft power.

Brazil's involvement in peaceful missions also has an impact on its global influence. In many instances, Brazil has made diplomatic interventions in an effort to restore peace in various countries. At the same time, it has also frequently dispatched diplomatic and military personnel to help in restoring peace and resolving conflicts, as in Haiti in 2004.[68] This has contributed to forming a positive image of Brazil on the international scene, again promoting it as a potential global power. Currently, the country is enhancing on its military capacity to enable it to protect its sovereignty and boundaries more effectively, as well as preparing its army to deal with possible attacks from international criminal organizations.

Participation in Global Security Issues

Brazil plays a very active role in the formulation and implementation of the multilateral system of rules that govern the activities of nation states in the fields of politics, trade and economics through its participation in international bodies such as United Nations, World Trade Organization and Missile Technology Control Regime (MTCR). The country is also involved in spearheading regional integration through its involvement in Mercosul.[69] Brazil has always taken a very clear position on various contentious global security issues, and has taken steps to persuade other nations to adopt its views. A Brazil's participation in global issues, especially those to do with security, is illustrated by the country's position on UN Security Council reforms, and the role Brazil has played in global security issues, including opposition to the propagation and use of weapons of mass destruction. The country has also recently participated in military interventions attempting to restore peace to war-torn regions.

Brazil's Position on United Nations Security Council Reforms

Brazil is of the opinion that the UN Security Council should be expanded to incorporate additional permanent members as well as non-permanent members. The new permanent members, according to Brazil, should be drawn not only from

---

67 Luiz Felipe Lampreia, *Brazilian Foreign Policy: Continuity and Renewal*: http://www.un.int/brazil/brasil/brazil-un.htm (accessed 16 January 2012).

68 Larry Rohter, 'Brazil is Leading a Largely South American Mission to Haiti', *New York Times*, 1 August 2004: http://www.nytimes.com/2004/08/01/world/brazil-is-leading-a-largely-south-american-mission-to-haiti.html (accessed 19 June 2013).

69 Lampreia, *Brazilian Foreign Policy.*

the industrialized world, but also from among developing countries.[70] It is Brazil's view that increased permanent and non-permanent membership of the Security Council is the key to reforms that would lead to equal representation which are desired by countries all over the world. Brazil also objects strongly to expanding the Security Council by allocating full permanent seats to industrialized countries, but only rotating permanent seats to developing countries, viewing this as discriminatory. According to Brazil, regions that decide to rotate their permanent seats should not insist that other regions follow suit.

Concerning the veto rights of new permanent members of the Security Council, it is Brazil's position that there should be no discrimination between the new and the old members, though it suggests that new permanent members should consider suspending the use of their veto rights to promote equality.[71] In fact, Brazil advocates for the eventual total abolition of veto powers, and in the mean time would prefer their use to be restricted to matters outlined in Chapter VII of the United Nations Charter. This approach to reforming the UN Security Council clearly indicates that Brazil is very active on global issues and is advocating strongly for equal representation and non-discrimination in the global arena.

Brazil's Stance on Contentious International Issues

International Criminal Court   One of the most outstanding reflections of Brazil's participation in international security issues is its advocacy for the establishment of an International Criminal Court to complement national justice systems. Brazil strongly condemns the violation of internationally recognized humanitarian laws through such inhuman acts as genocide. It is the position of the country that the perpetrators of such crimes should be promptly subjected to justice, and if found guilty of the alleged crimes, they should be made to face the judicial consequences of their actions.[72] Brazil was therefore in favour of the establishment of an International Criminal Court to effectively handle such crimes whenever necessary.

Brazil is concerned that international bodies whose mandate does not include jurisdiction over criminal activities nevertheless assume such powers. The position of the country is that the authority of such international bodies is delegated rather than a self-constituted, so they should not exceed the authority delegated to them. To avoid such situations, the Brazilian government supported the establishment of an International Criminal Court through a multilateral treaty to serve as an independent judicial body whose jurisdiction would be limited to very serious crimes that would raise concerns among the whole international community. The Brazilian government stressed that the jurisdiction of the court should be confined

---

70   Mission of Brazil to the United Nations, 'Security Council Reform, Brazil's Position'.

71   Ibid.

72   Ibid.

to crimes that are clearly and explicitly defined, given that the court was likely to operate without a penal code.

The operation of the court system suggested by Brazil would serve to complement national criminal justice systems, mainly in instances where the latter have inadequate trial procedures, or where such systems are deemed unable to handle cases. Finally, Brazil feels that states' acceptance of the court's jurisdiction should be voluntary rather than compulsory. These clearly articulated positions vividly reflect the country's concern for and participation in international security matters.[73]

Nuclear Suppliers Group   Brazil joined the Nuclear Suppliers Group (NSG) in 1996 as a demonstration of its commitment to full transparency in the peaceful development of its nuclear and space programmes.[74] The 34 countries of the NSG share the common objective of promoting non-proliferation of nuclear materials as well as nuclear technology by exerting control over exports, striving to ensure that nuclear materials that are being exported are covered by safeguards that comply with specific safety standards.

The credibility gained by Brazil through joining the NSG may enable the country to have better access to nuclear-related services and goods. It has also joined, signed or ratified a number of international agreements and control regimes to counter the spread of weapons of mass destruction.[75] This demonstrates Brazil's full commitment to participate in international security issues.

Nuclear weapons-free zones   Brazil's active participation in international security issues is further revealed through the country's clearly demonstrated commitment to bringing about a nuclear weapons-free global environment, beginning in the southern hemisphere and its adjacent area. This was manifested when the Brazilian delegation, accompanied by 67 co-sponsors, tabled a Draft Resolution entitled 'The Nuclear-Weapon-Free Southern Hemisphere and Adjacent Areas' at the First Committee of the 51st Session of the UN General Assembly. Its purpose was to persuade the UN to acknowledge the nuclear weapons-free status of the southern hemisphere and adjacent areas.[76]

The Draft Resolution presented by the Brazilian delegates indicated that 114 nations covering about half the globe, with a population of more than 1.7 billion people, had made a legally binding commitment of their own free will to abolish the use of atomic energy for military purposes. Currently, virtually the entire southern hemisphere is a nuclear weapons-free zone, conforming to the various treaties banning the deployment of such armaments.

---

73   Ibid.
74   Lampreia, *Brazilian Foreign Policy*.
75   Ibid.
76   Ibid., para. 8.

The Brazilian government believes that establishing nuclear-weapons free zones is a vital step towards achieving global nuclear disarmament, increasing pressure on those states that have yet to adopt such a policy to do so in due course. It feels that regional bans on such weapons help to drive home the principle that the possession of nuclear weapons is in no way justifiable. The Brazilian delegation sought the support of the General Assembly for its Draft Resolution to encourage such efforts, both at the international and regional levels, especially in the fields of non-proliferation and disarmament.[77] This is another clear indication that Brazil is an active participant in global security issues.

Biological weapons Brazil ratified the Convention on the Prohibition of Biological Weapons in 1973, barely one year after the convention had been opened for signature. At the time of its establishment, the convention failed to provide the necessary mechanisms to verify compliance, so an ad hoc group was established by the Special Conference of the States Parties in 1994 with the mandate to consider the most appropriate measures to strengthen it, including verification measures, and to draft proposals to be incorporated into a legally binding document to be submitted to the states parties for consideration. Brazil has been an active participant in this ad hoc group,[78] and was one of the countries that submitted proposals pointing out the links between compliance with provisions dealing with non-proliferation and disarmament (as provided for in Article I) and those dealing with technological and scientific co-operation for the purposes of peace (as provided for in Article XI).

Chemical weapons   In 1993, Brazil played a very active role in the negotiation on the Convention for the Prohibition of Chemical Weapons, in line with the country's consistent stances on disarmament. Together with Chile and Argentina, two years before the Convention for the Prohibition of Chemical Weapons was adopted, Brazil signed the Mendoza Declaration, committing the three countries to refrain from the production, use, acquisition, development, transfer and stockpiling, either directly or indirectly, of biological and chemical weapons. The countries also supported the negotiations over the Convention for the Prohibition of Chemical Weapons that were then in progress.[79] The other countries in South America have since joined the Mendoza Declaration.

In another initiative, Brazil has been an active participant in the meetings held by the Organisation for the Prohibition of Chemical Weapons (OPCW),[80] which was established to monitor whether various nations had complied with the provisions of the Convention for the Prohibition of Chemical Weapons.

---

77   Ibid., para. 4.
78   Ibid.
79   Ibid.
80   Ibid.

Brazil's Participation in Peacekeeping and Human Rights

From the early post-Second World War period, Brazil has played a very active role in the restoration of peace in different parts of the globe.[81] To begin with, the country took part in the first ever peacekeeping mission carried out by the UN, in Suez and Gaza in the 1950s. In 1965, barely a year after the country had been through a military coup, Brazil contributed soldiers to participate in a US-led intervention in the Dominican Republic. However, the resulting accusations that Brazil appeared to be acting as a puppet of the US led it to refrain from participating in similar military actions for most of the two decades when the country was under military rule.

President Cardoso, who took power after the fall of the military regime, focused more on trade, democracy and eliminating nuclear weapons rather than being vocal in the international security scene. However, he also strove to increase Brazil's prominence in non-trade discussions. The country assumed a very active role in resolving various conflicts in South America, including assisting in the resolution of a brief war between Ecuador and Peru in early 1995, even contributing military forces to participate in the border pacification mission that lasted four years. Brazil also helped to counter the coup d'état in Paraguay in 1996. Since then, Brazil has made many military contributions to various peacekeeping missions in different parts of the globe.[82]

A more recent instance in which the country demonstrated immense concern for international security through its military power was its 2004 peacekeeping mission in Haiti. After several failed attempts by different American administrations to restore peace in Haiti, Brazil stepped in to employ unconventional diplomacy as a complement to the frequently used military power. The *New York Times* reported that the Brazilian government had sent 1,200 military personnel to Haiti to take assist in restoring peace – a much larger force than was sent by other South American countries.

Seemingly in an effort to improve its image among those countries which were still suspicious about its intentions, Brazil also sent its football team for an exhibition match against Haiti while diplomats and the military attempted to restore peace in the country. *The New York Times* quoted a prominent Brazilian political scientist as saying that Brazil had strongly criticized the US invasion and occupation of Iraq, so it intended to use the situation in Haiti to demonstrate that it was a credible mediator.[83]

Apart from the military interventions, the Brazilian government, together with the various civil agencies in the country, has made many contributions to promoting international human rights. This may be attributed to the fact that the imprisonment of the last two presidents of the country, President Cardoso and

---

81 Sotero and Leslie, 'Brazil: To Be or Not to Be a Bric?', pp. 2 and 4.

82 Rohter, 'Brazil is Leading a Largely South American Mission to Haiti'.

83 Ibid.

President Lula da Silva, during the military regime made them more sensitive to the abuse of human rights due to political activity.

Concluding Remarks

This section makes it clear that Brazil is a very active participant in matters pertaining to international security. Although the country mainly employs its soft power through treaties and peaceful negotiations to promote security, the country's military has also participated in a number of UN peacekeeping missions. As has been observed, Brazil has been at the forefront in promoting conventions and treaties that would help to sustain global peace and security. The country has also been keen to foresee situations that might lead to discontent among some of the countries on the international scene, such as discrimination against developing countries, hence threatening international security, and has tried to take steps to avoid them.

Military Power

Military power in Brazil is vested in an integrated military organization referred to as the Brazilian Armed Forces, comprising the Brazilian Navy, the Brazilian Army and the Brazilian Air Force.[84] It was brought under presidential authority by the country's Constitution which came into force in 1988.

Brazil currently has about 327,710 officers and troops – the largest armed forces in the whole of Latin America. Since the country is not subject to any serious internal or external threats, the armed forces have taken on new roles, including participation in the provision of healthcare, education, the construction of structures such as bridges, roads and railways, and other civil programmes. The Brazilian Army has also joined peacekeeping forces that have been sent to five different countries by the UN, and has been spearheading the UN Stabilization Mission in Haiti since 2004.[85]

The Organization of Brazilian Military

As mentioned above, the Brazilian Armed Forces are organized into three distinct branches: the Brazilian Army (which incorporates the Army Aviation Command), the Brazilian Navy (which incorporates the Naval Aviation Command as well as the Marine Corps) and the Brazilian Air Force. The country also has reserve and ancillary forces of the army made up of the Military Firefighters Corps and the Military Police. All the branches of the military fall under the Ministry of

---

84   CIA, 'World Facts: South America, Brazil': https://www.cia.gov/library/publications/the-world-factbook/fields/2055.html#br (accessed 4 January 2011), para. 9.

85   Rohter, 'Brazil is Leading a Largely South American Mission to Haiti'.

Defence. It has been a common practice for countries to consolidate their armed forces under a single defence agency, which is often answerable to the head of the executive. Brazil adopted this course when the armed forces were subsumed under one ministry in 1999, after a long history of failed attempts to unite the branches.[86]

Brazilian Army   The most influential of all the branches of the military in Brazil has been the army. This has been attributed to a number of factors, including its historical development, its size (in 1997, an estimated 200,000 personnel) and its deployment. During 1964–85, a number of senior army generals found their way into the presidency and cabinet posts, contributing to the branch's current influence. The Brazilian Army is organized such that all promotions up to the position of colonel are determined by its internal command structure. To promote a general, the High Command presents to the president a list of three candidates to choose from. The retirement age for colonels is 59, while that for four-star generals is 66, or after serving as a general for 12 years.

Handling powerful and sophisticated modern weapons requires a supply of skilled and literate young personnel, so the army trains a large reserve force. The Brazilian Army emphasizes thorough training and professional development for its officers. Just over one-third of its officers are non-commissioned officers (NCOs) whose role in the army is less well developed, so they have little authority or autonomy. Roughly half of the NCOs hold the rank of sergeant, helping to deliver commands between officers and the higher ranks, while some of them are mid-level technicians. The army underwent major generational and structural changes between 1980 and the 1990s, in line with the modernization campaign to prepare the army for more effective rapid mobilization.[87]

All major decisions concerning the Brazilian Army are taken by the High Command, which was formally established in 1964, the task formerly being performed by a group of generals based in Rio de Janeiro. Since the restructuring of 1986, the High Command consists of the Chief of Staff, seven serving regional commanders and the Minister of the Army.

Brazilian Navy   The Brazilian Navy can be traced back to the mercenary fleet of Admiral Cochrane and the Portuguese crews and their small ships that served to protect the earliest colonies in the coastal regions from being attacked by seaborne marauders. This branch of the country's armed forces is considered the most conservative and aristocratic. In fact, most of the officials in the navy are drawn from either the upper class or the upper middle class. Although the navy usually participates in 'brown-water' operations, it has an ambition to be a successful 'blue-water' navy with the capacity to assert its authority on the high seas. This inclination towards 'blue-water' operations puts the navy at a disadvantage

---

86   Paulo Wrobel (ed.), *Global Security in a Multipolar World*, Chaillot Paper no. 118 (October 2009).

87   Ibid., p. 24.

in getting involved in such activities as counter-drug operations compared to other branches of the armed forces. In 1997, the navy hand an estimated 64,700 personnel.

Brazilian Air Force   Brazil has the largest air force among all the South American countries, comprising well over 50,000 personnel and 800 aircraft. This branch of the Brazilian military is divided into four different operational commands for effective operation. The Aeronautics Ministry was established in Brazil in 1941, and incorporated the former navy and army aviation commands to form the Brazilian Air Force. The air force soon had its first experience of war when it joined the Allied forces in Italy in 1944 and took part in operations there for roughly nine months. The establishment of the Ministry of Defence in 1999 resulted in the conversion of the Aeronautics Ministry to the Aeronautics Command, though with little change in the structure of the air force, if any. The Brazilian Air Force is currently actively involved in the protection of the Amazon Rainforest together with its resources.[88]

Military industry   The Brazilian Armed Forces have been pursuing the goal of self-sufficiency in weaponry since the beginning of the twentieth century. Rather than acquiring a large arsenal, the forces have aimed to develop the technological capacity to produce the weapons required for the country's military.[89] This drive for self-sufficiency stems from the First World War, when the Brazilian Navy, large as it was, was rendered a paper navy due to a shortage of weapons such as large shells.

After 1930, there was rapid industrialization in Brazil, thus providing the necessary infrastructure for the development of the arms industry. This was boosted by the development of a steel mill in Brazil just after the Second World War. The mill flourished rapidly, and soon Brazil emerged as the largest steel producer in Latin America. The country started producing its own automatic pistols in 1954. The Brazilian military also underwent large-scale technological development and set up industries and institutions to facilitate this.

Activities of the Brazilian Armed Forces

The Brazilian Armed Forces have played a vital role in the development of the country from the time they assisted in ousting the imperial power in 1889. They asserted a moderating influence and carried out frequent interventions in various

---

88   Ibid., p. 19.

89   Gareth Evans, 'NATO and Russia, the International Crisis Group', statement to the Shadow Globalsecurity.org: http://www.globalsecurity.org/military/world/brazil/intro. htm (accessed 29 November 2011).

political processes during 1930–64. The military overthrew the serving civilian government in 1964 and took it upon itself to govern the country for 21 years.[90]

The military regime in Brazil was guided by a national security doctrine that had two main elements: (1) it defined security as including both countering external threats and domestic defence against communism and insurgency, putting this element of the doctrine into practice during 1968–73 by successfully suppressing a number of internal insurgencies, and (2) it advocated for economic development. During the military regime, the state assumed a more active role in the development of the country's economy, and even undertook an expansion of its industrial base. The country's high economic growth rate during 1968–73 served to legitimize the military government.

The military regime gave up power in 1985. Since then, the armed forces have continued to assert themselves politically, though a number of factors mean that their influence on the country's political scene has significantly diminished. One such factor is that there have been concerted attempts to consolidate democracy in the country, so the civilian ministries and the National Congress have gained more influence over security matters. Another is the fact that the military has had to compete with the civilian ministries for limited resources. In addition, the military was placed under presidential authority by the Constitution that entered into force in 1988, although its external and internal roles were preserved.[91] As a result, the fact that the Brazilian Armed Forces were not in a position to effectively promote or even finance their pet projects in the missile, nuclear, space and armaments fields eroded their political influence even further.

Fernando Collor de Mello, the country's president from 1990 to 1992, revealed that Brazil had a nuclear weapons programme that had been sponsored by the military, exposing most of Brazil's nuclear programmes to international scrutiny. He placed the country's space programme, which had been controlled by the Brazilian Air Force, under civilian supervision.[92] The Brazilian government declared in 1994 that it planned to join the Missile Technology Control Regime, and a year later it did so. Although the state did not intervene directly to dismantle Brazil's armaments industry, the industry ended up collapsing anyway. All these factors contributed to reducing the political influence of the military over the Brazilian government.

Brazil's security interests could have been diverted by geopolitical changes that took place in the country and the civil–military balance that it faced. In the 1990s, for, instance, the country transformed from a bipolar to a multipolar orientation in the context of the international system. There was also greater integration between

---

90 Adriano Nervo Codato, 'A Political History of the Brazilian Transition from Military Dictatorship to Democracy', transl. Miriam Adelman, *Revista de Sociologia e Política* 2, Selected Edition (November 2005), pp. 83–106.

91 Adriano Nervo Codato (ed.), *Political Transition and Democratic Consolidation: Studies on Contemporary Brazil* (2006), p. 68.

92 Ibid., p. 87.

Argentina and Brazil.[93] In 1995, there were also some economic and political uncertainties which ended up influencing the military's conception of Brazil's national security.

Since the 1950s, Brazil has had one of the lowest rates of military expenditure in the world. In fact, the country's military expenditure dropped to 1.1 per cent of its total national product in 1993. This trend serves to demonstrate the low level of external threats experienced by the Brazil. The country enjoys a cordial relationship with the ten countries neighbouring it, and there are no threats to its internal security. Nevertheless, it still has the largest armed forces in Latin America.

Brazil has no history of congressional supervision of its military, the country traditionally had no major bureaucracies in its armed forces, and Brazilian civil society has been relatively uninterested in defence-related issues, so the armed forces' attempts to revise their structure, role, strategies, tactics and doctrines were carried out in a vacuum. The establishment of the Ministry of Defence was seen as a necessary step towards bringing the military under civilian control. The first effective civilian initiative to mandate modernization of the country's armed forces only came about in 2008, when the country started to consider security issues as an important element of its foreign policies.[94]

Currently, Brazil has demonstrated a great desire to develop its ability to manufacture military equipment, and a great aspiration to reconstruct its military, and more specifically to strengthen the country's air defences. These developments have been motivated by the country's concern over its sovereignty as well as its border security. Although Brazil does not have any current problems with border disputes, Brazilians view their borders with ten different countries as vulnerable, and hence requiring the maintenance of a strong defence force. They are more particularly concerned about possible attacks by non-state actors, such as international criminal organizations whose operations extend across national boundaries.

Brazil also regards the international community with a good deal of suspicion, especially with respect to intentions regarding the Amazon, so as a result it has strengthened its security forces in order to assert sovereignty over the area. The rebuilding of the military in Brazil has also been attributed to the country's ambition to occupy its 'rightful' position among the world powers, and to demonstrate that it deserves a permanent seat on the UN Security Council.[95] Brazil's policy makers regard this as at the forefront of its foreign policy objectives, which has contributed to its recent focus on developing nuclear submarines.

---

93   Ibid., p. 204.
94   Codato, 'A Political History of the Brazilian Transition from Military Dictatorship to Democracy', p. 148.
95   Ibid., p. 168.

Summary

Brazil is a continent-sized country with a large population of around 160 million. The size of the country, its population, its natural resources and other factors have led the country's elites to believe that it has what it takes to be a world power. This ambition has been the central focus of most of the country's trade and foreign policies, which have been purposefully formulated to help the country achieve its goal.

Due to its geopolitical location, Brazil has never had a history of external security threats, giving the country ample time to concentrate on its economic development. In fact, Brazil is one of the very few continent-sized countries that managed to demarcate its borders peacefully and diplomatically. This diplomatic tradition can be traced back to the time when Brazil freed itself from Portuguese rule without getting involved in an armed struggle. In striving for global influence, Brazil has spearheaded diplomacy, persuading a number of nations to give up weapons of mass destruction, such as nuclear, biological and chemical weapons. The country has also promoted diplomacy as means of conflict-resolution, and has discouraged the use of military power in such instances. However, where it has deemed necessary, Brazil has been ready to commit its military to participate in the restoration of peace.

Due to the lack of external threats, Brazil prioritized factors other than investing in the military, allocating it just a small proportion of its national production. However, Brazil's military still remains the largest in Latin America, and the country is currently increasing its military investment in the face of concerns about the vulnerability of its borders.

Brazil has also joined a number of international unions with other developing countries in pursuit of its dream of becoming a world power. By uniting the developing countries, Brazil aims to counterbalance the established global powers. Brazil courts loyalty and favours from the developing countries by offering them loans, aid and other financial assistance. It also seeks to serve as a spokesman to promote their interests, especially in international organizations such as the UN. All these efforts aim to bolster support among the developing countries to enable Brazil to achieve its ambitions.

Chapter 5
Russia

Introduction

Russia is a federation of 83 federal subjects in the north of Eurasia. From southeast to northwest, countries that share their borders with Russia include North Korea, Mongolia, China, Kazakhstan, Azerbaijan, Georgia, Ukraine, Belarus, Poland, Lithuania, Latvia, Estonia, Finland and Norway. It also shares a maritime border with Japan in the Sea of Okhotsk and the United States in the Bering Strait.

Russia is the largest state in the world, spanning a massive 17,075,400 square kilometres, occupying well over 12 per cent of the Earth's land area and spanning nine time zones. Its population of 143 million means that it ranks eighth in the world. Forty per cent of Russia is located in the continent of Europe, it spans the entire north of Asia, and its environment encompasses a wide variety of landforms. Its energy and mineral reserves are the largest in the world, and it is the world's foremost producer of oil. It also has the lion's share of the world's forestry and a quarter of the Earth's fresh water in its lakes.

Its economy ranks eleventh in the world in terms of nominal GDP, and sixth in terms of purchasing power. Its military budget is the fifth-largest in the world, it is one of the five states acknowledged to possess nuclear weapons, and it has the world's largest stockpile of weapons of mass destruction. Russia can rightly be described as a great power, and is a permanent member of the UN Secretary Council, a member of the World Trade Organization, the Organization for Security and Co-operation in Europe (OSCE), the Eurasian Economic Community, the Shanghai Cooperation Organisation, the Asia-Pacific Economic Cooperation forum (APEC), the Council of Europe, the G20, the G8 and the leading member of the Commonwealth of Independent States (CIS) Council.

Russian Foreign Policy

Russia is still a state in transition, but since the upheavals of the previous decade it has garnered more confidence in terms of international relations, although it is regarded with suspicion in some quarters. Russia can also be said to have communication problems, as it has consistently failed to clarify its activities and views. This has led to a stereotypical view of the country among the Western countries that sometimes impedes pursuit of its policies. Russia is often regarded as a twenty-first-century reincarnation of the USSR rather than a contemporary, progressively more dominant global player. Russia has also been characterized as exploiting the law to its own advantage.[1]

Russia has grown more radical towards foreign businesses and capital, and has managed to familiarize itself with the use of soft power instruments to promote its influence. Although Russia's foreign policy is based on its ambitions to achieve an international status that reflects its economic growth and development and become a force to reckon with in a multipolar world, this should not be mistaken for an attempt to revive the Cold War. The new doctrines of the Russian military also have to contend with NATO's suspicions and the deployment of missile defences, and nuclear proliferation and expansion.

Experts estimate that Russia possesses about 6,700 strategic nuclear weapons and 5,400 tactical nuclear warheads.[2] The latter play a significant role in Russia's deterrent posture, and also reflect NATO's Cold War policy of deploying them as a shield against conventional attacks under the Russian Doctrine of 2003. Disarmament treaties such as START I and SALT I, which sought bilateral reductions in the two major powers' nuclear arsenals, repeatedly omitted tactical nuclear weapons.

New Aspects of Russian Foreign Policy

The year 2006 was a prestigious one for Russia. It presided over the G8, and in May it took over from Romania as chair of the Council of Europe. Russia is a key player in Europe, not least because one fifth of the Russian population is Muslim, which makes it easier for it to institute meaningful dialogue with the region's Muslim actors. In furtherance of this dialogue, Russia also supports the 'Alliance of Civilizations' initiative in Europe, proposed by the prime ministers of Spain and Turkey and adopted by the UN.

Russia was admitted into the G8 in 2002, which it took as an acknowledgement of its growing importance in the modern-day world. Russia feels it crucial that the three European countries comprising the G8 in addition to Japan, the US and the EU should co-ordinate to address key global problems.

Vladimir Putin has managed to develop effective personal relationships with most of the democratic leaders of the industrialized nations. He has also to some extent been able to alleviate the ill feelings caused by some Russian policies in the recent past. Russia has since made the G8 a hub for pursuing its foreign policy interests, backing initiatives such as combating contagious diseases and promoting education and energy security. Every party involved in the G8 summit hosted in St Petersburg in 2006 deemed it a success. It is also important to mention that the twin colossal forces of Asia – India and China – were in attendance when all this

---

1   Andrew Wilson, *Virtual Politics: Faking Democracy in the Post-Soviet World* (2005), p. 5.

2   Hans Kristensen, 'Nuclear Notebook: Russian Nuclear Forces 2008', *Bulletin of the Atomic Scientists* 64:2 (2008).

was happening. Despite the fact that India and China are not formal members of the G8, they held an unprecedented tripartite meeting with Putin.

The St Petersburg G8 summit held constructive discussions on every item on its agenda. When the conference was coming to a close, Putin observed that Russia's perception of the current global state of affairs was no longer bipolar, but contrary to some expectations, it did not intend to seek a unipolar world run by a solitary superpower. He highlighted that since the end of the Cold War, the world had become neither more stable nor any safer, and that it was now much more unpredictable. The entire structure of international relations over recent decades was geared to serving a bipolar world, and there was a lack of mechanisms to provide solutions to all the current threats and challenges.

It therefore goes without saying that over the past few years there have been notable changes in Russian foreign policy. It remains a complicated issue, although its eastern component is developing and the entire approach currently seems to be well balanced, coping with integration while overseeing positive economic developments such as the growth in Russia's GDP, its early repayment of foreign debts and active investment abroad. Russia has entered the new century with a degree of confidence. It has been seeking new allies while consolidating its relationships with its older ones, and also as a form of reward for those countries that act in a friendly way towards Russia, which in the past has tended to retaliate for perceived slights. This has enabled Russia to develop a degree of self-criticism. To sum up, it is now more advantageous for countries to co-operate reliably with Russia and develop friendly relations with it, as when dealing with any influential, strong and major actor in the global arena.

Russia's Policy towards Europe

The rapid expansion of the European Union presents a significant challenge to the influence of Russia, in particular in terms of the EU's unified international policies. On the other hand, the majority of the Russian populace understand the advantages of the EU's independence and the fact that its scale provides a counterbalance to the US, helping to promote stability. Seeking positive relations with the entire European community could promote the interests of Russia, both economically and politically. However, this approach also carries risks to cohesion because of lingering tensions between Western and Eastern Europe. Some Eastern Europeans still have fresh memories of the oppressive and heavy-handed conduct of the USSR while being highly dependent on the energy Russia produces, so they have reasons to fear Russia's influence. Whether or not this wariness towards contemporary Russia is justified, it continues to be a sensitive issue which has an impact on relationships between Russia and the other European states. The Baltic nations are particularly susceptible to this power asymmetry as they try to develop foreign policies that further their own interests.[3]

---

3   Janina Sleivyte, *Intellectual Excellence in Defense: Russia's European Agenda and the Baltic States*, The Shrivenham Papers no. 7 (2008), p. 1.

A recurrent bone of contention for Russia has been the hosting of NATO tactical nuclear weapons in Italy, Germany, the Netherlands, Belgium and Turkey. Russia is currently bitterly opposed to these arrangements, claiming they contravene the Nuclear Non-Proliferation Treaty (NPT). Addressing this will go a long way to improving relations between Russia and the other European countries. In recent years, US Assistant Secretary of the State Rose Gottemoeller has repeatedly expressed the US's willingness to enter into negotiations with Russia concerning these deployments, and the US was ready to begin negotiations as early as December 2009.

Russia's Policy towards NATO

The perception that NATO was founded to keep the Russians out, the Germans down and the Americans in is still widespread. Nevertheless, some complaints about the expansion of NATO have focused not so much on the fact that it has encroached on Russia's borders, but rather that it has stopped there.[4] According to this view, if NATO consulted, co-operated with or even incorporated Russia into its security objectives, Russia would no longer feel so threatened by NATO's expansion.

The Impact of Russian Foreign Policies on Issues of Global Concern

This section aims to shed some light on Russia's foreign policy influence on a wide range of matters of global concern, including environmental issues such as climate change, health and mortality, international debt, globalization, false shortages and economic manipulation, unjust wars, oil, human rights abuses, overpopulation, the disposal of waste, consumerism, terrorism and worldwide.

Mediation of foreign international conflicts   Russia has been heavily involved as a go-between in quelling a number of international disputes, in particular engaging actively to promote peace in the aftermath of the Kosovo conflict. On 25 February 2008, the Russian Foreign Minister claimed that the European Union and NATO were seriously contemplating employing force to prevent Serbs from leaving Kosovo following Kosovo's declaration of independence.

Russia co-sponsors the Middle East peace process, and also supports UN and multilateral initiatives in Haiti, the former Yugoslavia, Angola, Burma (Myanmar), Cambodia and the Persian Gulf. It is noteworthy that Russia is a founding member of the Contact Group, has been member of the G8 since the Denver Summit in June 1997, and joined APEC in November 1998. Russia has also proclaimed its respect for OSCE principles and international law, and welcomed the involvement of the OSCE and the UN in regional disputes within its neighbour states. It has also contributed troops to the NATO-led peacekeeping forces in Bosnia and

---

4   Evans, 'NATO and Russia, the International Crisis Group'.

dispatched observers to Nagorno-Karabakh, Tajikistan, Moldova and Georgia. On 16 May 2007, Russia threw its weight behind instituting an international tribunal to bring to trial suspects charged with murdering the Prime Minister of Lebanon, Rafiq Hariri.

In terms of health and mortality, HIV/AIDS is the main concern globally. As of March 2011, there were 592,110 diagnoses of HIV/AIDS in Russia. According to the statistics, 58,663 new AIDS-related illnesses were recorded in 2010, a negligible increase over the 58,448 cases registered in 2009. Slightly over 40 per cent of the new reported cases were females, indicating that transmission via heterosexual contact is rapidly increasing. The Russian government has enforced laws on HIV prevention and treatment via the Federal Targeted Programme and National Priority Health Project. HIV treatment programmes are estimated to cost the Russian government approximately $250 million annually, and the state devoted $42 million to vaccine research in 2007–2010. The number of patients on anti-retroviral medications was projected to increase to 100,000 by the beginning of 2012. The Russian government should also be credited with sending anti-retroviral therapy drugs to poverty-stricken regions of the Third World, especially Africa, where treatment is scarce.

Environmental issues such as climate change have also drawn Russia's attention, and its policies have had a tremendous impact on conservation matters. In September 2004, despite strong opposition from the Russian Academy of Sciences (part of the Ministry for Industry and Energy) and Putin's adviser Andrey Illarionov, Putin and the Russian cabinet expressed support for the Kyoto Protocol. In return for EU support for Russia's accession to the WTO, Putin formally endorsed the protocol on 4 November 2004, and the Russian parliament's subsequent ratification of it on 18 November 2004 meant that the protocol complied with the membership threshold, allowing its entry into force on 16 February 2005.

To comprehend the impact of Russia's signing of the Kyoto Protocol, it is necessary to clarify its impact. It limits signatories' permissible greenhouse gas emissions to a specific percentage increase over baseline 1990 levels. Russia was not subject to compulsory reductions because its greenhouse gas emissions fell drastically following the break-up of the Soviet Union.[5] Although Russia has not signed up to the next phase of the Kyoto Protocol, its emissions are currently still below the 1990 baseline. Although Russia is sometimes referred to as 'the Saudi Arabia of carbon credits', it is not yet clear whether it will gain from trading emission credits with other states bound by the Kyoto Protocol.[6]

5   Toni Johnson, 'Backgrounder: G8's Gradual Move toward Post-Kyoto Climate Change Policy', Council on Foreign Relations, 25 January 2008: http://www.cfr.org/europerussia/g8s-gradual-move-toward-post-kyoto-climate-change-policy/p13640 (accessed 22 January 2012), pp. 5–6.

6   'Press Conference with Presidential Economic Adviser Andrei Illarionov', Moscow World Climate Change Conference, October 2003: http://www.sysecol.ethz.ch/Articles_Reports/Illarionov_Press_Conf.pdf (accessed 22 January 2012), pp. 2–3.

Individual abuse of humans by humans, human rights and Russia   Human rights arguably qualifies as the most pressing issue of global concern, since it affects people in a direct manner on a daily basis. Cases of bullying are widespread in Russia and all over the globe. In some of the countries, there is a conspicuous absence of social agencies to deal with such oppression. The abuse takes various forms, including medical, spiritual, financial, gender, sexual, psychological/ mental, physical and verbal. Russia's human rights record has been poor and patchy in some regions, and although there have been tremendous improvements in conditions in the post-Soviet era, problems persist. The Russian government's policies in the North Caucasus region have been of primary concern and have generated international friction. Despite the Russian government's acceptance of the validity of international human rights standards, the implementation of policies to protect these standards has been slow. However, the future looks more promising, as legal avenues are progressively opening up for individuals concerned with safeguarding human rights.

Unlike many other countries, the Russian judiciary does not enjoy total independence and freedom, but is rather vulnerable to political pressure, and enormous backlogs of cases and long trial periods persist. Although Russia abolished the death penalty in 2001, the Russian prison population (613 of every 10,000 of the population) remains the highest in the world. There are verified reports that detainees and inmates are being beaten and tortured by Russian law enforcers and prison officers, and such acts are even being carried out by other prisoners who have been given authority to maintain order within the prison system. It is disappointing to note that Russia has not complied with international standards and its prisons are extremely overcrowded. There are reliable reports that the Russian government may be still in the habit of breaking its undertakings to the European Council, especially in terms of prison conditions and control. Although a law passed in 2008 to set up an independent association of prison supervisors was implemented in 2009, the outcome has been mixed, with some prison officers co-operating while others have been obstructive. Pressure is piling up on the Russian authorities, especially after the death of lawyer Sergey Magnitsky in November 2009, apparently because of denial of medical care during detention before trial. Such highly publicized cases are forcing Russia to improve its monitoring of prisons.

There are authenticated reports from the North Caucasus that both non-governmental and governmental factions are involved in infringing humanitarian laws and international human rights. Despite counter-terrorism activities in Chechnya officially ceasing in April 2009, violence has risen dramatically in the North Caucasus since the beginning of 2009, especially in the Republic of Dagestan. The authorities have attempted to bring about some positive changes, for example ensuring that civilian observers are present during all large-scale military activities and following search operations. According to non-governmental and humanitarian rights organizations, the leaders in the region maintain that some cases are being swept under the carpet, so some of those responsible are going unpunished and violence in the region has escalated alarmingly.

In April 2011, Chechen President Ramzan Kadyrov won a second five-year term. In 2010, Kadyrov had imposed strict Islamic laws on Russian women, including the compulsory wearing of headscarves and many other restrictive dress codes and workplace policies, leading to attacks on some women simply for failing to wear headscarves despite being otherwise modestly dressed.

Despite its separation of state and Church, the Russian Constitution guarantees freedom of religion and stipulates that all religions are equal under the law. Nevertheless, statistics show that 70 per cent of the Russian population belongs to the Orthodox Church, and Jews, Muslims and other religious minorities are regularly subject to discrimination and prejudice. Although high-ranking federal officers have expressed disapproval of anti-Semitic hate crimes, this is not always reflected in enforcement of the law. Some religious minorities have reported that local officials and the Federal Registration Service have impeded them from local registration and acquisition of property and harassed them, including Scientologists, followers of Said Nursi and Jehovah's Witnesses. These three minorities have also had their religious literature denounced as extremist by the courts in the region.

Although the Constitution guarantees freedom of expression, the government continues to exert pressure on the media in contravention of these rights. Large private corporations affiliated to the government control or influence the major media outlets, especially television, either through self-censorship by journalists and editors, or directly. This restricts access to information on issues regarded as sensitive, including coverage of political opposition movements and parties. Some murders of journalists have gone unsolved, including that of highly regarded investigative journalist Anna Politkovskaya in October 2006. This has attracted international concern and increased the disinclination of journalists to cover subjects that are controversial. In another unsolved mystery, environmental journalist Mikhail Beketov was beaten to near death in November 2008 following his publication of an article critical of local authorities' plans to develop the Khimki forest. In 2010, President Medvedev had to intervene after *Kommersant* reporter Oleg Kashin was beaten up. Subsequently, more than 200 journalists signed a formal request to the president for protection.

The law on NGOs enacted in 2006 imposed registration procedures that were burdensome for every NGO, with firmer requirements for NGOs that were reliant on foreign donors and more flexible ones for religious organizations. Since January 2007, the Russian authorities have also used laws against radicalism to shut down media organizations and NGOs opposed to the government. The State Duma has since approved a law relaxing the registration requirements for NGOs, though it has faced criticism that this is largely symbolic as it has not reinstated tax exemption for foreign donors.

The Constitution grants citizens the right to freedom of choice of residence and overseas travel. However, some large city governments have limited these rights though local statutes that are almost as restrictive as those of the Soviet era. Nevertheless, these measures are widely flouted, as evidenced by the number of undocumented alien employees in these cities. Opportunities for emigration and overseas travel may be restricted for persons who have had access to state secrets or those who have been served with court orders for default of debts. Nevertheless, according to the US, Russia complied fully with the conditions of the Jackson-Vanik Amendment, a legal provision (repealed in December 2012) which restricted US trade with countries that imposed barriers to emigration and committed human rights violations.

Military Power

The Russian government has expressed a bold aspiration to professionalize its army, though progress has been slow to date. Attempts by Russia to convert the military legacy of the USSR into a more streamlined and agile force have been hindered by an ossified military leadership, demographics, limited funds, corruption, violations of human rights and problems with discipline. Russia's clash with Georgia in August 2008 focused attention on the need to modernize its armed forces, which the leadership of the General Staff estimated at 850,000 personnel.

Russian Defence Minister Serdyukov announced implementation of a 'New Look' reconstruction of the Russian military, including a reduction of the officer corps by more than 60 per cent, the development of a combined operational command structure, a reduction in the number of operational and support units, institution of a new NCO corps, improvements in housing and pay, and enhanced education and training. At the same time, the Kremlin announced a wide-ranging modernization and rearmament scheme under the State Armament Plan, with Putin committing spending of US$670 billion up to 2020 – a threefold increase in military expenditure. It is highly questionable whether Russia has the capacity to fund such a programme, especially since it is competing with other national priorities.

At the beginning of 2008, the tour of duty for conscripts was reduced to one year (previously it had been 18 months), in an attempt to make military service more attractive, and there were increases in pay and benefits to encourage professionalization while reducing the officer corps. At present, Russia is seeking to diversify its military so that 70 per cent of its personnel will be professional soldiers, including elite units, and the remaining 30 per cent will be conscripts. Russia's attempts to develop an NCO corps are being hampered by problems attracting candidates and a lack of resources to support it. Russia's military expenditure continues to rise, the government recently announcing that it would be spending more than $650 billion on hardware improvements despite the severe lack of investment in its civilian infrastructure.

Russian military personnel are known to be poorly paid. The government has apparently promised increases of up to three times the current wages, though this has not been confirmed. In theory, the military should provide everything its personnel might require, although food and housing shortages are constant and widespread. There are also problems that encourage draft evasion and do nothing to improve the military's image, such as brutal 'hazing' and disciplinary issues, as well as problems with petty crime, low standards of education and a high prevalence of communicable diseases. For instance, the Russian Army's HIV infection rate is estimated to be two to five times higher than that of the general population, and tuberculosis is a persistent problem.

The Kremlin remains resistant to transforming the Russian military into a force with the capacity to deal with the challenges of modern warfare and current threats. Russia's worldwide ambitions require the ability to project power through highly skilled expeditionary forces with modern equipment that can be dispatched at short notice to any region in the world, while prolonged conflict in the North Caucasus calls for a military with the ability to engage in asymmetric warfare. The current schemes for military reform are unlikely to be able to meet these disparate demands.

Continued resistance to change among the military elite and the mismatch between Russia's security concerns and its armed forces' capabilities and structure will continue to hinder any ambitions it may have to become a superpower, unless there is a change of leadership.

Arms and Equipment

Most of Russia's military equipment and weaponry are out of date, and investment in the acquisition of new hardware is not keeping pace with the rate of obsolescence. Advanced military hardware accounts for only 10–20 per cent of its complement: for instance, of the army's 23,000 tanks, only 15 are relatively recent acquisitions. Similar problems afflict its naval, air and ground forces.

This lack of investment in conventional armaments is caused by a number of factors. The first concerns Russia's inefficient military-industrial complex, which places a huge burden on the military budget because employment considerations hamper restructuring. The sheer size of the armed forces is a second explanation. Sustaining even a recently reduced force of over one million personnel is only possible with ample funding, not just for bottom-level pay schemes, but also for to support active operations. Last but not least, the lion's share of tangible investment is not being directed to conventional forces, but rather to nuclear ones.

Russia's current political leaders are faced with a choice between reforming its military into a modern expeditionary, high-tech, professional conventional force – the trend in other Western armed forces – or carrying on with its huge but outmoded conventional forces in tandem with its advanced nuclear strategic deterrent forces to maintain relevance in the global scene.

Personnel

Social conditions in the armed forces remain so dire that Sergei Ivanov (currently Putin's Chief of Staff after having held various administrative posts) has conceded that the low levels of pensions and salaries have led to severe problems and have contributed to the increasing suicide rate among the military. Moreover, there is a constant problem with conscripts deserting, partly as a result of widespread hazing of new recruits (a practice that has a long history, but has gone grown in severity in recent times), insufficient qualified officers, low motivation levels and inadequate training, which all contribute to a general lack of preparedness for combat.

Any moves to modernize the military to develop high-tech conventional expeditionary military forces would demand a transformation from the traditional largely conscript force to a much smaller professional one. The reduction in the mandatory term of service for conscripts from 18 months to 12 months on 1 January 2008 is a noteworthy step which may have sought to reduce the incidence of hazing, but the severe lack of qualified recruits means that Ivanov's ambition that the Russian military will be made up of 70 per cent professional personnel is unlikely to be achieved.

Ivanov has admitted in previous statements that the overall size of the complement – currently approximately one million personnel – will not be subject to radical cuts. Conscripts are very poorly paid (currently US$3 a month, roughly equivalent to 100 rubles, depending on the exchange rate), so employing a large number of professional soldiers would drain most of the military budget. Because the army is dogged by negative stereotypes resulting from its poor rates of pay, the conflicts in the Caucasus and hazing, not to mention a general population that is rapidly diminishing, there is a high probability that Ivanov will not succeed in his endeavours to increase the proportion of professional personnel. The overall impression of the current human resource plans is that – as with the plans for arms investment – the Kremlin is not in a position to achieve authentic reform of the armed forces to prepare them for modern warfare and current threats.

Ground Forces

In accordance with Russia's traditional doctrine on large-scale land combat, its ground forces still possess the largest arsenal in the world. For example, it has the 23,860 battle tanks, more than all the NATO states combined. However, approximately 80 per cent of these tanks (the T-72, T-64 and T-55 models) can be considered obsolete as they were built in the 1960s and 1970s, and the remainder consist of the T-80 series, dating from the late 1970s, and the T-90 series, in production since 1993, but numbering only 250–300.[7] Russia would have to purchase 1,000 tanks a year to achieve its goal of modernizing the existing arsenal to 70 per cent of the reserve by 2020, but there are minimal chances of achieving this goal as only 149 T-90s were purchased during 2004–2008.[8] Structural

---

    7   International Institute for Strategic Studies, 'Russian Armored Personnel Carriers', *Military Balance 2009: Annual Assessment of Global Military Capabilities and Defense Economics* (2009), p. 218.

    8   Mikhail Barabanov, 'Russian Tank Production Sets a New Record', *Moscow Defence Brief* 16 (2009): http://mdb.cast.ru/mdb/2-2009/item4/article1/ (accessed 22 January 2012), pp. 10–11.

modernization can only be attained through considerable reductions in the number of tanks in the arsenal, and this appears to be the current course being followed. Reports in the Russian press suggest that over the next ten years the army intends to cut the number of battle tanks by approximately 75 per cent to approximately 6,000 tanks, of which only 2,000 will be ready for deployment at any one time.[9] In order for Russia to realize its 2020 vision of 70 per cent of its projected 2,000 tanks consisting of rebuilt or new models, existing rates of production will need to be increased.

Although there is still a substantial need for modernization in other armament categories, the state of affairs is to some extent better. As a consequence, for example with reference to medium-range air defence systems, the ground forces have the Buk (SA-11) and Tor (SA-15) systems, which are deemed fit for purpose. Russia also possesses the most advanced air defence missile system in the world, the long-range S-400 Triumf (SA-21), far superior to the US Patriot missiles.[10] However, unquestionable modernization accomplishments such as these cannot obscure the reality that the re-equipping of ground forces with new systems is lagging behind. A perfect illustration of this is the fact that only two military regiments have been supplied with S-400 missiles.[11]

Air Force

Most of Russia's military aircraft are out of date as well as poorly serviced. One of the classic examples of this is the MiG-29, where corrosion was cited as the reason for the crashing of two of these aircraft in October and December 2008. As a result, all Russia's MiG-29s were checked for airworthiness, and 70 per cent were declared non-operational. The fact that this included relatively new aircraft with fewer than 150 flight hours indicates design faults or bad servicing regimes.[12]

The Russian Air Force has been undertaking a modernization programme from the beginning of the twenty-first century, re-equipping its existing aircraft of all types with higher-precision weapons and modern avionics, but also developing new aircraft. This is bound to enhance the air force's ability to conduct special operations against terrorists or in inter-state clashes close to the Russian borders.

---

9 Ilya Kramnik, 'Tank Force Reductions or Statistical Juggling', RIA Novosti (July 2009): http://en.rian.ru/analysis/20090703/155424380-print.html (accessed 22 January 2012), pp. 10–12.

10 Sergey Ivanov, 'The Armaments Order is Reliably Protected from the Crisis', *Rossijkaja Gazeta*, 26 February 2009.

11 'The State Armament Program for the Period 2007–2015 Envisages the Equipment of 18 Regiments with the New S-400 Systems: Second S-400 Air Defense Regiment Put into Service in Russia', RIA Novosti (March 2009): http://en.rian.ru/russia/20090317/120604177.html (accessed 22 January 2012), pp. 2–4.

12 'Russian Fighter Jets Become Obsolete', *Kommersant*, 16 March 2009.

Similar to the ground forces, progress on modernizing the air force has been slow. For example, the air force has only very limited numbers of the Su-34 fighter aircraft, and it is very doubtful whether the T-50, MiG-35 and the Su-35 will be built.[13] In addition, by the beginning of 2009, only 6 per cent of the air force's 1,743 combat aircraft had been significantly re-equipped or were new. The remaining vast majority of the aircraft thus cannot be operated in bad weather conditions or at night, or are incapable of deploying precision weapons. Russia will have to modernize or purchase 95 aircraft per year if it is to achieve its goal of re-equipping 70 per cent of its air force by 2020, but only 116 acquisitions of new aircraft are provided for in the 2007–15 armaments programme. At this rate, it would take well over seventy years to achieve the target. In the medium term, insufficient modernization plus a reduction in the size of the air force are likely. The same applies to the air force's fleet of helicopters: so far, only a small number of the new helicopter models (the Mi-28N and Ka-52) have been produced.

The Navy

The Russian Navy was worst affected by the decay of the country's conventional armed forces during the 1990s. The Russian Navy consists of four fleets: the Caspian Flotilla, the Northern and the Black Sea Fleet, the Baltic Fleet and the Pacific Fleet. The Pacific and the Northern Fleets have the most advanced vessels, including submarines equipped with tactical nuclear weapons. Unlike the air force and ground forces, the navy was barely involved in the post-Soviet-era conflicts in regions beyond Russia's borders, and not at all in the wars in Chechnya.

The navy fared so badly because it is very cost-intensive compared to the other armed forces. Russia largely stopped building naval ships in the 1990s, but the political leadership has reversed this course from the beginning of the twenty-first century, reflecting its wishes to further its ambitions to be seen as a great power through a much more noticeable presence on the high seas, safeguarding the economic and security interests of a state bordered by the Black and Caspian Seas in addition to a two oceans, and propping up its claims on energy resources in the Arctic.

This naval resurgence is evidenced by increased budget allocations, efforts to rejuvenate the Russian ship-building industry, and the number of modernization programmes. Ship renovation projects and others begun in the 1990s have almost come to fruition, and there are plans to build new ones. However, these measures are insufficient to counteract the reductions in the fleets. Many ships will inevitably be decommissioned as obsolete in the coming years, and one Russian military expert claimed that only 15 of Russia's 61 surface ships are currently operational, mainly due to lack of servicing.[14] It is also likely that this contraction will continue

---

13   Reuben Johnson, 'Sukhoi's T-50 PAK-FA Fighter Enters First Stage of Assembly', *Jane's Defence Weekly*, 14 January 2009, p. 7.

14   'Press Conference with Presidential Economic Adviser Andrei Illarionov'.

to worsen, as ship-building in Russia is an extremely slow procedure. A good example of this is the Yasen Class of submarines, whose construction began in 1993, and whose first of class is still being fitted out. It is therefore highly unlikely that Russia will be able to build the 14 new ships set out in the 2009–11 reforms, and the navy is likely to continue to atrophy.

The New Face of the Armed Forces

The Russian Army can be said to have undergone a transition from a mass-mobilization army to combat-ready forces. The military potential of a state depends on its equipment, but other factors that also have to take into account include the leadership qualities of its officers, the education level and training of its soldiers, as well as its organizational structure. Under modern operational concepts, well-led and well-trained personnel are essential to be able to deal with the modern, high-tech systems that enable effective action and rapid reaction to events.

The war in Georgia highlighted the flaws in the Russian conventional forces and provided new momentum for reform efforts, leading to re-scrutiny of previous proposals. If put into practice, the reforms will spearhead the achievement of the 'New Look' for the military that the president guaranteed in March 2009, bringing to an end the old Soviet model of a mass-mobilization military prepared for large-scale combat on land. The resulting army is likely to be more professional, more flexible and more mobile, with the capacity to react more effectively to regional and conflicts, as well as asymmetrical ones.

Changes in organizational structure and force deployment concepts At the moment, Russian military reform endeavours are founded on the understanding that future military threats are likely to arise, grow and end rapidly.[15] For this reason, the main aim of the military reorganization is to secure the operational preparedness of the Russian armed forces.

To meet this objective, it is essential to alter the organizational structure and power concepts concerning the deployment of the military, both of which stem from the Soviet era. As described above, Russia's military is subdivided into three armed forces. It is also divided into three branches which are directly subsidiary to the General Staff: the airborne forces, the space forces and the strategic forces. This structure is likely to remain unaltered, but not so the armed forces commands. In the future, there will be only three levels of organization – military district, operational command and brigade – compared to the previous system of military districts, armies, divisions and regiments. These anticipated changes reflect the abandonment of traditional force deployment concepts. The burdensome divisions were well suited to large-scale operations along a front line extending many

---

15 'The Russian Army Revealed Itself Not to be Ready for the Wars of the Future', *Izvestiia*, 16 December 2008.

kilometres, such as in inter-state conflict, but the smaller brigades will allow more rapid deployment and reaction in asymmetric, regional and local conflicts.

The Ministry of Defence's turn away from traditional force deployment concepts is also reflected in the reduced reliance on reserve forces. Currently, the Russian Army is able to draw on over 20 million reservists, but in future, especially during combat, its complement will consist of at most 1.7 million personnel, as announced by then Chief of General Staff Makarov in December 2008. The military reforms will see the number of personnel reduce from the current 1.13 million to 1 million by 2016, while the reserve forces will be reduced to 700,000 personnel, only 3.5 per cent of the current complement.

To compensate for the diminished potential for mass mobilization, President Medvenev declared that all military formations and units should achieve permanent operational readiness. The conflict in Georgia also proved that there was a pressing need for this reform. Makarov also made the public aware that during the Caucasus deployment, only 17 per cent of the total units were able to carry out their duties.[16] However, this was a marked improvement in comparison to the combat in Chechnya in 1999, where only 5 per cent of the military were operational. During his annual Federal Assembly address in May 2006, Putin complained that at the beginning of the second war in Chechnya in August 1999, only 55,000 of the required 65,000 personnel had been available.[17] It was also known that 83 per cent of units are currently in substandard states of readiness with regard to equipment and personnel. These 'paper' forces were remnants of the mass-mobilization forces, and have been disbanded in favour of fully equipped and staffed units. The Ministry of Defence also plans to deploy airborne brigades in all military districts to enable rapid response to emerging threats.[18]

Improvements in training   The training and skills of personnel are vital to the operational readiness of the military, and to address this, the approaches of the 1990s have been abandoned. In May 2006, President Putin pointed out that the armed forces were only carrying out paper exercises, naval craft were not leaving the dockyards, and the air force seldom undertook any flights. The proposed restructuring aimed to improve the Russian military's ability to respond effectively to local conflicts such as that in Georgia, to suppress insurrection and to conduct anti-terrorist operations. It also sought to maintain a balance of forces with the other NATO states.

---

16   'Top Russian General Reaffirms Key Role of Ground Troops in Year-end Interview', BBC Monitoring Global Newsline – Former Soviet Union Political File, 1 January 2009.

17   Vladimir Putin, 'Address to the Federal Assembly of the Russian Federation', Official website of the Kremlin (May 2006): http://www.kremlin.ru/appears/2006/05/10/1357_type63372type63374type82634_105546.shtml (accessed 22 January 2012), pp. 1–3.

18   'Russian CGS Meets Military Attaches, Discusses Army Reform, Other Issues', BBC Monitoring Global Newsline – Former Soviet Union Political File, 12 December 2008.

Since that time, the number of military exercises and manoeuvres have continued to increase. The autumn of 2008 saw the largest military manoeuvres since the dissolution of the Soviet Union, Stability 2008, involving 8,500 personnel over 11 time zones for approximately one month.[19] In this combined Russian-Belarusian operation, out of the 79 Russian bombers, only 20 were seeing action for the first time since 1984, launching cruise missiles. In February of that year, a Russian naval unit had staged the longest exercise since the end of the Cold War; in July, manoeuvres involving 8,000 Russian personnel took place in the Caucasus, and in September, 6,000 Russian personnel participated in the combined Russian-Kazakh exercise Center 2008. In addition, Russian naval vessels were deployed to the Caribbean, Latin America and Asia for port visits, also engaging in counter-piracy operations off the Horn of Africa.[20]

While the complexity, duration and scale of manoeuvres may have grown, the overall state of personnel training is still very much in need of improvement. For example, transport plane pilots have only 60 flight training hours per year, helicopter pilots 55 hours and tactical air force pilots 20–25 hours, compared to the average of 189 hours per year for US fighter pilots. The penalties for this lack of training among the tactical air force were noticeable during the Georgian conflict. Makarov, Chief of Staff at the time, stated that it was possible to count on one's fingers the number of pilots who were able to complete combat missions under the most straightforward circumstances.[21] The navy is also still suffering from deficiencies. Essential training missions cannot be undertaken because many ships are so poorly serviced.

To sum up, while current attempts to address the shortcomings of Russia's armed forces may reassure the public, they should not mask concerns about their current weaknesses and state of readiness.

Efforts to create a professional armed forces   Russia's efforts to develop a military in a state of permanent readiness depend on the deployment of high-tech weapons and limiting the reliance on reserve forces, since mass mobilization is of less military importance nowadays. As a result, there is a greater need for professional soldiers who have undergone proper training. The current military reforms fall short of providing real solutions to questions that have been hotly debated since the 1990s about whether conscription should be abandoned. The three main reasons for retaining conscription seem to involve Russia's large geographic extent, recruitment problems and military leaders' resistance to its abolition, despite recent reductions in the length of mandatory military service for conscripts.

---

19   Putin, 'Address to the Federal Assembly of the Russian Federation'.

20   Ilya Kramnik, 'Restoring the Tradition: Russian Navy on Long-distance Tours of Duty', RIA Novosti (December 2008): 1-2. http://en.rian.ru/analysis/20081215/118867561.html (accessed 22 January 2012).

21   Mikhail Zubov, 'The Officers are Being Retrained for Duty in Administration', *Moskovskii Komsomolets*, 18 December 2008, p. 10.

Nevertheless, the professionalization of the Russian military begun under Putin has continued. There have been efforts since 2002 to staff selected units entirely with personnel under contract, in particular those units that are essential to rapid deployment or are stationed in conflict-ridden areas, including the 201st Motorized Rifle Division in Tadzhikistan, the 42nd Motorized Rifle Division in the Northern Caucasus and the 76th Airborne Division in Pskov. Future plans include the formation of such elite units in the southern regions of Russia, where it shares borders with countries that are prone to conflict.[22] However, recruitment problems are hampering these attempts at professionalization. There have been suggestions in the Russian press that as an alternative to under-equipped and under-staffed 'paper' units, reservists should only be called up when required.

The Georgian conflict also exposed the fact that officers were unable to lead their troops. Makarov deplored the fact that the ability to lead troops was not an essential requirement for progressing to the rank of general, colonel or lieutenant-colonel. As the five-day war unfolded, it became increasingly obvious that staff officers who spent most of their time dealing with paper divisions in offices were unprepared to cope with the issues that arose during actual conflict.

Russia is burdened with a swollen officer corps, but lacks a professional NCO corps, historically being notorious for under-using NCOs as a human resource in the army.[23] Soldiers in Russia generally receive inadequate training. Apart from personnel who work under contract, recruits usually just go through a crash course lasting three to four months.

The lack of non-commissioned officers and professionalism plus the imbalance in its officer corps may explain why the discipline in the armed forces is extremely poor. Another factor that cannot be overlooked is *dedovshchina* (literally, 'grandfather's rules), the systematic hazing, humiliation, abuse and exploitation of new recruits by superiors and other personnel. It is widely believed that the numerous cases of suicide in the army stem directly from this system. A report from the Ministry of Defence in 2008 stated that 23 soldiers had died as a result of manslaughter or murder, while 215 had committed suicide. Other independent organizations, such as the Committee of Soldiers' Mothers, have come up with higher estimates, and claim that victimization is among the major reasons for 50,000 soldiers per year going absent without leave. *Dedovschina* obviously does nothing to promote operational readiness of the armed forces while worsening the recruitment difficulties. Disciplinary problems also manifest themselves in high crime rates among both conscripts and volunteers. In 2008, military service personnel were convicted of 15,390 crimes, according to official data, corruption accounting for the largest proportion. During 2007–2008, the crime rate increased

---

22   'Russia CGS Says No Plans to Give Up Conscripts', BBC Monitoring Global Newsline, Former Soviet Union Political File, 17 December 2008.

23   Zoltan Barany, 'Resurgent Russia? A Still-faltering Military', *Policy Review* 43147 (2008), pp. 4–6.

by a third and the monetary loss amounted to 2.2 billion rubles, equivalent to the cost of 30 T-90 battle tanks.[24]

A number of factors, including the Georgian conflict, have led to serious efforts to reform the upper and middle echelons of the military leadership. The initial efforts include a drastic reduction in the number of officers. The plans to shrink the military's complement from 1.13 million to 1 million soldiers by 2016 include the abolition of 195,000 officers' posts, 55 per cent of the current total. This process will have wide-ranging effects, altering the staffing profile from 'an egg, swollen in the middle, to a pyramid'.[25]

Another initiative involves the creation of a professional corps of non-commissioned officers by putting staff sergeants and sergeants through 34 months of training, with a special emphasis on the management of high-tech weapons.[26] This can almost be described as a revolutionary measure, since it calls for the abandonment of military institutional traditions, and it will inevitably extend to the curricula for training and instruction. Nevertheless, so far, there has been scant interest in the novel career alternatives opening up in the Russian armed forces. The first course for sergeants had to be postponed from February to autumn 2009 because it had proven impossible to find enough applicants who had met the requirements.[27]

Whether the goal of creating a volunteer professional military supplemented by conscripts serving for a year, transforming the institutional traditions and improving the armed forces' public image can be achieved will be heavily reliant on the provision of sufficient funding.

Capabilities for Power Projection with Conventional Forces: Russia as a Regional Power

As mentioned in the previous sections, Russia's military reforms aim to transform the burdensome mass-mobilization army that was a legacy of the USSR into a modern armed forces. If the initiatives succeed, Russia will be in a better position to deploy its military effectively and rapidly beyond its own territory, but its abilities to project its conventional military power worldwide are unlikely to improve. This

---

24   'Military Corruption Costs Russia Almost $80 Million in 2008', RIA Novosti (December 2008): http://en.rian.ru/russia/20081202/118637765.html. (accessed 22 January 2012), pp. 5–8.

25   Pavel Felgenhauer, 'A Radical Military Reform Plan', *Eurasia Daily Monitor* 198: 5 (2008), p. 13.

26   Nikita Petrov, 'Russia to Start Training Professional Sergeants Soon', RIA Novosti (20 January 2009): http://en.rian.ru/analysis/20090130/119894538.html (accessed 22 January 2012), pp. 1–2.

27   Deniz Tel'Manov, 'Participants in Non-Commissioned Officers' Training Courses are No Comrades' GZT.RU (March 2009): http://gzt.ru/politics/2009/03/25/223011.html (accessed 22 January 2012), pp. 1–4.

may be illustrated by examining the crucial aspects of power projection: the range of weaponry systems, coherent capabilities and the existence of military bases abroad.

With reference to the first two factors, the Russian armed forces have access to conventional; weapons with a broad variety of ranges. Like the US, Russia is re-equipping a number of its tactical and mid-range bombers with conventional precision weapons, such as Kh-555 cruise missiles (with a range of 3,500 km) and the Kh-101 (range 5,500 km), and the air force received the first Tu-160 strategic aircraft installed with the Kh-555 in the summer of 2006. The Kh-101 is currently undergoing trials.[28] The Russian Air Force also possesses 293 transport aircraft, used to carry personnel, weapons and equipment, but the fleet is ageing and plagued by operational problems.

Russia lacks the logistical capabilities to engage in military operations distant from its territory, and this is particularly so in terms of the navy, whose only aircraft carrier, the *Admiral Kuznetsov*, is in a parlous state. An aircraft carrier task force is made up of a combat unit consisting of a number of escort vessels, plus an aircraft carrier. A rule of thumb states that projecting power on a worldwide scale requires at least three aircraft carrier groups, assuming that one aircraft carrier will be undergoing servicing, another will be on a training mission and the third will be carrying out operational duties.

In terms of military bases abroad, Russia currently has none beyond the area of the former USSR. Following end of the Cold War, its bases in Africa, the Caribbean, Latin America and Asia were all closed, and after 11 September 2001, its last bases, at Cam Ranh in Vietnam and Lourdes in Cuba, followed suit.

It is therefore obvious that Russia has few capabilities for the projection of power globally. This has driven it to attempt to portray itself as a militarily powerful nation through such measures as deploying strategic bombers on flights over the Pacific and Atlantic regions and naval units to the Indian Ocean and Caribbean. In addition, a range of non-official and official spokesmen occasionally hypothesize about grandiose projects, such as building a number of new aircraft carriers and setting up military bases in Cuba and other far distant places, none of which do anything to further Russia's prospects of becoming a great power.

However, within the territory of the Commonwealth of Independent States, Russia does have the potential for effective power projection. It has more than twice as many soldiers as the nations that make up the former USSR combined, its closest rival being Ukraine, whose armed forces are a tenth of the size. In terms of weaponry, both qualitatively and quantitatively, Russia is also far ahead of its neighbours. For this reason, Russia's deficits and other problems have had less impact on its military supremacy in this region, and it has gradually built up its military presence since 1993, when it opened its first military base abroad after the collapse of the Soviet Union. Following the conflict in Georgia, Russia greatly increased its number of troops in the Caucasus. South Ossetia and Abkhazia also

---

28 'Russian Air Force to Develop "General-purpose Forces" Commander', BBC Monitoring Global Newsline, Former Soviet Union Political File, 11 February 2009.

signed treaties with Russia that allow it to deploy about 7,600 soldiers – equal to one-third of Georgia's army.

The CIS provides a vital buffer for Russia, and it may try to promote its political agenda through greater dependence on military resources. Russia has regarded the CIS as its primary field of influence, in which it desires to maintain dominance. On 31 August 2008 Medvedev re-emphasized that point when he termed the post-Soviet geographical area a zone of 'privileged [Russian] interests' and proclaimed the protective power of Russia in the region.[29] Given the wide range of political, economic, territorial and ethnic tensions that persist both within and among states in this region, Europe should focus on reviving and promoting conventional arms control accords.

Russia's Nuclear Capabilities: 'Great Power' Attribute and Instrument of Deterrence

Nuclear weapons serve a dual function for Russia. First and foremost, they provide a link to the USSR's former status as a superpower and justify the nation's permanent seat on the UN Security Council, the final remaining legacy of superpower status. In this forum, Russia is accorded equal status to the US, setting it apart from other states that are seeking a much larger role in world affairs, such as China. Russia has the largest nuclear arsenal in the world, with 114,000 nuclear warheads, and in 2009 it was estimated that of that total, 2,787 strategic and 2,050 tactical nuclear warheads were operational.[30]

In addition to their symbolic value, since the mid-1990s the role of nuclear weapons in Russia's national security has increased because of the decline of its conventional armed forces. The USSR's conventional forces were two or three times larger than those of the NATO. In the years following 1991, that ratio was reversed.

Participation in Global Security Issues

Russia has engaged in a number of activities designed to promote global security, mainly involving collaboration with other countries. Russia's major partners in working to curb threats to global security are the US and China.

Since 1992, Russia has been involved in the Nunn-Lugar Cooperative Threat Reduction (CTR) programme under the auspices of the US Defense Threat Reduction Agency. One aspect of this is the US Department of Energy's Initiatives for Proliferation Prevention (IPP), which co-ordinates activities by bodies such as

---

29   Dimitri Medvedev, 'Russia, First Channel, and NTV TV Channels Interview', official website of the Kremlin, 31 August 2008: http://www.kremlin.ru/appears/2008/08/31/1917_type63374type63379_205991.shtml (accessed 22 January 2012).

30   Robert S. Norris and Hans M. Kristensen. 'Nuclear Notebook: Russian Nuclear Forces 2009)', *Bulletin of the Atomic Scientists*, 65:3 (2009), pp. 55–64.

the non-profitmaking International Science and Technology Center (ISTC) and its sister organization in the Ukraine to help scientists who formerly worked on weapons of mass destruction to find alternative employment through collaboration with Western partners.

The Nuclear Cities Initiative, set up in 1998, focused on providing assistance to the communities and nuclear scientists in Russia's former closed cities to avoid their expertise being channelled to proliferation. The programme met with some success, but was criticized for its allocation, implementation and management of funds, which led to its being merged with the IPP in 2002.

Another initiative is the Materials Protection, Control and Accounting (MPC&A) programme, which seeks to address nuclear proliferation issues by instituting security systems in the hundreds of Russian facilities that house weaponry and nuclear materials. A study by the US General Accounting Office indicated that Russia had been generally co-operative, though it had been slow to provide sensitive information and access to some of its facilities.

The plutonium disposition programme aims to dispose of surplus US and Russian weapons-grade plutonium by converting it into spent nuclear reactor fuel that cannot easily be used in nuclear weapons. Many critics have questioned the size and cost of this endeavour, and it is feared that these efforts may take a very long time to complete and verify.

The CTR programme is a complex effort. Its main objective is to assist in the elimination of surplus offensive weaponry in the former Soviet Union, including strategic bombers and sea-launched ballistic missile (SLBM) platforms, SLBMs themselves, and inter-continental ballistic missile (ICBM) silos and their missiles. The programme has contributed to the non-nuclear weapon states of Kazakhstan, Belarus and Ukraine, while efforts are being stepped up to bring in Russia on board to supplement existing arms reduction agreements. The programme has also collaborated with other bodies to find alternative employment for the biological weapons scientists through links with Western commercial partners.

A number threat reduction initiatives over the past decade have been successful, including the withdrawal of nuclear weapons from the non-Russian states of the former USSR, assisting Russia to accelerate strategic arms reductions, controlling and securing nuclear warheads and nuclear materials, and the establishment of the Mayak fissile materials storage facility to securely house a significant proportion of the plutonium from decommissioned nuclear weapons. The rest of this section will provide further details of the role played by Russia in improving global security.

Withdrawal of Nuclear Weapons from Non-Russian States of the Former USSR

After the disintegration of the USSR, there were concerns that Kazakhstan, Belarus and Ukraine would retain the approximately 3,000 nuclear armaments they had inherited, giving birth to three new nuclear weapon states. Fortunately, through the CTR programme, Russia and the US succeeded in convincing these countries to surrender the nuclear arms to Russia. The US assistance to Russia included the provision of emergency support equipment, security enhancements for railway wagons, secure containers and whatever else was requested, and ensured that the materials were safely consolidated in storage facilities on Russian territory.

Russia and the US in Accelerating Strategic Arms Reductions

The CTR programme has helped Russia to dispose of its surplus strategic arms, including 21 ballistic missile submarines, 260 SLBM launchers and 174 SLBMs, 366 ICBM silos, 419 ICBMs and 5,288 warheads.

Hastening Strategic Arms Reductions

The USSR had a highly effective security system to safeguard its nuclear weapons and nuclear materials. The Russian Ministry of Defence in collaboration with the US Department of Defense has increased security at sites belonging to the 12th Main Department of the Ministry of Defence, upgrading approximately half of its 123 nuclear storage buildings and facilities. A Security Assessment and Training Centre has been established outside Moscow at a location named Sergiev Posad to appraise new physical security technology and equipment and to train personnel in warhead security.

The Mayak Fissile Material Storage Facility

One of the main problems with dismantling nuclear warheads is providing adequate storage for the highly enriched uranium and plutonium recovered from the weapons. To address this issue, the US helped the Russian Ministry of Atomic Power (Minatom) to build a new high-security facility in the Mayak region. The first section of the facility is expected to enter operation in 2013, providing safe storage for nearly 8,000 warheads.

Arms Transfers

The Russian military-industrial complex has suffered badly since the dissolution of the USSR through the reduction in internal orders for armaments. To address this, Russia has engaged in the sale of weaponry to Iran, India and China, its three primary customers, as well as a number of other smaller states. Unlike the USSR, Russia prefers cash rather than strategic advantage or political influence in exchange for its weapons.

Nevertheless, Russia introduced arms export controls in the early 1990s to block the transfer of certain categories of armaments to specific countries, and it has signed up to a number of international agreements, including the Chemical Weapons Convention, the Wassenaar Agreement on Export Controls for Conventional Arms and Dual-Use Goods and Technologies, and the UN Weapons Register. In the aggressive international arms market, Russian defence industrialists tend to see the US as a ruthless and powerful competitor to their efforts to focus on sales to Western companies and other governments. One example of this is Minatom's attitude to US opposition to Russian nuclear contracts with Iran. This leads to inevitable global security tensions, but these are tempered by the co-operative initiatives described above.

Retrenchment and Reintegration in Asia

Russia's security interests in Asia are related to the large proportion of its territory in Siberia (particularly landlocked eastern Siberia) and the Russian Far East, between Lake Baikal and the Pacific coast, and its borders with the US (in the Bering Strait), Japan, Korea and China. Unless Russia follows a regional development model geared to the new market environment, both within its borders and in the face of globalization, its Asian territories are likely to suffer from depopulation, de-industrialization and general dilapidation. The fear among the general population and the leadership is that if Russia cannot prove conclusively that it has the ability to develop and sustain this region that has ample natural resources, another country is bound to do so – most likely China.

To address this situation, Russia cannot rely solely on traditional security arrangements. Any Chinese influx is more likely to take the form of peaceful workers and settlers rather than a military invasion. China is growing increasingly interested in Russia's energy resources in Russia, but this is manifested through business contracts rather than any attempts at occupation.

Some of the Major Strengths and Weaknesses of Russia

Positive Attributes

Russia possesses a large number of nuclear weapons, and more importantly, the capacity to deploy them to any region in the world. Although this is usually seen as a tactical advantage, critics feel that the more powerful a weapon is, the less likely it is to be used, considering the fact that the Cold War ended without any of the missiles being launched. This remains a controversial issue.

Secondly, Russia has more unexploited wealth in terms of untapped mineral resources than almost any other country. This factor will gives Russia the advantage of rapidly boosting its economy once it develops a strategy to ensure efficient management of the resources.

Thirdly, currently Russia currently receives a lot of revenue from oil. However, there are fears that this revenue stream will be directed mainly to upgrading its under-funded armed forces rather than investing in its economy.

Analysts and the general public generally feel that Russia's growth rate, currently stagnant and not projected to improve much in the near term, makes it highly unlikely that it will become a superpower in the foreseeable future.

However, it is difficult to predict the future of Russia's petrochemical revenues since energy conservation has become a global issue. The price of crude oil is increasing rapidly by the day as a consequence to diminishing oil resources, and there is no telling how much a litre of crude oil could cost in the near future. Russians comment light-heartedly that when oil was at US$15 a barrel, Russia was an appendage to the world economy, but when it is US$70 a barrel, it is an imperial nation.[31]

Modern-day Russia is more likely to develop superpower status as it becomes more integrated into the rest of Europe, which excites some unease in the West and among its neighbours. Nevertheless, although some states have expressed concerns about Russian aggression, they still seek to maintain friendly relations with it.

However, nations such as Canada have questioned whether this attitude is sustainable, since it often condones criminal behaviour. Corruption is rife among Russian businesses. Most of Russia's wealth is controlled by oligarchs whose activities usually serve the state's interests, and in return it turns a blind eye to human rights abuses. A classic example is Boris Berezovsky, a businessman who had to flee the country because he had crossed the oligarchs.

Russia's situation as it transitioned from the former USSR has obvious parallels to that of postwar Germany, which was described as being in no position to negotiate terms. Nevertheless, a number of people (Stalin's term for the USSR's Western apologists was 'useful idiots') lobbied hard to bring an end to Russia's apparent humiliation and campaigned for its independent claim to a new 'near abroad' empire. Kazakhstan and Ukraine were threatened with the withdrawal of aid if exclusive control of the USSR's nuclear arsenal was not transferred to Russia. Although close to 70 per cent of the population of Ukraine were in favour of joining NATO, the Western democracies took Russia's side instead of admitting Ukraine – the largest European state, a fledgling democracy which sought to adapt to the West's economic system – into its fold. This pattern continued: there was lukewarm international concern instead of outrage when Putin threatened Georgia and Ukraine with nuclear obliteration if they joined NATO.

Appeasement of Russia continues as short-term interests obstruct strategic goals and principles. French expertise is contracted to assist Russia's expansion of its maritime fleet. Chancellor Angela Merkel of Germany – originally from East Germany, where Putin was a KGB operative – strives to communicate in Russian at bipartite conferences and constantly accommodates Russia's energy policies. For the time being, Russia's strategic goals are gaining ground. It is increasing its domination over its neighbours, collaborating with Europe on matters of security, seeking to increase its sea power, and is seeking to join the WTO.

Ukraine has a vital role to play in Russia's future. It is the largest state in Europe, with enormous assets in terms of aerospace, agriculture and metallurgy, not forgetting its ready access to the rest of Europe via the Atlantic and the

---

31 Georgi Derluguian, *The Fourth Russian Empire?*, PONARS Policy Memo 114 (2006), p. 5.

Mediterranean via the Black Sea. Its current president, Viktor Yanukovych, is providing Russia with an alternative example of how it could be run, while the West is obsequiously giving in to Russia's demands. From an impressive level of 90 per cent support for independence from the USSR in 1991, Ukraine has gradually grown closer to Russia, which exercised its influence on the 2010 Ukrainian elections by denigrating Ukraine's politics, declaring it 'politically unstable' and complaining of 'Ukraine fatigue' to ensure the outcome was as it desired. Instead of resisting this vigorously, the West capitulated, and Ukraine has gradually been drawn further into Russia's region of influence. Western enterprises and politicians do not merely agree to play by Russia's rules, but serve as lobbyists for Russia's brand of capitalism. This reinforces Russia's self-confidence and supports the belief that the West is always susceptible to being corrupted or blackmailed.

Pro-Russian attitudes are obvious internationally. Despite its lawlessness, it is a member of the G8 and G20, and it is being courted by NATO. According to Christopher Westdal, more Russian adjustments are in the pipeline. He suggests that the world should be wary in its perception of Russia as the boundaries of Europe and Russia are redrawn. He also highlights the fact that the Caucasus is not and has never been European, and the same applies to Ukraine. If history is any guide, the West may yet permit Russia to be triumphant.

Russia and NATO   More than sixty years after its founding, NATO has arrived at a crucial turning point. The fear that gripped the world during the Cold War has since largely faded away, and the shifting global balance is bringing new hazards and challenges. The latest Strategic Concept for a so-called 'modernized alliance' is bound to play a significant role in laying the groundwork for its long-term plans.

To some extent, NATO is dogged by an image problem. It was set up in 1949 with the aim of safeguarding both security and freedom. It has experienced tremendous success, making an outstanding contribution to the establishment of security, peace, prosperity and stability for its member countries. On the other hand, ever since the conclusion of the Cold War, a number of people have wondered why the organization still exists. In a world where constant budget reductions are the norm, taxpayers are inquisitive about how their money is being spent and want to know what NATO can provide that other organizations cannot. It is essential that NATO provides convincing answers to these questions.

The role of NATO's Public Diplomacy Division needs to be expanded. Currently, the division devotes too much attention to specialist matters and very little to public outreach, though NATO's NewsMarket project is a step in the right direction. At this point, it imperative to emphasize that NATO has an important role in civilian life. For instance, the Euro-Atlantic Disaster Response Coordination Centre and Civil Emergency Planning Committee have both provided assistance following numerous natural catastrophes.

During the Cold War, NATO's massive build-up of its armed forces was a reasonable tactic: it served a deterrent role and signalled a readiness to engage in warfare to protect the territory and interests of its member states. However, nowadays military operations are more often than not out-of-area undertakings, and modern threats call for armed forces that are technically advanced and flexible. Interoperability is as significant as considerations of tactical logistics. The NATO Response Force (NRF) was established to address these new demands, though it suffers from a number of problems.

The NRF's complement of 25,000 personnel falls far short of the numbers required, and few of the states that contribute troops meet the requirements for interoperability and technological compatibility. It is essential for member states to break with the tradition of maintaining large standing armed forces which are unsuited to modern combat. NATO members, particularly the European ones, should reduce the size of their armed forces significantly (as has recently happened in Germany), diverting resources to providing the best possible equipment and training. There are also financial issues. In the past, US Defense Secretary Donald Rumsfeld called for joint financing of NATO undertakings and an equitable distribution of costs. However, NRF military procedures are still not funded on this basis, and NATO often fails to meet its financial aid obligations.

There have been moves towards greater collaboration through the NATO-Russian Council, although in the long term, NATO must seriously consider granting Russia membership. However, this is unlikely to happen soon, especially in view of the Georgian conflict and remarks made at the 2010 Munich Security Conference which revived old enmities. There is no doubt that Russia and the NATO member countries hold divergent views on a number of issues. Nevertheless, there are areas where Russia and NATO share strategic priorities and face similar challenges: counter-terrorism, counter-narcotics, the expansion of radical Islamism, the non-proliferation of weapons of mass destruction, among many others. Also, in countries such as Afghanistan, Russia's geo-strategic position and its historical knowledge give it an edge in dealing with developments, President Barack Obama's Global Zero non-proliferation initiative can only come to fruition with Russia's support, Russia's NATO membership would be likely reduce the perceived need for nuclear deterrence, and NATO's eastern development will depend on Russian collaboration. Russia is currently delaying a contract it signed with Iran in 2007 to supply the sophisticated S-300 air defence system, valued at US$800 million, using it as a bargaining chip with the West. This sort of scenario is characteristic of a state being reliant on a superpower for protection and aid. Another classic example occurred in August 2007, when Russia cut its oil supplies to Germany as a bargaining ploy.[32] Finally, in dealing with the emerging potential superpower China, NATO could do with Russia on its side.

Industrialization and population growth To illustrate how factors such as industrialization and population growth can enhance the chances of a country

---

32   Vladimir Socor , 'Shortfalls in Russian Oil Deliveries to Germany', *Eurasia Daily Monitor*, 5 September 2007.

becoming a superpower, we will briefly examine the cases of the UK and Japan before drawing comparisons to Russia.

Industrialization can be described as a process of economic and social transformation in the course of technical improvements and mass production. England was the primary pacesetter of the Industrial Revolution, which began in its North-West and Midlands in the eighteenth century. It extended to North America and Europe during the nineteenth century, and to the remainder of the globe in the twentieth century. In the pre-industrial era, the availability of food was a critical issue. The UK enjoyed the benefits of a massive rise in agricultural productivity by means of mechanization. Food abundance was followed by population growth, which ultimately provided the labour essential for the recently created industries while development was under way. The specialization of skills and the division of labour plus the introduction of assembly lines made it possible to produce a wide range of equipment, some of it devoted to modernizing the armed forces.

Japan provides a prime example of how a superpower may behave towards a less-developed country, imposing its will and showing a lack of respect. At the Kanagawa Conference in 1854, Japan reluctantly signed an 'unequal treaty' with the US to open up the ports of Shimoda and Hakodate to American trade on terms extremely favourable to the Americans. Such punitively one-sided arrangements were a standard feature of Asia's relations with Western countries at the time, and the Japanese government resolved that it was essential to take steps to prevent such humiliation by the West in future. As a result, it abolished the feudal system and initiated military reforms which amounted to industrialization of the state. During the 1870s, the Japanese government vigorously supported industrial and technological developments that eventually transformed Japan into the powerful state it is today.

Russia was dealt a similar blow during the Allied involvement in the Russian Civil War. Allied forces from 14 states entered Russia in 1918 to support the Czechoslovak Legion, secure supplies for the armed forces in Russian ports, and re-institute the Eastern Front. At the conclusion of the First World War, apprehensive of Bolshevism, the Allies got involved in the Russian Civil War, supporting the pro-Tsarist, anti-Bolshevik White forces. It took an all-out rebellion against the Allies to drive them out of Siberia and Northern Russia in 1920. This led the Soviet Union, with its centrally controlled economy, to invest a large proportion of its resources in its infrastructure and industrialization to guarantee that such events would never happen again.

Negative Attributes

There are a number of reasons for concluding that Russia will be unable to attain superpower status in the near future. The first is Russia's history. It is obvious that Russia commanded much more respect during its membership of the USSR, and it has fallen far from the supremacy of that era. In terms of its foreign policies, Russia's conduct can be characterized as rather harsh and self-centred, and both under the imperialist and the communist systems, it treated its populace appallingly. These factors present disadvantages, given that future dominance is likely to rely on combined armed forces.

Past performance is a good indicator of future behaviour. For example, Canada and the US are likely to carry on having a healthy relationship against a background of 200 years of prosperity and peace. The future in the regions surrounding Russia and the rest of the world, however, is likely to bring conflict unless Russia is encouraged and pressurized to change its ways. In the twentieth century, Russia invaded a number of states, including Czechoslovakia, the Baltic states, Poland, Georgia and Hungary. Russia has also interfered in Transnistria and Armenia, as well as Estonia and Kyrgyzstan. The unjustifiable massacre in Chechnya offers a sharp contrast to the approach adopted by Canada, for example, in dealing with Quebec's ambitions for independence. Moreover, through Gazprom's dominance over gas exports from Turkmenistan, Kazakhstan, Uzbekistan, Russia is seeking to compensate for its own shortages while reinforcing Europe's reliance on Russian gas.[33]

Russian aggression should be restrained rather than being rewarded. In April 2011, Russia and the US signed the New START Treaty, aiming to reduce both states' nuclear weaponry. There are fears that this may lead to a situation where the US can no longer provide a counterbalance to Russia, and Russian Foreign Minister Sergei Lavrov has since highlighted that Russia retains the right to withdraw from the treaty if it feels that US missile defence strategy in Europe presents a threat to its security.

Population is also another attribute that could prevent Russia from becoming a superpower, as its diminishing population cannot be compared to those of China, India, the US, and in future that of the European Union. Having a large population is considered to be an important aspect of superpower capacity, conferring a wide range of advantages. A growing population will ensure that there are sufficient numbers to defend the country in the case of a combined attack. A sizeable population is also advantageous to a country in terms providing a large enough workforce that there is no need for outsourcing, and allowing labour costs to be kept low.

Summary

Russia's foreign policy, based on the legacy of the USSR, can be characterized as highly self-centred, focusing on courses of action that bring it the greatest benefits while making every effort to satisfy its political, economic and territorial interests at the expense of other states. As mentioned above, Russia is a permanent member of the G8, and the lingering perception is that Russia is using this status to wield undue influence over other states' decisions. Russia's foreign policies have had

---

33   Keith C. Smith, 'Russian Energy Pressure Fails to Unite Europe', Centre for Strategic and International Studies, January 2007, p. 3.

both positive and negative impacts on the rest of the world. On the positive side, it is an active participant in the major organizations and positive initiatives described in this chapter, but it has also infringed a number of agreements in an effort to move towards superpower status.

Although Russia has the largest military in the world, its armed forces have more problems than any of the other potential superpowers. Russia is attempting to transform its massive, outdated armed forces into a much smaller, professional, modern military that is constantly ready for combat and can be deployed easily to any part of the world, but this process is, perhaps inevitably, not going smoothly. Apart from chronic health, social and structural issues among its personnel, most of its equipment is obsolete, and programmes to update its weaponry are hampered by lack of funding. Recruitment is also problematic, the main issue being the fact that the Russian population is rapidly diminishing, meaning that there are insufficient numbers of recruits to allow professionalization to proceed as rapidly as required.

Nevertheless, Russia has the capacity to achieve all the aims it has set itself, although analysts have predicted that this may take far longer than anticipated because of the issues this chapter has highlighted.

Chapter 6
India

Introduction

Globalization is increasingly expanding the world market, and India is one of the developing giants in Asia. In analysing whether India is likely to become a future superpower, it is important to look at the long-term effects of its foreign policies on the rest of the economies of the world. Even though economic power plays an important role in influencing the decisions and directions taken by other countries, it is also important to consider other factors, such as political relations, military power and cultural influences that may directly result in a nation becoming a dominant superpower. Foreign direct investment, gross domestic income as well as the scale of goods and services of a country can also serve a predictive role.[1]

Unlike other nations considered to be potential future superpowers, India has been slow to develop into an industrial powerhouse, focusing instead on scientific research, art and culture. Colonization by the British bestowed a legacy of cultural diversity on India which endures to the present. In recent years, India has focused on technological advancement and service industries, which has increased its GDP and expanded its global market.[2] However, it faces similar problems to other nations, such as unemployment, corruption, overpopulation, pollution, poverty, fluctuation in interest rates, high oil prices, inflation and high commodity prices globally, all which threaten India's economy. However, its technological and service industry base have helped it to deal these challenges more effectively than other nations.[3]

Despite India's past experiences and current potential, it is difficult to predict whether it is likely to become a future superpower. Having undergone major transitions, India has transformed into a major developing economy, mainly due to its ability to generate higher income and attract direct foreign investment, which have boosted its GDP over time and mean that it is likely to be a highly influential force in years to come. This chapter will analyse India's economic power, foreign policies, political relationships, military power and cultural make-up to determine its prospects of becoming a future world superpower.

---

1   Tanvi Madan, *The Brookings Foreign Policy Studies Energy Security Series: India* (2006), p. 11.

2   Ibid., p. 12.

3   Varun Sahni, 'India and the Asian Security Architecture', *Current History* (April 2006), p. 161.

Foreign Policy

India has been sidelined in international politics for very long time. In 2005, US Secretary of State Condoleezza Rice addressed this when she stated that 'international institutions are going to have to accommodate India in some way'.[4] The hesitant steps India has recently taken to participate in international affairs have largely been prompted by the US. Despite the country's tendency to be inward-looking, the Indian government realizes that it will be very difficult to achieve its economic objectives without engaging with the international community,[5] but its policies are still confused and relatively vague.

Despite this recognition of the importance of participating in international affairs, India has continued to pay lip service to the policy of non-alignment instigated by Nehru. However, the conduct of its economic and diplomatic agencies does not always reflect this. As India's economic power increases, it is likely to take a more active role in world politics. This may include expansion of its military forces, supported by its strong economy and partnership with other more powerful nations. The current volatility, threats and uncertainty in most parts of the world have emphasized the benefits of developing strong international relations in terms of trade, security and development.

Proponents of the classical realist theory argue that the current system of international relations stems from the need to engage with other nations to deal with conflicts or to bring warring nations to the negotiating table.[6] There is a need for a forum to resolve conflicts and settle disputes,[7] and the United Nations was created to fulfil this role. India's recent attempts to participate more actively in international politics stem mainly from security considerations.

Geographically based groups are the central points and actors in the system of international relations. There is a general agreement among classical realists that some states behave rationally, while others behave irrationally.[8] In this view, some states contribute to resolving problems through general agreements as positive actors in international relations, while others tend to aggravate them. The interplay between these two types of actors is a major focus of the classical realist theory of international relations. The theory also holds that some states can be viewed as unitary actors, responding to international issues in ways that show more concern for pursuing goals beyond their borders than political considerations.[9] Many of the developed countries, especially those of the West, demonstrate this, taking

---

    4   Timothy Dunne, *International Relations Theories: Discipline and Diversity* (2007), p. 89.
    5   Ibid., p. 91.
    6   Ibid., p. 96.
    7   Sahni, 'India and the Asian Security Architecture', p. 166.
    8   Ibid.
    9   Dunne, *International Relations Theories*, p. 96.

a keen interest in other nations' affairs, but mainly with an aim to gaining and consolidating power, rather than focusing on social issues.

India's major external threats come from Pakistan and China, both of which have in the past attacked India in one way or another.[10] However, while India has been relatively dormant on the world scene, it has been very active in suppressing internal militancy. The fact that, despite having the largest population of Muslims in the world outside Indonesia and Pakistan, India has never served as a base for the Taliban or Al-Qaeda is a clear indication of the success of its stringent anti-terrorist policies. This is likely to promote the country's prospects for international partnerships and prosperity in its business objectives, especially among the Western nations. India has been described as an island of peace, security and democracy among the authoritarian or weak and conflict-ridden governments, militant strongholds and neighbours constantly at war or afflicted by very acrimonious relationships that surround it.[11] In order to protect itself from impact of these, India has developed what most analysts call 'strong democracy'.

The Indian government's growing role in the United Nations is reflected in its efforts to maintain peace in Nepal, Sri Lanka and Bangladesh. It obviously has a vested interest in ensuring stability in the region, but beyond this, the Indian prime minister has pointed out: 'India continues to pay ... a heavy price to fulfil our UN obligation to support the lawful government of Nepal and Bangladesh .... We pay with the resources of Indian taxpayers ....'[12] This statement can be interpreted as implying that India has only intervened in the affairs of its neighbours because of the wars being waged on their territory. One of the principles of classical realism is that countries seek to further their own interests and increase their power by imposing their political policies on other nations. Deploying military force is one of the more extreme means of intervening in other countries' affairs, and India's moves to act beyond its own borders in an attempt to keep the peace may eventually result in it emerging as a superpower.[13]

India and Terrorism

Nationalist terrorism involves committing violence in an effort to achieve self-determination in some form, perhaps by establishing a sovereign state.[14] Such acts are therefore aimed at opposing what are considered illegitimate or imperial powers of the existing government. A very good example of this is the Liberation Tigers of Tamil Eelam in Sri Lanka. The group was formed in 1976, waging a

---

10   Ibid., p. 97.

11   Madan, *The Brookings Foreign Policy Studies Energy Security Series: India*, p. 13.

12   Manmohan Singh, 'Prime Minister's Independence Day Address', speech, Delhi, 15 August 2007: http://pib.nic.in/release/release.asp?relid=29937 (accessed 27 July 2013).

13   Ibid.

14   'Indian Retailing: Mall Rats – Reliance Moves into Low Fashion', *The Economist*, 18 October 2007: http://www.economist.com/node/9998869 (accessed 19 June 2013), p. 87.

secessionist terrorist campaign with the main aim of making the north of Sri Lanka an independent state.[15] Regarded as the longest-running nationalist conflict in the world, it was defeated by the Sri Lankan military in May 2009.[16]

The Tamil Tigers carried out a number of high-profile attacks, some of them targeting government and military officials of the government of Sri Lanka. The height of the campaign saw the assassination of several politicians, including President Ranasinge Premadasa in 1993 and ex-Indian prime minister Rajiv Gandhi in 1999.[17] Other assassinations followed, including a member of the parliament in 1999, the Industry Minister in 2000, the Foreign Minister in 2005, and in 2008 another member of parliament. The group's tactics included the use of suicide bombers and light aircraft, and it engaged the Sri Lankan military in the fiercest exchange of fire ever witnessed with nationalist terrorists in any part of the world. At times they took control of the north of Sri Lanka when government forces were unable to contain them, especially in the north-east.

At the beginning of the peace talks in 2002, the Tamil Tigers had placed an area of about 15,000 square kilometres under their authority.[18] When the peace talks failed in 2006, the Sri Lankan government was left with no option but to launch a major military offensive throughout Sri Lanka, and by May 2009 it had regained control. When the Tamil Tigers' founder and leader, Volupillai Prabakaran, was later killed by government forces, his assistant, Seyarasa Pathmanatham, took over, but he was subsequently arrested and interrogated.[19]

The Olson hypothesis proposes that those who participate in any kind of revolutionary violence resort to it on rational terms based on a cost–benefit calculus, believing that violence is their best available course of action in a particular set of social, political and economic circumstances. Apart from the idea that a group rationally chooses a strategy of terrorism being questionable, such a decision is often divisive, sometimes resulting in factionalization among the group. This was the case with the Tamil Tigers when faced with the loss of members and some of their leaders.

India has also played an important role in partnering with other religious countries to restore peace, making a significant contribution to the stabilization of Iran, with which it has a close relationship despite the religious differences. Iran has often been accused of supporting religious terrorism: violent activities by terror groups, individuals or organizations motivated by certain religious influences or characteristics that are predominant within a group of people or a society, often related to geopolitical pressures.[20]

Iran has also been accused of state-sponsored terrorism, in which a government sponsors certain terrorist groups to further its international objectives, and it

15   Singh, 'Prime Minister's Independence Day Address'.
16   Dunne, *International Relations Theories*, p. 147.
17   Ibid., p. 156.
18   Stefan M. Aubrey, *The New Dimension of International Terrorism* (2004), p. 213.
19   Ibid., p. 216.
20   Ibid., p. 221.

has been widely criticized for this by a number of countries,[21] including Israel, Yemen, the US and the UK. The latter two countries in particular accused Iran of sponsoring Shia forces in Iraq, which attacked coalition troops, civilians, the Sunni militias and other forces that supported the new Iraqi government.[22]

Iran remains the sole supporter of many religious groups opposed to the peace process in the Middle East, including the Islamic Revolutionary Guard and its faction the Qods Force, the Palestinian terrorist group Hamas and other smaller movements. Iran has also provided funds and training to the Lebanese Hezbollah and other religious groups that have killed many civilians in the Middle East as well as UN peacekeepers in Iraq and Afghanistan.[23] Iran is also accused of refusing to transfer some of the terrorists in its custody, especially Al-Qaeda leaders and other top-ranking leaders of militia groups.

Iran is alleged to have been involved in the 9/11 Al-Qaeda attacks on the World Trade Center and the Pentagon, widely believed to have been masterminded by the religious leader Osama bin Laden. The theory that the attacks were motivated by Islamic beliefs have been supported by some notes found written in books among the attackers' luggage, one copy of the Koran carrying the inscriptions 'You're doing a job which is loved by God, and you will end your day in heavens where you will join the virgins' and 'I pray to you God to forgive me from all my sins, to allow me to glorify you in every possible way.'[24] This lends credence to the idea that this type of terrorism is not motivated by political calculations such as those suggested by the Olson hypothesis, but rather by certain extremist spiritual beliefs.

India is currently the only country that enjoys close ties with both Iran and its bitter enemy, the US, one of the major bones of contention being the Iranian nuclear programme.[25] It has maintained friendly relations with the US despite being a key Iranian ally. It is in India's interests to ensure stability among its neighbours, not only to safeguard its own security, but to promote its own international objectives. Despite the need to provide for its own economy and population, the support India has provided to neighbouring countries has been estimated to amount to hundreds of millions of dollars – a clear indication of its commitment to international affairs and its influence on nations beyond its immediate borders.

Impact of Indian Foreign Policies on Issues of Global Concern

In analysing the impact of Indian foreign policies, it is important to also consider the reactions of other nations, since international relationships are multilateral. One of most significant and unexpected developments in recent times has been

---

21 Tore Bjørgo, *Root Causes of Terrorism: Myths, Reality and Ways Forward* (2005), p. 147.

22 Aubrey, *The New Dimension of International Terrorism*, p. 222.

23 Ibid., p. 236.

24 Bjørgo, *Root Causes of Terrorism*, p. 148.

25 Ibid.

the improvement in relations between India and the US,[26] which have progressed from what has been described as 'estranged democracy' to 'engaged democracy'.[27]

It is believed that the US is mainly pursuing a strategic relationship which not only endorses India's position and stature, but also seeks to exploit its potential in the region as well as in the world as a whole. In this partnership, India expects to benefit from open trade and increased markets for its products. The collaboration is seen as part of the US strategy to improve its influence in the Middle East, where it has had long and troubled relationships with many countries. However, India has a different agenda, seeking to use this opportunity to expand its economic reach.[28] Another factor of the detente between the US and India relates to India's nuclear ambitions. The US-India Civil Nuclear Agreement instigated in 2005 provides clear evidence of US recognition of India as a legitimate nuclear power.

However, what is important in this kind of partnership is whether it will bring lasting benefits for India, or whether it will mainly benefit the US. While India and China are two nations that are currently in the ascendancy on the international scene, India is pursuing its agenda through political and economic models for growth that differ from those of China. Its main advantages over China are its closer proximity to the Western countries and its status as the largest non-Western democracy. This gives India the potential to serve as an example to its Asian neighbours.

India's engagement in international issues is seen as intrinsically serving its national interests, and those interests include promoting stability in Eastern Asia, which is why it has chosen to extend its participation in UN initiatives. Political analysts agree that India wants to see a more multilateral international system. It is clear that the country's political and economic power along with its relationships with current superpowers like the US will be critical in determining the future of global politics and governance, and increase the likelihood of India taking its 'rightful position'.[29] Because India's foreign policies look far beyond its immediate neighbourhood, it is more likely to secure not only its political interests, but also its economic interests. Access to raw materials and energy are major areas of concern for India, and this is likely to lead to competitive tensions with its neighbours, such as China, Africa and the countries of Southern Asia.

Although India and China are the major emerging powers in Asia, many political analysts question whether they will seek to impose their own order, or whether they will endorse the existing state of affairs. However, critical analysis of Indian foreign policy shows that India is concerned to enhance its influence and power by cementing its relationships with the US, Europe, Russia and China. India is skilfully using its soft power to enhance engagement as well as participating in

---

26   Ibid.

27   Gus Martin, *Understanding Terrorism: Challenges, Perspectives, and Issues*, 3rd edn (2009), p. 217.

28   Ibid., p. 218.

29   Ibid., p. 221.

foreign affairs through international organizations.[30] The most interesting aspect of this is its growing co-operation with Israel and the Arab world, through which India is keen to boost its already formidable military power. As outlined above, because India is very much preoccupied with its own security and seeking stability within its neighbourhood, it has built a strong military and devoted a great deal of resources to promoting peace beyond its borders and in the wider world.

India's Military Power

The growth in India's soft power due to its young population and rapid pace of technological development command respect throughout the world, even among the Western nations. As mentioned above, India is viewed as an island of peace in its region.[31] The support it has offered to other nations over the decades, and the material and financial support it continues to provide to promote peace among its neighbours in a very unstable region enhance its strategic power in its region in terms of military strength, diplomacy and economic influence.[32]

India is bordered by two nuclear weapons states, China and Pakistan, and the most significant aspect of India's military power is its large stockpile of nuclear weaponry, which is viewed as a threat to international security and is one of the reasons India has never been granted a permanent seat on the UN Security Council despite several attempts. India only acknowledged that it had a nuclear weapons programme after many years of denial. It has had a patchy record of co-operation with nuclear regulatory bodies such as the IAEA, and has resisted signing up to the NPT.[33] This has hampered its relationships with other nations, particularly those of the West, and it is also a waste of resources that could otherwise be used to improve the lives of its population and its neighbours who are languishing in poverty.

India recently embarked on a major research programme to develop its expertise in the fields of environmental, physical and life sciences and engineering to cater for its long-term security needs.[34] The scale of investment in its Department of Defence to develop more effective and sophisticated weaponry is controversial because some people feel that it is unwise and unnecessary to commit so much government funding to military systems at the expense of other areas of the economy. In response, India's Finance Minister has argued that the project will

---

30   C. Raja Mohan, 'Nine Ways to Look West,' *The Indian Express*, 8 January 2007, http://www.indianexpress.com/story/20387.html (accessed 27 July 2013).

31   Martin, *Understanding Terrorism*, p. 221.

32   Ibid., p. 229.

33   Alexis Madrigal, 'Nuclear Power to Explode in India, but China Prefers Coal,' *Wired*, 25 October 2007: http://www.wired.com/science/planetearth/news/2007/10/nuclear_report (accessed 27 July 2013).

34   Ashish K. Vaidya, *Globalization: Encyclopedia of Trade, Labour and Politics* (2006), p. 187.

bring a number of benefits, both direct and indirect. The direct benefits claimed include technological innovations and the encouragement of competition between suppliers that will eventually reduce defence spending. However, weapons development is a notoriously unpredictable field in terms of cost, schedule and performance, so ongoing monitoring of acquisition programmes is being conducted both within and outside the Department of Defence to ensure cost-effectiveness and more responsive support for the nuclear weapons programme in the future.[35]

The government reported that the Department of Defence would spend more on developing fewer nuclear weapons during 2005–2009, focusing on quality rather than quantity.[36] The increased cost of spending on this particular project has been questioned because it diverts funds from other federal programmes which are competing for scarce resources, and there are fears that it may never come to fruition.[37]

Like any other nation, India's major security priority is to protect its borders and citizens from external attacks, and to do so it has constructed the world's fourth-largest navy, its seventh-largest air force and its third-largest army, developing a well-trained and well-equipped military that is a match for the forces of most other countries in the world. Despite this, India still faces a number of threats and challenges, not only from Western nations, but also its neighbours. Pakistan has been a constant threat to India due to its support for terrorist activities. An attack on India's parliament in 2001 led to a major military stand-off between the two countries.[38] Although India has superior military forces to Pakistan and other nations in the Middle East, the topography of its western border is very mountainous, and hence restricts the number of troops India can deploy at any given time. Tensions between India and China have also been evident since 1962, when the two nations fought a war that India lost, leading to lasting mutual distrust.[39]

India's focus on economic trade is a significant reason for modernizing its air force and expanding its blue-water navy, which it has reinforced with a modern submarine force, in order to ensure safe passage for goods to and from its trading partners. The Bay of Bengal and the Straits of Malacca in particular are hotbeds of piracy, so India has striven to take control of these waters. The expansion of the blue-water navy is also intended to counter any threats from China and prevent a repeat of past conflicts. Statements from the ex-Chief of the Indian Naval Staff Admiral Suresh Mehta indicated that India was not building up its army for offensive purposes, but to develop a 'mutual respectful partnership that ensures the stability of the Indian Ocean'.

In recent times, India has been very wary of armed conflict with other nations or its neighbours. Apart from Pakistan and China, India's only recent engagement has

---

35 Ibid., p. 192.
36 Sahni, 'India and the Asian Security Architecture', p. 167.
37 Ibid.
38 Ibid.
39 Madan, *The Brookings Foreign Policy Studies Energy Security Series: India*, p. 21.

been its intervention in the internal conflict in Sri Lanka. Other than this, the Indian military has never intervened directly in the region to stem conflicts between its neighbours, relying instead on its soft power, diplomacy and economic influence. India has provided a role model for its neighbours through its development of a strong democracy, as was evident when India collaborated with the UK and US to persuade the King of Nepal to abandon the country's military ambitions in 2005. India's singular status in the region enhances its influence outside the Middle East. However, some political analysts have argued that India's activities, including its continued provision of support to its neighbours in terms of funding and resources, threaten the other countries' political sovereignty by increasing their dependence on it. On the other hand, India's neighbours such as Afghanistan have key strategic roles in the region, so it cannot just ignore their economic and political difficulties. In the case of Afghanistan, providing assistance to help it to stabilize and grow its economy provides direct benefits to India, and the same applies to other nations in the Middle East, such as Iran and Pakistan.

In addition to its substantial military investments, India is also expected to increase its provision of humanitarian aid, enhancing its relationships and acceptance among the international community. If the Indian military continues to grow as it has in recent times, it may eventually overtake those of other developed nations such as the US, making it a major player in international affairs.

India's modernization of its navy will enable the nation not only to dominate the Indian Ocean, but to extend its sea power to the south, an area of great strategic importance to China. Political analysts believe this is part of a strategy to give India a competitive edge in the region, both in terms of trade and international relations. If it succeeds in these ambitions, the southern part of Asia, where China enjoys most advantages in terms of trade with and influence over other nations, will fall under India's control, However, managing and controlling the Indian Ocean would come at a high cost. India has drawn up a strategic plan to acquire 103 new warships worth over US$45 billion over the next twenty years, including modern submarines and destroyers. However, a report released by the Department of Defence in January 2011 revealed that the government of China planned to spend approximately US$135 billion on 135 new naval vessels.

During President Barack Obama's tour of East Asia in 2012, it was clear that the US supports India's ambitions to emerge as the leader of the region rather than China, which has held supremacy there since the Second World War, and this was borne out in the Asian and East Asian summits in November of that year. Recent years have seen a shift from India's traditional defensive posture to an offensive capability. This was emphasized in 2009, when the army chief of the time indicated in a media briefing that India was reviewing its strategy with regard to fighting wars on two fronts, with Pakistan and China. In August of the same year, the development of roads in the border areas was also seen as a major initiative to improve the Indian Army's mobility in these regions.

The Indian Air Force has also drawn up strategic plans to dominate the Indian Ocean, as reflected in the military build-up at its Tezpur air base and its acquisition of powerful radar systems and AWACS aircraft. However, India's investments in its air force and army in response to rising Chinese power are secondary to its naval developments, including the acquisition of several nuclear submarines from Russia. These are only a few of the military projects planned for the next ten to fifteen years that are expected to put India at a strategic military advantage in the region.[40] However, this depends on the reactions of its neighbours and the rest of the world.

Finally, a major weakness of India's ambitions for regional dominance is that unlike other nations in the region, it is reliant on US support, which could always be withdrawn.

Participation in Global Security Issues

India has recently stepped up its involvement in global security issues and relations with the international community and the United Nations. Despite its lack of success in becoming a permanent member of the UN Security Council, it has frequently responded to calls for humanitarian aid and peacekeeping forces. Over the years, major organizations of the international community, including the European Union, the US, the African Union and the Association of Southeast Asian Nations, have frequently sought the involvement of India in a number of international peace and security issues, but until recently India has been very reluctant to respond.

India's moves to engage in many international security and trade forums, such as its prominent role in the WTO's Doha Development Round, have increased its international profile and gained respect from the major world powers. India's engagement in security issues can be seen in its membership of the UN Peacebuilding Commission, its role in East Asia and its new neighbourhood policies, which seek to establish a stable base for its economic and political ambitions by using its economic advantage to promote peace in Sri Lanka, Bangladesh, Nepal and other East Asian nations.[41]

India faces a number of challenges on its borders and in its wider neighbourhood. As mentioned above, India is a unique example of a strong democracy in East Asia, but its ascendancy is likely to be short-lived if it does not act decisively to counter the rise of China. India has become part of the global consensus on peace and security, which requires nations to act to protect their neighbourhoods.[42] India's growing relationship with the US has been promoted by increasing tensions between Pakistan and India as a result of India's vital role, along with the European

---

40   Ibid., p. 214.
41   Stephen Lucarelli, 'The European Union in the Eyes of Others: Towards Filling a Gap in the Literature, *European Foreign Affairs Review* 12:3 (2007), p. 249.
42   Ibid., p. 251.

Union, in supporting the US mission in Afghanistan. China, on the other hand, is providing support to Pakistan to counterbalance India's prominence in the region.[43]

However, India's continued contributions to promoting international security will depend greatly on the Western nations providing assistance to ensure its own security against the threats it faces, especially from the countries that surround it, as a result of its partnership with the US. Nevertheless, India is still optimistic about its ambitions to develop stable and peaceful coexistence with its neighbours, especially if it is finally granted a permanent seat on the UN Security Council.[44] However, this does not seem likely in the near future without the support of the European Union, since the Obama administration shows no signs of putting Security Council reform on its agenda. Given the changing dynamics of East Asia, in which India plays a key role as a bridge between the region and the rest of the international community, an international consensus on security will only be possible with the full involvement of India.

India's Economic Power

India's action plan for 2010 called for large-scale investment, including up to US$3.2 billion on personal income tax relief, more than US$4 billion on creating and protecting employment, US$7.7 billion on infrastructure with the aim of job creation, US$1.9 billion on nurturing the economy, and US$2.2 billion on supporting India's industries and the communities.[45] Investment on this scale is likely to promote economic growth in a number of sectors and the economy in general, driven by India's large human labour resources in the service industries, which is the largest sector, followed by the manufacturing industries, a combination of other industries, and lastly, agriculture.

Worldwide, the major indicators of a healthy economy are foreign trade and growth in the industrial sector, so India's investment in these sectors is likely to boost the performance of its economy.[46] Despite recent setbacks, India has made progress in terms of economic growth, which at 3 per cent over the last decade is slightly less than that of the US.[47] This shows that it has the potential for even greater expansion, but only if it sustains investment.

A number of factors have contributed to the growth of India's economy, including foreign trade and exports, which have made resources available for investment. The trend is likely to continue if more resources are directed to India's major industries. India's economic growth has long been characterized

---

43   Ibid., p. 263.

44   J. Holslag, *Europe's Normative Disconnect with the Emerging Powers*, BICCS Asia Paper 5:4 (2010), p. 1.

45   Lucarelli, 'The European Union in the Eyes of Others', p. 263.

46   Lucarelli, 'The European Union in the Eyes of Others', p. 4

47   Ibid.

by net capital flows and low interest rates, direct investment and a focus on capital formation, direct foreign influences, especially on prices and the wages, adjustments to exogenous capital flows and rapid responses to domestic policies, all of which have proven that it is capable of performing beyond expectations.

India has focused strongly on reducing impediments to economic growth, especially in international competition in professional services.[48] There are nowadays lower barriers to foreign ownership and competition in network industries, and fewer disincentives to work because income support provisions have been cut. However, some of India's economic policies have almost led it to become a failed state, and have not united and strengthened the nation.[49] Nevertheless, India's high rate of investment in sectors such as health, education and urban development is laudable.

In 2004, India's prospects for economic growth depended on macroeconomic developments.[50] Some of the challenges anticipated included competition in product markets, hiccups in economic performance and the need to enhance productivity. This meant that India had to change some of its policies in an effort to maintain the trend of continuous growth it had been experiencing for the past decade. India's regional development policy originated in attempts to improve standards of living, especially in its nine maritime provinces. The nation should be given credit for avoiding some of the worst effects of the recent global financial crises since, unlike many countries, it had anticipated them and had instituted measures to mitigate their impact, especially on its banking system.

India has adopted a number of strategies to deal with pressures such as these and remain competitive with other countries in the face of the perennial problems that afflict virtually all the nations in the world. Strong service sectors are among the most important factors in spurring economic growth. More than two thirds of India's GDP is generated by its service industries,[51] so its strategy has involved focusing on this sector to ensure growth and prepare it for economic challenges. Other factors include reliance on home markets and a strong partnership with the US, since most of the production plants of American motor manufacturers are based in India.

Imposing corporation taxes is one of the most effective means of enhancing growth and generating revenue, and India's tax regime has done so for a long time, categorizing corporations as persons or legal entities that are liable for default.[52] Another strategy adopted by India has involved devolution to federal governments. One of the areas which has benefited from this strategy is India's infrastructure, since the federal governments invested more than US$960 million

---

48   Holslag, *Europe's Normative Disconnect with the Emerging Powers*, p. 267.

49   Ibid., p. 271.

50   Lucarelli, 'The European Union in the Eyes of Others', p. 4

51   David A. Smith, Dorothy J. Solinger and Steven C. Topik, *States and Sovereignty in the Global Economy* (1999), p. 186.

52   Ibid.

in infrastructural development during 2000–2007,[53] and this has brought benefits to all the sectors which directly or indirectly depend on it.

Another factor that has enabled India to weather the global financial crises has been India's job creation policies.[54] The government has enacted strong measures to ensure that levels of employment remain high, including offering students jobs, especially through summer programmes. India's high productivity levels have also been a contributory factor.

India's economic action plan can be defined in terms of two major approaches or ideologies: nationalism and monetarism. The nationalism is manifested through reforms throughout the country that focus on developing strong local economies, indicating that India is keen to develop the nation as a whole.[55] In terms of monetarism, most major nations have adopted it as a way to pursue economic progress.[56] The amount of investment in the economy stipulated in the action plan is evidence that India is aiming to follow this trend in an effort to strengthen the state and help to reduce its dependency on other countries in order to achieve a greater degree of autonomy.[57]

This drive for nationalism and autonomy faces challenges from economic globalization and the trend towards increasing cross-border trade. This means that countries are becoming increasingly interconnected, to the extent that they exert a growing influence on each other. Sovereignty, on the other hand, implies that a state is independent, competent and has legal equality with other states.[58] It encompasses each state's authority to make its own decisions without interference from other sovereign states about matters related to economy, politics, foreign policy, and social and cultural issues, limited only by international law.[59]

Some researchers argue that this autonomy is threatened by globalization in a number of ways. Due to increasing capital mobility, many nations have adopted neo-liberal policies. Intensified international competition has also led to increased government spending, which has reduced revenue-generation.[60] Each state tries to adapt to these trends to further its own interests, but this exacerbates inequality, since developed countries have more influence on the process than less-developed countries.

One of the major problems of economic globalization is the threat it poses to democracy,[61] since it can impede the ability of citizens to exercise their political,

---

53   Ibid., p. 191.

54   Ibid., p. 201.

55   John D. Montgomery and Nathan Glazer (eds), *Sovereignty Under Challenge: How Governments Respond* (2002), p. 45.

56   Ibid.

57   Ibid., p. 51.

58   John Agnew, *Globalization and Sovereignty* (2009), p. 221.

59   Ibid., p. 227.

60   Ibid., p. 228.

61   Ibid.

economic, social and other rights, compromising national sovereignty. In other words, globalization can erode the ability of states to exert political control, and it can also eliminate social correctives to the market economy.[62] These kinds of phenomena lead to increasing social inequality, where the rich become richer and the poor become poorer. These are threats to the very foundations of contemporary democracies, imposed through external pressures and changes in the domestic social structure that are unfavourable.[63]

Globalization has increased the potential for mobility of goods and services, financial capital, real investments and skilled labour. Mobile economic actors are free to avoid dealing with states whose regulations they regard as unfavourable. This means that countries are driven to compete with each other for personnel or the resources they control, which reduces their control over the conditions under which their economies operate.[64] In general, globalization has challenged the ability of states to govern autonomously, including in the domain of public policy. States are therefore losing control over information and financial flows and the transnational organization of production.

Control over the transmission of information is a vital issue that affects national sovereignty. The increasing growth of international media coupled with the inability of individual governments to exercise control over outlets is a major issue. If a nation hosting a media outlet is able to impose control over the information it propagates beyond its borders, it provides a powerful tool for manipulating public opinion on important issues that may affect how people think about their own countries, which interferes with sovereignty. National control over information concerning a country's government is very important in protecting the sovereignty of the nations that are interacting as a result of the global integration of economies.[65] Financial flows and the transnational organization of production may also hinder democratic governance at the national level. Constraints on the financial abilities of nation states is the most frequently identified threat as far as sovereignty and democratic decisions are concerned.[66] All this points to the fact that economic globalization tends to favour developed countries in terms of competition.

A sovereign state also has the right to set its own economic development objectives and to develop and run a taxation policy to finance them, as well as to participate independently in international tax regimes.[67] It has been alleged that economic globalization erodes this national tax sovereignty. The first form of

---

62   Ibid., p. 237.

63   Smith et al., *States and Sovereignty in the Global Economy*, p. 231.

64   Montgomery and Glazer, *Sovereignty Under Challenge*, p. 67.

65   Ibid., p. 75.

66   Mikael Mattlin, 'Thinking Clearly on Political Strategy: The Formulation of a Common EU Policy toward China', in Bart Gaens, Juha Jokela and Eija Limnell (eds), *The Role of the European Union in Asia: China and India as Strategic Partners* (2009), p. 95.

67   Mattlin, 'Thinking Clearly on Political Strategy', p. 99.

erosion results from the formation of regional economic groupings of nations.[68] These usually have a governing body that manages the grouping's affairs and with whose rules member states must comply, and this may include taxation policies. National tax policies may also be compromised by the operations of multinational companies in different countries.[69] Economic globalization can also increase international competition over tax regimes, because certain countries may try to attract foreign investment by offering low tax rates or other concessions.

There is an urgent need for nations to co-operate in addressing these issues to protect tax sovereignty.[70] This applies particularly to developing countries, which are the worst affected. For the developed countries, the nature of the economic globalization process and their economic strength already afford them a degree of autonomy and protection, often at the expense of the developing countries. Under the guise of giving grants and other financial assistance to these developing countries, they can impose their will on very important social, economical and political decisions, hence threatening the democracy and sovereignty of these poorer states.

On the other hand, some scholars argue that economic globalization may have positive effects in terms of democratic governance and the representation of the people. If certain groups do not feel that their interests are adequately represented by traditional political institutions, perhaps because their needs are not a priority or because of corruption, the influence of other nation states may be very helpful. Their contention is that economic globalization may exaggerate the structural weaknesses of democratic regimes, but there is no evidence that it has an adverse effect on democratic governance at the national level, and it may also reduce the opportunities for unconstructive political populism, since global institutions can promote emerging social interests and help to overcome the divisions that globalization gives rise to.

There is still no convincing evidence that the future will be so optimistic, so the developing countries – including India – need to take account of the need to protect their sovereignty in their economic development strategies while seeking ways to maximize the benefits of economic globalization.

Summary

India's principal strategic interests include maintaining a strong military, especially its navy, promoting peace and security among its neighbours, developing a strong economic base, and maintaining productive relationships with US, EU and UN. All these factors give India the potential to become a powerful force for transformation, not only in Eastern Asia, but the whole world.

---

68 Ibid., p. 109.
69 Ibid., p. 120.
70 Agnew, *Globalization and Sovereignty*, p. 238.

A critical analysis reveals that India's potential to become an agent of change in the short term is evident in a number of areas. While its success in this will depend on the reactions of other nations, India's advantages include its strong democracy, considerable economic power and powerful military. It is also important to note that India has recently shown more interest in international relations than in the past. However, despite this, it is difficult to predict what the future may hold for India.

India's current foreign policy is characterized by a strong focus on security in East Asia, improving relations with Western nations, especially the US, and active participation in UN initiatives, which have extended India's influence beyond the Asian region. However, it still faces various challenges, the major one being threats from its immediate neighbours such as Pakistan, Iran and China. In order to continue as a dominant force for peace and humanitarianism in the region, India needs to develop its collaboration with the US and fulfil its long-term ambition to gain a permanent seat on the UN Security Council.

In conclusion, India's acquisition of superpower status will depend on how it deals with challenges from the other significant powers in its region, including China, Iran, Russia and North and South Korea. While India continues to build a strong navy, the North Korean and Iranian nuclear weapons programmes are potential threats that will have to be dealt with. Despite the many economic challenges it faces, China has also continued to expand its military infrastructure and its defence budget is quite high, and Russia is considered to have the most powerful air force in the region in terms of weaponry and combat capabilities. While the BRICs countries are emerging as a political force to be reckoned with in world governance, it is the balance of power among these nations that will determine whether any of them, or the bloc as a whole, will emerge as the next superpower.

Chapter 7

China

Introduction

China has experienced a substantial growth in its GDP for the past three decades. For this reason, there has been a rapid transformation of China from a demoralized, isolated and impoverished country to a confident, prosperous and dependable global trading power. With its GDP of about US$4.4 trillion and total foreign trade of about US$2.6 trillion, the international community has recognized China as an economic powerhouse. Among the BRICs countries, only India's economic growth is comparable to that of China.

Since the founding of modern China in 1949, its foreign policies have developed substantially. As witnessed in the 1950s and 1960s, China's policy of self-reliance seriously restricted its foreign contacts. However, this changed in the 1970s, after the rapprochement under President Nixon and the decision to grant the People's Republic of China (PRC) full membership of the UN.[1] China adopted new policies that focused on economic development and diplomacy, spearheaded by its leader at the time, Deng Xiaoping, in 1978.[2] The objective of the policies was to obtain access to technology, expertise and foreign investment. This did not take long, as China increased its participation in international institutions and organizations and embraced international norms and regulations championed by the US. In view of this, China has gradually increased the quantity and quality of its diplomacy. It has been able to attract the support of foreign governments through diplomatic exchanges, cultural understandings, tourism, investment agreements and trade initiatives.[3]

Foreign policies and their impact on issues of global concern, military power, and the participation of a country in global security issues determine how powerful and influential a country is, so this chapter will focus on China's foreign policies, its military power and its involvement in international security issues. China plays a very important role in the world community, and analysis of these topics will reveal China's overall position internationally and allow us to evaluate the international community's attitudes towards it. China's increasingly prominent role has focused the attention of powerful countries such as the US and international organizations such as the European Union.

---

1   State Council Information Office White Paper, *China's National Defense*, July 1998. See full text at: http://english.peopledaily.com.cn/whitepaper/2.html (accessed 27 July 2013).

2   Bates Gill, *Rising Star: China's New Security Diplomacy* (2007), p. 3.

3   Kerry Dumbaugh, *China's Foreign Policy: What Does it Mean for U.S. Global Interests?*, CRS Report to Congress, 18 July 2008, p. 5.

China's Foreign Policy

The Chinese government's domestic agenda, with a major focus on the nation's economic and political transformation, is the major driving force behind China's foreign policy. It is geared to enhancing the integrity and stability of the country, securing development of its economy, and improving its standing as an influential player in global decision-making. In recent years, China has adopted a less confrontational, more constructive and more confident stance regarding regional and global issues,[4] and it has engaged in numerous bilateral trade agreements, participated in addressing global security concerns and signed up to a variety of security and trade accords. As a result, China has moved closer to compliance with the norms and rules of the international system and the international organizations of which it is a member in an effort to promote its national interests. Accordingly, any political opposition which may hinder the achievement of these goals is deemed a threat. For instance, North Korea's nuclear brinkmanship is one of the difficulties China is facing in its foreign policy.

It is worth noting, however, that China's foreign policy largely depends on a multilateral approach except for matters that might limit its sovereignty. This multilateral stance is apparent in the country's preventive shuttle diplomacy, its participation in multilateral arbitration of the North Korean issue, and its provision of both medical and technical assistance for the UN's peacekeeping missions.

The Chinese government's foreign policy is heavily influenced by traditional balance-of-power politics, with the primary aim of safeguarding the country's territorial integrity and sovereignty in a multi-polar world. This approach is driven by China's unease at the fact that the US is currently the only world superpower, and its hopes that eventually other spheres of influence will arise to serve as a counterbalance. The US-led invasion and occupation of Iraq was one of the catalysts for this reaction.[5] As argued by many scholars, China's current foreign policy has enabled it to be envisaged globally as an emerging superpower due to the various interests it is pursuing and the various international responsibilities it is undertaking.[6]

The transformation of China's foreign policy dates back to the late twentieth century, when the Chinese government expanded its bilateral links, in particular during 1988–94.[7] Later, China normalized relations and engaged in diplomacy with 18 countries, including the US. The major motivation for these moves was to limit the US strategy of forging regional alliances through the partnerships it had established with a number of countries to facilitate co-ordination of security and economic interests.

---

4   Evan S. Medeiros and M. Taylor Fravel, 'China's New Diplomacy', *Foreign Affairs* 86:2 (2003), p. 6.

5   Knut Dethlefsen, *China's Foreign Policy in Transition*, FES Briefing Paper (May 2004), p. 1.

6   Medeiros and Fravel, 'China's New Diplomacy', p. 22.

7   Ibid., p. 24.

In 2001, China's objective of stemming the US's influence was evident in the signing of the Treaty of Good Neighborliness and Friendly Co-operation with Russia.[8] During this period, China also moderated its opposition to many multilateral institutions that it had hitherto seen as determined to suppress its economic and military growth, and embraced them as avenues to secure its security and trade interests, and above all its chief aim of limiting US dominance.

The Association of South East Asian Nations (ASEAN) was one of the multilateral institutions with which China formed an alliance in the second half of the twentieth century, when it helped to introduce annual meetings between the ASEAN countries plus Japan, South Korea and itself, dubbed the ASEAN+3 mechanism. ASEAN+3 rapidly gave way to ASEAN+1, headed by the prime minister of China.

Also in 2001, China intensified its participation in international economic policy by hosting the ninth leaders' meeting of the Asia-Pacific Economic Forum in Shanghai. In the mean time, China facilitated the establishment of the Shanghai Cooperation Organization, the first multilateral institution in Central Asia, whose major purpose was to resolve disputes and demilitarize borders in the region. Currently, the organization's main focus is the expansion of regional trade, and it has joined the rest of the world in advocating against terrorism. Other Asian organizations that China has joined include APEC and the ASEAN Regional Forum (ARF).

China's efforts did not stop at strengthening its ties in Asia, but also extended to Europe, evident by the fact that it is one of the founding members of the Asia–Europe Meeting instituted in 1996, which organizes twice-yearly meetings between heads of states and annual meetings between ministers of foreign affairs. In 1998, China instigated a political dialogue with the European Union, and the Chinese prime minister sought to develop this relationship during his visit to Europe in May 2004, concentrating on the need to shape the strategic political partnership between Beijing and other European capitals.

The most unanticipated move was China's dialogue with NATO, since it marked the end of China's tradition of condemning the alliances led by the US. The major issues discussed were NATO's involvement in Central Asia and developing strategies to resolve past and future differences.

Latin America has also not been neglected by China, which is a member of the Organization of American States, in which China has been granted full observer status since 2004, and the Forum for East Asia–Latin America Cooperation (FOCALAE), which was formed in 1994, and of which the US is not a member.[9]

During the twentieth century, China also took initiatives to resolve territorial disputes which were a major cause of tension and conflict with its neighbours. It is worth noting that despite China's interests in the territories under dispute, it generally compromised, laying claim to half or less of the territory and ceding the

---

8 Ibid., p. 25.
9 Robert Sutter, *Chinese Foreign Relations* (2008), p. 62.

majority of it to the counter-claimant, as was the case with Kyrgyzstan, Russia, Kazakhstan, Tajikistan, Laos and Vietnam.

During this period, tensions between China and its arch-rival India reduced dramatically, even though there was still no formalized agreement between the two countries. Regarding China's offshore territorial disputes, it embraced a more realist approach which ensured that peaceful means were used to resolve issues. In fact, in 2002 a code of conduct aimed at settlement of such disputes was arrived at, the majority of its terms drafted by ASEAN rather than China.

As outlined above, regionally, China has embraced the themes of peace and development in a bid to secure its own development. This is evident in the Chinese Foreign Ministry's efforts to ensure that peace is maintained between China and its neighbours. As a result, China has welcomed the advice of experts who have recommended political and economic co-operation between the countries in the region to form a stronger front against the numerous security threats that confront them. By striving to implement these policies, China has enhanced its reputation as a dependable regional power and as a motor for growth.

Surprisingly, in 2003 China started to back US security initiatives, for example by proposing a new security summit at the ASEAN summit meeting. This followed another major foreign policy initiative in 2002, when China voted for UN Resolution 1441, which was directed towards the search for nuclear weapons in Iraq. This was in sharp contrast to its abstaining from the UN resolution authorizing the use of force in the case of non-compliance, on the grounds that it contravened national sovereignty. Its increased participation in controversial decisions of the UN Security Council is evidence of China's readiness to co-operate with the UN.

In November 2004, the PRC established the Confucius Institutes, a non-profit programme to promote Chinese languages and culture to enable easier communication with the countries with which China has engaged in bilateral relationships. The first was opened in Seoul in Korea, and by 2007, 207 others had been established worldwide, with 40 in the US alone.[10] In addition, the extension of Approved Destination Status (ADS), a bilateral tourism arrangement, has also helped to strengthen China's bilateral relationships.[11]

Experts and scholars argue that in the 2000s, China adopted the projection of soft power as a key strategy in its foreign policy in a similar way to the US, aiming to improve its economic development, especially in terms of catering for its growing needs for energy and raw materials, and enhancing China's image internationally to enable it to compete more favourably with the supremacy of the United States. Joseph Nye observes:

---

10   Tang Shiping and Zhang Yunling, 'China's Regional Strategy', in David Shambaugh (ed.), *Power Shift* (2005), p. 14.

11   ADS status means that local Chinese package tour operators are able to sell tours in the designated ADS country. Authorization of group tours tends to increase the number of tourists to ADS-designated countries.

Soft power rests on the ability to shape the preferences of others. It is the ability
to get what you want through attraction rather than coercion or payments. It
arises from the attractiveness of a country's culture, political ideals, and policies.
When our policies are seen as legitimate in the eyes of others, our soft power is
enhanced. America has long had a great deal of soft power.[12]

This soft power has mainly been manifested in the unconditional and attractive
loan and investment packages that China has offered to many foreign governments
on terms more favourable than Western countries offer. Although there is a danger
of these giving rise to short-term losses, this strategy is likely to lead to long-
term profits for China. It is also apparent that China has continued its policy of
diplomatic isolation of Taiwan, with which it has long been embroiled in disputes
over sovereignty.[13]

China has participated in the formation of a number new multilateral institutions
that do not include the US, such as the East Asia Summit (EAS), the Shanghai
Cooperation Organization (SCO) and Forum on China–Africa Cooperation
(FOCAC). Although the formation of the SCO has already been outlined above, it
is worth noting that it was formed without any participation from the US, as was
the EAS in 2005, and it was China that hosted its first summit meeting. The EAS
consists of the 10 ASEAN members plus New Zealand, Australia, India, South
Korea, Japan and China. FOSAC, a multilateral institution comprising China and
45 African states, is a forum that aims to promote economic development and co-
operation through meetings held every three years.

Impacts of Foreign Policy on Issues of Global Concern

The global economy crisis   As outlined above, China's current assertive foreign
policies aim to balance the pursuit of economic development with considerations
of stability among its partners, and this has enhanced its power and economic
influence. During the recent global economic crisis, many countries have looked
to China for help to deal with their problems, but there are concerns that China has
put its own economic interests above the need for global economic stability, for
instance in its policies towards the European Union. China seeks the transfer of
technology and access to European markets, while the EU and other countries are
bearing the major share of expenditure on measures to combat climate change, and
China has also demanded that the EU abstain from talks and criticisms concerning
its conduct towards Taiwan and Tibet.[14] Shi Yinyong, a Chinese international
relations expert, feels that 'China's demands of the EU are feasible, limited and

---

12   Nye, *Soft Power*, p. 10.
13   Sutter, *Chinese Foreign Relations*, p. 10.
14   John Fox and François Godement, *A Power Audit of EU–China Relations* (April
2009), p. 5.

realistic', yet the question remains whether China has offered the EU anything in return for these demands.[15]

China takes advantage of the EU, since it prevents it from penetrating its own market while gaining full access to the EU market. This is facilitated by the mismatch between China's system of government (centralized authority) and the rule-based system under which the EU operates, since there is lack of distinct boundaries between China's central, regional and local authorities. As a result, Chinese state-owned firms and local people have limited autonomy in relation to foreign trade as the central government has the final say in these matters, making it easier for the government to take control of issues in which it has a strategic interest. In addition, under the WTO agreement, China reserves the right to protect newly formed industries from competition from foreign entities, enabling it to close its market to outsiders.

China has limited the pressure from the EU by allowing discussions of key issues, such as human rights, then using the EU's preoccupation with these at the annual meetings as a tactic to distract it from addressing the high trade deficits between the EU and China. These dialogues frequently favour China, as it exploits the Western tendency to seek win–win outcomes in order to restrict anti-dumping measures and keep the American and European markets susceptible to its economic exploitation. Another deflection tactic involves accusing the US and EU of being guilty of double standards on sensitive issues.[16]

It is most notable that not only does China exploit divisions between EU member states, it actually seeks to provoke them. Although divisions within the EU have also been taken advantage of by the US, for instance during efforts to seeks support for its military intervention in Iraq, China ruthlessly exploits this opportunity by identifying member countries which are particularly vulnerable and pressurizing them to support China's stance on issues such as the granting of Taiwanese independence, also rallying the ideological free-traders to support China over the controversial issue of maintaining a market economy rather than tolerating both assertive industrialism and mercantilism.[17] This is illustrated by a statement from a diplomat of one of the EU member states, who said that his country could not afford to be politically critical of China because its trade was too dependent on its government's decisions.[18]

China's impact on issues of global concern is apparent from the fact that the EU has continued to ignore belittling remarks from Chinese scholars and experts who boast about China's dominance over it. Shi Yinyong, a neo-authoritarian Chinese academic, regards the EU as weak, politically divided and militarily non-

15   ECFR interview with Shi Yinyong, Chinese international relations expert, Beijing, 3 June 2008.

16   Fox and Godement, *A Power Audit of EU–China Relations*, p. 35.

17   Ibid., p. 36.

18   ECFR interview with Feng Zhongping, European Studies Analyst at the Chinese Institutes of Contemporary International Relations, Beijing, 6 June 2008.

influential: 'Economically, it's a giant, but we no longer fear it because we know that the EU needs China more than China needs the EU.'[19]

Environmental concerns   China's foreign policies do not favour the environment, as is evident from the fact that its economic growth comes at the price of unacceptable ecological degradation as a result of inadequate government regulations and management policies, coupled with the Chinese public's lack of awareness of environmental issues.[20] In light of the above, China has faced a significant loss of agricultural land, and the rest of its land is suffering from soil erosion, increased salinity, deforestation and desertification. Due to this, the Chinese population's demand for food has been increasing, as the country is consuming more than it can produce. The international community is therefore concerned about how China is going to meet these challenges while ensuring that there is effective management of its environmental resources. The concerns focus on a number of areas:

- *Land* – Apart from the issue of land loss, China's rapid rate of development has led to serious problems of pollution from the country's manufacturing industries, both in terms of industrial waste and the by-products of energy production. This is exacerbated by the fact that energy costs in China are currently very low, so there are few incentives for conservation measures. Despite the fact that China has huge reserves of water, oil and coal, current rates of consumption are likely to lead to energy shortages in the near future.
- *Energy* – Although China has made some efforts to improve the conservation of its resources and environmental impact, it still faces many problems. For example, China's attempts to reduce the use of coal and adopt alternative sources of energy have been hampered by its continuously growing population's demands for more energy and resources. China is the largest consumer of coal in the world, relying on it for most of its energy. It is also the second-largest consumer of electricity and oil in the world, so it is clear that China cannot survive for long solely by exploiting its own resources, but will have to rely on imports of oil and other forms of energy in the near future.
- *Water* – China's agriculture is highly dependent on water, and the continuous emphasis of its policies on economic development rather than environmental protection mean that water pollution has become a major issue of concern. This has been caused by increased dumping of industrial waste into its rivers, coupled with inefficient use of the resource. In an attempt address these issues, China embarked on the building of the Three Gorges Dam. However, international concerns about the project's effects on China's cultural heritage, human habitat and historical relics led the World Bank to refuse to provide funding for it.

19   Ibid.
20   Li Xiaofon, 'Environmental Concerns in China: Problems, Policies and Global Implications', *International Social Review* (Spring/Summer 2006), pp. 1–10.

- *Regulations* – China's economic growth has been remarkable in recent years. However, it lacks adequate laws and policies to protect its environment, and what laws do exist are subject to interference from bureaucrats and local authorities, in the face of which Chinese courts have little autonomy. Given the inescapable evidence of increased environmental degradation, the Chinese government has begun to increase the environmental focus in most of its national policies.

Military Power

China is an economic powerhouse with the ability to convert its economic power to military power. Its military doctrine focuses on its capability to defeat an enemy and its indirect ability to exert influence to achieve the country's interests.[21] China's military power derives from a number of factors, such as the nation's geography, industrial capacity, national resources, its armed forces' intensive training, effective control and leadership, experience in combat and the technological characteristics of its weaponry and equipment, and the country's willingness to wield this power.[22]

Modernization of the People's Liberation Army and the PRC's Strategic Direction

It has been established that China is spending billions of dollars on modernizing its military, a fact that has spurred controversy both regionally and internationally. In light with this, there are speculations that China is on the brink of establishing a modern force that would be capable of joint service offensive operations.[23] Assessments by experts have revealed that the PRC is striving to enhance its military capabilities to further its strategic and political interests in a variety of ways.[24]

Strategic coercion and strategic denial   Improving its strategic coercion and denial capabilities is one of China's reasons for modernizing its military. It is believed that the main motivation is to deter the US from the use of military force against China, as can be inferred from the remarks of Chinese General Zhu Chengdu in response to a question posed by the editor of the *Wall Street Journal*

---

21   Larry M. Wortzel, 'China Pursues Great Power Status', *Orbis* (Spring 1994), pp. 157–76.

22   On the definitions of what constitutes natural power, see John M. Collins, *U.S. Defense Planning: A Critique* (1982), p. 1.

23   'China's Military Power: An Assessment from Open Sources', testimony of Richard D. Fisher Jr, International Assessment and Strategy Center, before the Armed Services Committee of the US House of Representatives, 27 July 2005, p. 2.

24   Dennis J. Blasko, *The Chinese Army Today: Tradition and Transformation for the 21st Century* (2006), p. 78.

about what tactics China's would adopt if an all-out conventional war erupted over Taiwan: 'If the Americans interfere in the conflict, if the Americans draw their missiles and position-guided ammunition into the target zone on China's territory, I think we will have to respond with nuclear weapons that would lead to destruction of about a hundred or two hundred American cities.'[25] To counter this threat, China has embarked on the deployment of longer-range mobile ICBMs and SLBMs, in addition to developing new air, space and naval warfare capabilities. This includes direct-assent anti-satellite ground-based lasers installed with the intention of shooting down key US space assets, and new naval assets such as the Chinese-made Xian JH-7A fighter bombers, conventional attack submarines and Russian-made Su-30MKK2s have also been strategically positioned.[26]

Forcing unification with Taiwan   China's opposition to Taiwanese independence provides a major impetus for enhancing its military power, developing the capability to achieve unification with Taiwan through intimidation, or possibly even invasion. In 2006, the US estimated that China had deployed a further 120 short-range ballistic missiles (SRBMs) and 200 land attack cruise missiles (LACMs), and predicted that by 2010 China would have deployed approximately 2,300 missiles against Taiwan. Coupled with the sudden doubling in the number of tank landing ships, amphibious assault ships and mooted plans to purchase or engage in the co-production of Zubr assault hovercraft, these developments foster fears of a Chinese invasion of Taiwan.

Preparing for regional military ascendancy and extra-regional influence   China has historically promoted the adoption of a 'peaceful rise' ideology among its supporters in pursuit of its global interests. However, it seems to be acting in contravention of this principle, since some of its actions suggest that its intent is to displace US power in Asia in defence of its strategic global interests.

Staffing Trends

Currently, China's military is the largest in the world, comprising four major branches – the People's Liberation Army (PLA), the People's Liberation Army Air Force (PLAAF), the People's Liberation Army Navy (PLAN), incorporating the marines and naval aviation, and the strategic missile forces of the Secondary Artillery – supplemented by the paramilitary People's Armed Forces and reserves. China's forces, estimated at over 3.2 million personnel, are evenly distributed throughout the country's seven military regions. In addition, China has approximately 10 million organized militia stationed at strategic locations throughout the country.[27]

---

25   Danny Gittings, 'General Zhu Goes Ballistic,' *Wall Street Journal*, 18 July 2005, p. 18.

26   'China's Military Power: An Assessment from Open Sources', p. 3.

27   Office of the Secretary of Defense, 'The Military Power of the People's Republic of China 2005', *Annual Report to Congress* (19 July 2005), p. 27.

Ground forces   The Chinese military structure is dominated by its ground forces, despite the fact that the strategic importance of its air, naval and missile branches is increasing. In readiness for a potential clash with Taiwan, China is improving its ground forces' rapid reaction and power projection capabilities.

China's has approximately 1.4 million ground forces personnel organized into eight branches: nuclear and biochemical defence, infantry, air defence missiles, signals, army aviation, engineers, armour and artillery. Other specialized branches include electronic warfare and the medical reconnaissance branch. Each of its seven military regions has a complement of 60,000 personnel, with a total of 18 army groups.

The PLA ground forces also include a special type of unit called the Rapid Reaction Forces, trained and maintained in a permanent state of readiness to carry out urgent missions outside China, and with superior equipment compared to the regular forces. However, it is difficult to compare the levels of efficiency, effectiveness and combat-readiness of the Rapid Reaction Forces and the regulars. In the recent past, China has supplied its ground forces units with armoured vehicles, more artillery pieces and tanks, including the ZTZ-99 (a third generation main battle tank) to units deployed in the Beijing and Shenyang military regions.

Air power   China has over 700 combat aircraft stationed within operational range of Taiwan, and has sufficient airfield capacity to expand their numbers if required. In order to improve its capabilities to support different types of aircraft in all weather conditions, China is enhancing its existing airfields with secondary radar, meteorological observation and microwave landing systems.[28]

The PLAAF has upgraded a number of its older aircraft, a perfect example being the re-engined B-6 bombers for extended-range targeting, but most of its inventory is made up of newer models, such as the F-10 multi-role fighter, the multi-role Su-30MKK/Flanker fighter bomber and the Su-30MK2. In addition, China's aircraft are armed with cruise missiles, laser-guided precision munitions, and a refined range of air-to-surface and air-to-air missiles, and it is improving the FB-7 fighter to facilitate night-time maritime strike operations and enable it to use conventional weaponry such as KAB-500 laser-guided munitions and Kh-31P (AS-17) anti-radiation missiles.[29]

Naval power   China's naval forces consist of 72 major vessels, about 58 attack submarines, approximately 50 medium and heavy amphibious lift vessels and 41 coastal missile patrol craft. In 2006, China took delivery of two Russian-made Sovremennyy II guided-missile destroyers (DDGs), improved versions of its earlier models which now include expanded air defence systems and anti-ship

---

28   Shanhe Wang, 'The Air Force Vigorously Promotes the Improvement of Aviation Field Station Supply System,' *PLA Daily*, 8 December 2008.

29   Office of the Secretary of Defense, 'The Military Power of the People's Republic of China,' *Annual Report to Congress* (2007), p. 4.

cruise missiles (ASCMs).[30] It has also focused on building Jin Class (Type 094) nuclear-powered ballistic missile submarines and Shang Class (Type 093) nuclear-powered attack submarines, which began sea trials in 2005.[31]

The PLAN possesses 12 Russian-made Kilo submarines, with the newest models equipped with wire-guided torpedoes, wake-homing torpedoes and the supersonic SS-N-27B ASCM. In addition, the PLAN will be acquiring a new ship of the Luzhou Class (Type 051C), a DDG designed to neutralize air threats by deploying the Russian SA-N-20 surface-to-air missile (SAM) system controlled by the Tombstone phased-array radar, significantly improving the PLAN's shipborne air capabilities by doubling the range of its current defensive systems.[32] Other developments include the Luyang II DDGS equipped with an air defence system and the Jiangkai II guided-missile frigate equipped with SAMs.[33]

Advances in Chinese Military Modernization

In order to evaluate China's military power, it is crucial to examine the advances it has made in military modernization in the following areas: expeditionary operations, air defences, ground forces, space, counter-space and anti-access measures, moves to protect lines of communication, computer network operations and nuclear deterrence.[34]

Nuclear deterrence   China is enhancing the quantity and the quality of its strategic missile forces to improve its nuclear deterrence and counter-strike capabilities. It has embraced the principle of 'no first use' of its nuclear weapons, but it is continuing to deploy survivable missiles that are capable of targeting the US, Australia, New Zealand, the Asia-Pacific region, Russia and India.

It is predicted that in the future, China's strategic force will consist of silo-based CSS-4 ICBMs, which are already deployed, road-mobile DF-31A ICBMs, sea-based JL-2 SLBMs and the DF-31. To support its regional strategy, China is expected to maintain a force composed of nuclear-armed CSS-5 medium-range ballistic missiles. In 2005, it was estimated that China had deployed a total of 20 silo-based liquid-propellant CSS-4 ICBMs which comprise its primary nuclear

---

30   Ronald O'Rourke, *China Naval Modernization: Implications for U.S. Navy Capabilities: Background and Issues for Congress*, CRS Report to Congress (18 November 2005), p. 4.

31   James C. Bussert, 'China Builds Destroyers around Imported Technology,' *Signal* (August 2004): http://www.afcea.org/signal/articles/anmviewer.asp?a=252 (accessed 20 January 2012).

32   'New-generation Warships for the PLA Navy', *Military Technology* 28:2 (February 2004), pp. 90–91.

33   Office of the Secretary of Defense, 'Military Power of the People's Republic of China', *Annual Report to Congress* (2008): http://www.defenselink.mil/pubs/pdfs/China_Military_Report_08.pdf9 (accessed 20 January 2012), p. 30.

34   Ibid., p. 32.

deterrent. Meanwhile, to sustain its regional nuclear deterrent, it is believed that China has supplied its Second Artillery with no fewer than 20 liquid-fuelled limited-range CSS-3 ICBMs, the aim being to keep the older missile in service until the more survivable road-mobile DF-31 ICBMs are ready in sufficient numbers.

The DF-31 series serves as a supplement to China's silo-based strategic force, its mobility allowing it to cover a wider area, making it more difficult for an enemy to locate and neutralize the missiles. The introduction of SLBMs on China's new ballistic missile submarines, along with the longer-range CSS-4 Mod 2 and the silo-based CSS-4 Mod 1, have substantially increased the survivability and operational capabilities of the strategic missile force. Finally, still under development are the JL-2 SLBM and the DF-31A ICBM launcher missiles, with ranges of 8,000 and 11,270 kilometres respectively. Currently, the US considers the DF-31 ICBMs as the primary threat.[35]

Precision strike　　China visualizes the use of precision strikes by its rapid reaction units that would be able to target ports, Western Pacific air bases, command facilities, land-based C4ISRs and air defence systems. To achieve this, objective China has 650–750 missiles available, the main types being conventionally armed SRBMs, whose later generations have been greatly improved in terms of accuracy and range, and the number is increasing by 75–120 per year. China is also in the process of developing conventionally armed LACMs in a bid to hit harder targets. The PLAN and PLAAF deploy a variety of ASCMs, ranging from the 1950s-era CSS-N-2/Styx to the Russian-made SS-N-22/Sunburn and SS-N-27/Sizzler, and China has also increased the pace of research, foreign procurement, production and development of ASCMs in the last decade. The PLA's current objective is to improve the ASCMs' stealth launch capabilities, standoff distances and closure speeds. However, it is believed that China possesses only a limited quantity of tactical ASMs, and to address this, it is stepping up foreign and domestic acquisitions in an attempt to enhance its airborne and anti- ship capabilities.

Finally, the scope and size of China's ARM deployments are currently unclear, although the nation has imported ARMs and the Harpy unmanned aerial vehicle (UAV) from Israel. China's military doctrine of 'electromagnetic superiority' is demonstrated by its acquisition of anti-radiation weapons, which locate targets through their own transmissions.

Expeditionary operations　　China's expeditionary forces consists of three airborne divisions, two amphibious infantry divisions, two marine brigades, about seven special operations groups and one regiment-size reconnaissance element in the Second Artillery.[36] In order to modernize these units, China

---

35　Office of the Secretary of Defense, 'The Military Power of the People's Republic of China' (2007), p. 42.

36　Office of the Secretary of Defense, 'The Military Power of the People's Republic of China' (2005), p. 30.

has focused on the procurement of more equipment, the co-ordination of joint operations and the improvement of unit-level tactics. To improve the lethality and the speed of seaborne assaults, China has supplied its ground forces in the Nanjing and Guangzhou military regions with tanks, personnel carriers, upgraded amphibious armoured vehicles and troop-carrying hovercraft. In addition, the PLAAF has also been supplied with modern transport aircraft similar to the IL-76/Candid, as well as modern air-mobile light-weight vehicles, as used by the Russians, and China has also embarked on the development of amphibious ships to address its force deployment problems. This modernization programme seeks to facilitate amphibious operations by special operations forces, enhance air defence capabilities, safeguard critical lines of communication, improve airfield seizure capabilities and improve the secondary deployment of infantry forces. It is also upgrading its Second Artillery inspection elements in order to improve the flow of information on the degree of damage on the battlefield. Although the Chinese military conducts some combined training of its forces in amphibious assault exercises, its capabilities in this respect remain unclear.

Air defence   China has moved from an air defence strategy based on protecting key industrial, political and military targets to a joint anti-air raid strategy that incorporates both effective offensive and defensive counter-air capabilities, relying on surface-to-surface missiles, long-range artillery, aircraft, special operations naval forces and guerrilla units to launch offensive air operations and to offer effective protection of its airspace. To pursue this, China has concentrated on the acquisition of foreign and domestic fourth-generation tactical aircraft and advanced ASMs, enabling the PLAAF to attack both external and internal targets with a high degree of accuracy. China is also equipping its new aircraft with advanced air-to-air missiles and electronic warfare systems that equal or surpass most of its adversaries in terms of technology.[37]

Anti-access   China has been particularly nervous about military invasion since the potential Soviet threat of the 1980s. To address this and in support of its geo-strategic ambitions towards Taiwan, China has significantly tightened security by shifting from deploying its the navy solely for coastal defence to including surface, air and sub-surface elements in its strategy. It is believed that China has adopted the Assassin's Mace programme to deny entry and neutralize the operations of adversaries, as well as enhancing its sea denial capabilities by deploying submarines, cruise missiles, special operations forces and naval mines.[38]

---

37   Roger Cliff, 'The Development of China's Air Force Capabilities', testimony presented before the US-China Economic and Security Review Commission on 20 May 2010, pp. 2–3.

38   'Securing Borders: China's Doctrine and Force Structure for Frontier Defense', *Journal of Strategic Studies* 30:4–5 (2007), pp. 705–37.

China has embarked on the production of the domestic Song Class submarine, acquiring more Kilo Class submarines from Russia, and the development of the Type 093 nuclear attack submarine to undertake missions that require endurance at sea. It has also increased research into the use of ballistic missiles and special operations forces against ships and their shore-based support infrastructure. In a bid to develop and enhance its space exploration and countermeasure capabilities, China is adopting a range of measures, including camouflage, high-tech lasers and space tracking systems

Protecting vital lines of communication   China has many gaps in the protection of its vital lines of communication. Despite the fact that the PLAN patrols its coasts, China is still susceptible to attacks from adversaries' air and naval forces due to its limited air defence capabilities. In addition, the limited operational range of the PLAAF and the PLAN's own air forces mean that the PLAN lacks long-range air support. To address this, China has assigned two destroyers, HHQ-7C SAMs, submarines and surface combatant units.

Joint logistics   Incorporation of the civil sector into the military procurement system is the major feature of China's reforms, involving the outsourcing of numerous logistics functions where the civilians can perform the same functions as its military at a lower cost. It has also emphasized mobilization of the civilian economy during times of both peace and in war in a bid to strengthen the nation's capabilities in commerce and trade, urban construction, agriculture, finance, medical care and health, and transport and communication. Despite the fact that China's command system is incompatible both with its support systems and its management of supply and planning, since 2000, China has striven to enhance the structure, efficiency and co-ordination of its joint logistics.[39]

Space and counter-space programmes   In recent years, China has focused on developing its infrastructure to support advanced command, control, communications, computers, intelligence, surveillance and reconnaissance (C4ISR) systems. China has numerous space-based programmes that may be integrated into its military developments. On 15 October 2003, China launched its first manned spacecraft into Earth orbit, and in September 2005 it sent two people on a five-day space expedition. In the same year, China launched its first satellite system, the Ziyuan-1 (ZY-1), and in October 2004 its second, the Ziyuan-2 (ZY-2). The ZY-2 provides worldwide digital imagery reconnaissance. In 2003 and 2004 China also tested small digital and film-based imagery satellites.[40] China has also

---

39   Keith Crane, Roger Cliff, Evan Medeiros, James Mulvenon and William Overholt, *Modernizing China's Military: Opportunities and Constraints* (2005), p. 109.

40   Office of the Secretary of Defense, 'The Military Power of the People's Republic of China' (2005), p. 35.

shown an interest in electronic and signals intelligence satellites, including data relay satellites to support global coverage for deployed military forces.

These small satellite programs have been an important aspect of China's military modernization programme. Since 2002, has launched a number of these, including an oceanographic research satellite, two imaging satellites and another two for conducting space research. Since 2000, it has also been developing micro-satellites weighing no more than 100 kilograms for the detection of electro-optical networks and radar satellites. Some of these programmes have involved collaboration with other countries, such as China's joint venture with the UK to build seven mini-satellites. Finally, China plans to launch weapons capable of tracking, disabling and destroying other countries' satellites.

China's spaceborne capabilities were evidenced in 2007, when it destroyed an old weather satellite orbiting at 862 kilometres with a ground-based missile equipped with a kinetic warhead. This was a great advance for China, as similar tests conducted in 2005 and 2006 had met with failure.[41]

A ground-based mid-range missile interception test was conducted by China in January 2010. Although the details of this have not yet been revealed, China stated that the test was consistent with its defensive strategy and that it would not alter its position on missile defences.[42]

Computer network operations China's computer network operations (CNOs) involve exploitation, defence and attack. Following the principle of 'electromagnetic dominance', the PLA perceives CNOs as vital to gain an early advantage against adversaries in force multiplication conflicts. The approach is described as integrated network electronic warfare, combining the use of CNOs and kinetic strikes to disrupt its adversaries' information systems in the battlefield. In pursuit of this, China has widened the role of CNOs role in military exercises, and as well training its forces in defensive measures, it has focused on integrated offensive operations to enable it to launch first strikes against its adversaries' networks.

Participation in Global Security Issues

China's participation in global security matters has increased greatly over the past decade, including programmes to prevent the spread of epidemic diseases such as AIDS, peacekeeping in war-torn areas, engaging in counter-terrorist activities and supporting nuclear non-proliferation initiatives. However, it has been resistant to arms control measures despite calls from the US and Russia to stop testing nuclear weapons.

---

41   National Institute of Defensive Studies, *NIDS China Security Report* (2011), p. 37.
42   Ibid., p. 38.

Counter-terrorism

The September 11th attacks on the US proved that global terrorism could pose a similar threat to China, so it has joined the rest of the world in the fight against terrorism, seizing this opportunity to crack down on separatists in the autonomous region of Xinjiang.[43] However, China's policy does not rely on military intervention alone, but incorporates identifying and addressing the root causes of terrorism.

China has been an active participant in the international alliance against the Taliban and Al-Qaeda, sharing intelligence, supporting Pakistan's anti-terrorist efforts, acting to prevent the outbreak of war between Indian and Pakistan that could have thwarted the anti-terror campaign in the region, and taking part in a range of activities to combat terrorist groups and organizations across national borders,[44] including its campaign against the East Turkestan Movement, a terrorist organization that has received funding, training and weapons from international groups such as Al-Qaeda.

China is also playing a major role in the UN's fight against international terrorism, including the formulation of an international anti-terror legal system. Even before the September 11th attack, China had ratified most of the international anti-terrorism conventions, and after it, China supported a number of UN Security Council anti-terrorism and enforcement resolutions. China is a signatory of the International Convention on Curbing Terrorist Explosions and the International Convention on Curbing Funding to Terrorism, and has been at the forefront in organizing negotiations and dialogues relating to anti-terrorism campaigns with a number of countries. It also made a significant contribution to Tadzhikistan's Afghan national reconciliation process and Afghanistan's reconstruction programme after the war. China made concerted efforts to find a sustainable solution before the eruption of the Iraq War, and offered considerable assistance to the UN in the reconstruction of Iraq.

China and Nuclear Proliferation

The proliferation of nuclear weapons has heightened China's sensitivity to these threats, and it has declared its readiness to support an effective global regime to control nuclear weapons and other weapons of mass destruction, not least because it is surrounded by nuclear-armed countries, including North Korea, India, Russia and Pakistan.[45]

China has taken a leading role in countering the expansion of the production of nuclear weapons, driven by the continued efforts in this field by North Korea despite

---

43   Dethlefsen, *China's Foreign Policy in Transition*, p. 2.

44   Pan Guang, 'China's Anti-terror Strategy and China's Role in Global Anti-terror Cooperation', *Asia Europe Journal* 2 (2004): http://www.irChina.org/en/news/view.asp?id=357 (accessed 21 January 2012), pp. 523–32.

45   Dethlefsen, *China's Foreign Policy in Transition*, p. 2.

criticisms and calls for a halt from the UN, China, the US and other countries. One of China's motives for opposing North Korea's nuclear weapons programme is the fear that if it proceeds, other Asian countries such as Japan will develop and deploy them in response. For this reason, China has offered strong support for the Global Initiative to Combat Nuclear Terrorism (GICNT), a programme launched by the US and Russia. China joined the GICNT in October 2006 at Rabat, where the founding preliminary meeting was held. In the same year, China joined the Implementation and Assessment Group, responsible for drafting GICNT's work plan and deciding what activities GICNT should sponsor.[46]

It is worth noting that since China signed the Nuclear Non-Proliferation Treaty in 1992, it is one of the few countries that has agreed to all the protocols referring to existing nuclear weapons-free zones. In addition, China's defence white paper emphasizes it position on non-proliferation, stating: 'China firmly opposes the proliferation of weapons of mass destruction (WMD) and their means of delivery, and actively takes part in international non-proliferation efforts.'[47]

China and Arms Control

Despite these efforts, China has also opposed certain arms control initiatives over the past twenty years, resisting reductions in its ballistic missiles and nuclear weapons.[48] China has justified this position by claiming that the US and Russia have colluded to ensure that China constantly lags behind in economic terms. Its selective approach to arms control is evident from China's active participation in the 1987 Intermediate-range Nuclear Forces Treaty prohibiting the US and Russia from developing, manufacturing and deploying missiles (both ground-based and cruise missiles) with ranges of 500–5,000 kilometres, despite Russia's has consistent complaints that other countries possess missiles that could reach its territory.

Peacekeeping Training and Exchanges

China has also expanded its engagement in peacekeeping operations, not least because they provide excellent learning opportunities for its security forces, and the benefits in return for other countries, for instance through Chinese medical

---

46   Conference on 'U.S.-China Strategic Nuclear Dynamics' co-organized by the Center for Strategic and International Studies, Institute for Defense Analyses, the Rand Corporation, and the China Foundation for International and Strategic Studies, 8–10 June 2008: http://www.csis.org/media/csis/pubs/081015_intro_and_key_findings.pdf (accessed 20 January 2012).

47   Information Office of China's State Council, *China's National Defense in 2008*, 20 January 2009: http://www.gov.cn/english/official/2009-01/20/content_1210227_16.htm (accessed 20 January 2012), ch. 14.

48   Alastair Iain Johnston, 'Learning Versus Adapting: Explaining Change in China's Arms Control Policy in the 1980s and 1990s', *China Journal* 35 (January 1996), pp. 27–61.

units participating in the UN Mission in the Democratic Republic of Congo have gained respect for PLA troops. Recently, Chinese personnel's engagement in joint peacekeeping training and exchanges has increased, as has its participation in regional and national security dialogues. These initiatives have gone some way to allaying China's neighbours' concerns about its strategic intentions, and increased their willingness to help China to be recognized as a positive global force by the international community.

As part of its efforts to acquire more military experience and knowledge of tactics, China has sent troops to take part in professional training and exchange programmes in a variety of countries, including Estonia, Germany, Mongolia, Australia, South Africa, Bangladesh, Canada, Indonesia, Switzerland, Hungary, India, Norway, Ireland, Italy, New Zealand, Sweden and Thailand. Chinese personnel have also taken part, both as active participants and as observers, in peacekeeping exercises organized by the UK and the French Reinforcement of African Peacekeeping Capabilities programme.[49]

China has increasingly organized and hosted numerous international seminars relating to peacekeeping issues, such as the annual UK-China Seminar on Peacekeeping Operations, which China has hosted since 2004, and China and Sweden have also engaged in similar arrangements. In addition, seminars and pre-deployment briefings on international humanitarian law for China's peacekeeping troops have been provided by the International Committee of the Red Cross.

China also takes a leading role in co-ordinating peacekeeping activities in the Asian region, as evidenced by its sponsorship and hosting of ASEAN's first peacekeeping seminar in 2007 in Beijing, where discussions took place on ways to improve co-operation and exchange ideas and experiences concerned with UN peacekeeping. Finally, in 2009, China's commitment to co-operation and peacekeeping was emphasized by senior military officials at the China–ASEAN High Level Defence Dialogue.[50]

Joint Military Exercises and Other Military-to-military Co-operation

Recently, there has been increased engagement between the PLA and other foreign forces in joint military exercises. Although some of these exercises are not directly related to UN peacekeeping operations, China dubs these exercises 'peace missions' since they are directed towards the fight against terrorism, extremism and separatism with the aim of enhancing regional stability and security and improving the level of trust between the Chinese military and others.

---

49   P. Zhang, 'Remarks on the People's Liberation Army's Participation in UN peacekeeping operations', speech delivered at the conference 'Multidimensional and Integrated Peace Operations: Trends and Challenges', Beijing, March 2007, pp. 26–7.

50   'Defence Ministry Touts Deepened China–ASEAN Security Cooperation', Xinhua Domestic Service, Beijing, 30 March 2009.

In October 2002 and 2003, China, in conjunction with its partners (Kazakhstan, Kyrgyzstan, Russia, Tajikistan and Uzbekistan) in the Shanghai Cooperation Organization, participated in what were labelled joint counter-terrorism exercises,[51] conducting similar ones with India and Pakistan in 2004. In September 2006, Chinese and Tajik troops simulated a hostage-taking scenario during a joint military exercise called Coordination 2006,[52] in July 2007, Chinese and Thai troops engaged in a two-week counter-terrorism training exercise named Strike 2007 in China's Guangzhou Province, and in June–July 2009, Chinese and Mongolian troops held a joint military training exercise called Peacekeeping Mission 2009.

China's joint naval activities have also increased since 2000. Canada, India, Thailand, France, the UK, the US and Pakistan are some of the countries with which the PLAN has engaged in joint naval exercises.[53] China also deployed ships to the Gulf of Aden in December 2008 after declaring its support for the multinational anti-piracy force. In September 2009, China was invited by Australia and the US to take part in a trilateral military disaster relief exercise, offering humanitarian assistance to victims of war and other disasters.

China and Russia engaged in a joint military exercise in August 2005 involving approximately 10,000 air force and navy personnel from both countries, consisting of the movement of ships to the Shandong Peninsula from Vladivostok, and command post and headquarters exercises, believed to simulate intervention in countries faced with political disturbances and instability. In 2007, China and Russia engaged in a counter-terrorism exercise involving about 4,000 troops and 80 aircraft in Uruqi, China and Chelybisk, Russia, and another joint exercise took place in 2009 in China's Jilin province and Russia's Khabarovsk, involving 13,000 air force personnel from each country.

Other Bilateral and Multilateral Developments

China has engaged in a number of bilateral and multilateral agreements with other countries and blocs regarding peacekeeping and the maintenance of regional and international security. This has led to increased co-operation between China and some member states of the EU in several security-related fields, including joint military exercises, peacekeeping training, port visits, strategic dialogues, military-to-military diplomacy and educational exchanges. A good example of this co-operation is China's engagement in formal consultative dialogues with the UK, Germany and on defence issues.[54] In 2005, China and the EU instigated regular

---

51   Bates Gill and Chin-Hao Huang, *China's expanding Role in Peace Keeping: Prospects and Policy Implications*, SIPRI Policy Paper no. 25 (2009), p. 18.

52   Ibid., p. 19.

53   Gill, *Rising Star*, pp. 63–6.

54   Bates Gill, 'European Union–China Cooperation on Security Issues', in D. Shambaugh and G. Wacker (eds), *American and European Relations with China: Advancing Common Agendas* (2008), p. 97.

ministerial strategic dialogues which emphasized international and regional issues.[55] This mechanism has been useful in addressing bilateral matters of concern between the countries, as well as regional and international issues.

China has also established bilateral anti-terrorism arrangements with Pakistan, Russia, India and the US. For instance, it co-operated with the US after the September 11th attacks, mainly focusing on tackling sources of funding for terrorism, supporting Pakistan's anti-terrorism efforts, preventing the escalation of conflicts between India and Pakistan and sharing information. In October 2001, China complied with a US request to seal its 90 kilometre border with Afghanistan to facilitate co-ordination with the US military, and subsequently participated in the interrogation of Chinese East Turkestan terrorists after the US subdued Afghanistan. Two meetings between the Chinese and US presidents and later meetings between China's premier and the US president resulted in the formation of an anti-terrorism working group, and in August 2002 the East Turkestan Islamic Movement was included in the list of terrorist organizations, with the UN affirming this decision through the combined efforts of Kyrgyzstan, Afghanistan, China and the US. In recent years, China has engaged in joint anti-terrorism search and rescue exercises with Russia, France, Australia, the UK and Pakistan.

In October 2008, the European Commission issued a policy directive outlining a trilateral dialogue and co-operation initiative involving the African Union (AU), the EU and China. The directive recognized that promoting peace and security in Africa would enhance the region's development and was an issue of common interest for the three partners. In addition, a proposal was made to the EU and individual member states to support China and the UN in strengthening the AU's African Peace and Security Architecture. A new organization, the African Support Force (ASF), was to be established, and EU member states were requested to offer assistance with training, capacity-building and AU peacekeeping operations.[56]

In March 2009, the UN Security Council met to discuss ways to strengthen co-operation between the AU and UN on peace and security matters, focusing on increasing the level of financial and logistical support from UN member states and African countries. The major objective of the meeting was to enhance the AU's capacity in terms of early warning, conflict-prevention, peace-building after conflicts, and intelligence. While deliberating on the matter, Chinese UN Ambassador Zhang stated that China 'supported more reliable means and funding for African Union peacekeeping operations … and enhancing the regional body

---

55　European Union, 'Joint Statement of the 8th EU–China Summit', Press Release no. IP/05/1091, Brussels, 5 September 2005: http://europa.eu/rapid/pressReleasesAction.do?reference=IP/05/1091 (accessed 21 January 2012).

56　European Commission, *The EU, Africa and China: Towards Trilateral Dialogue and Cooperation: Communication from the Commission to the European Parliament, the Council, the European Economic and Social Committee and the Committee of the Regions on Trilateral Dialogue and Cooperation between the EU, Africa and China*, COM(2008) 654 final, 17 October 2008, p. 5.

by scaling up personnel, institutional training and logistical support in order to implement the UN 10-year capacity-building programme for the AU.'[57] In the 2007–2009 Forum on China–Africa Cooperation action plan, China promised to co-operate with the AU in peacekeeping operations in Africa and to help to improve the AU's ability to respond to shifting security challenges by providing funding for the ASF.

China's promotion of international anti-terrorism co-operation is evident form its involvement in multilateral organizations such as APEC, the Asia–Europe Meeting (ASEM), the SCO and the ASEAN Regional Forum. Since 1996, the SCO has taken the lead role in combating terrorist activities in Central Asia. Three days after the September 11th attacks, a joint statement released by the SCO during a prime ministerial-level meeting expressed the organization's extreme condemnation of the attacks and affirmed its willingness to support any country and the international community in combating terrorist threats worldwide. China's commitment to anti-terrorism efforts was also apparent when its prime minister suggested the urgent establishment of a SCO anti-terrorism agency, which was an important factor in the success of the 2002 US Afghanistan offensive.

In June 2004, the SCO's Regional Anti-Terrorist Structure (RATS) was officially launched in Tashkent, which affirmed the SCO's commitment to counter-terrorist activities and engagement in non-conventional security issues such as drug trafficking. In 2001, China, Thailand, Myanmar and Laos signed a multilateral anti-drug co-operation agreement, and in November 2002, China and ASEAN confirmed this commitment and offered an assurance of full co-operation in anti-terrorism measures in the region in a joint statement at the sixth summit meeting.

It is believed that China will continue to engage in international anti-terrorism initiatives and numerous other coalitions in the future despite the fact that it did not side with the US in its unilateral decision to attack Iraq. However, China's strategy to combat terrorism differs from the US concept of global action. China's main aim is to enhance its security and eliminate terrorist activities within the region in order to make the environment conducive for economic development. Nevertheless, its influence and anti-terrorism efforts have had a global impact.

Summary

As this chapter has shown, China's foreign policies are geared to serving its domestic interests, and their major objective is to bring about economic development and political transformation. However, another important aim is to

---

57   UN, Department of Public Information, 'Security Council Underscores Importance of Supporting African Union's efforts to Improve Regional Peacekeeping Capacity', Press Release no. SC/9615, March 2009: http://www.un.org/News/Press/docs/2009/sc9615.doc.htm (accessed 21 January 2012), p. 18.

limit the influence of the US. To enhance its regional influence, China has engaged in bilateral and multilateral relationships with other countries in the region and formed regional organizations to promote free trade and economic development within Asia. It has also shown that in recent years, China has departed from its traditional self-reliance policies and taken an increasingly role in international organizations, abiding by their rules, regulations and policies, in order to improve the country's potential for development.

The overview of China's foreign policy offers evidence that China is indeed gaining soft power as the rest of the world grows more and more reliant on its role. Although it has not yet overtaken the US in economic terms, its growth rate and increasing economic power mean that its international influence may in time equal or surpass the US's. However, China's foreign policies also raise issues of concern since it is not immune from the effects of the global financial crisis, so some critics argue that it places too much emphasis on its own economic development at the expense of other countries. For example, China exploits the opening of markets in the European Union, but does not reciprocate. China has also shown a tendency to break bilateral agreements and fail to fulfil promises of formal dialogue meetings. Another issue of concern is that China's current economic policies are leading to severe degradation of its own environment and making a major contribution to global warming.

China has an extremely large military which it is in the process of modernizing to protect the country from attack, to deploy for strategic coercion and denial, and to force the issue of unification with Taiwan. The country's huge investment in defence and the continuous growth of its military power have led to suspicions among other world powers about China's real motives.

Finally, China's participation in issues of global security extends to areas such as arms control, nuclear weapons proliferation, peacekeeping and counter-terrorism initiatives, promoted through a range of bilateral and multilateral arrangements with other countries, including taking part in joint military exercises and other types of co-operation such as peacekeeping operations and training. Despite the fact that China has taken on key roles in its region, the UN and the international community in these ways, a major concern that remains is China's refusal to scale down or abandon its nuclear weapons programme.

Chapter 8

The BRICs and International Security

A succinct and comprehensive definition of international security is provided by Viotti and Kauppi:

> In [international security's] narrowest construction, the term refers to defence matters among states and their respective societies. In its broadest sense, it encompasses a very wide range of issues that affect the welfare of human beings-not just defence, but also economics, health, environment, human rights, and other social questions that cross national boundaries. Critics of broad definition argue that is security as a concept can be constructed to mean so many things, then as a practical matter it means nothing. They prefer to retain the more traditional distinction between security (and related defence issues) and welfare issues.[1]

From this, it is clear that there exist both narrow and broad perspectives on global security issues. The narrow perspective is limited to military security, while the broad one covers a wide range of issues concerning human welfare and development, such as the environment, economy and health. In this latter sense, the term 'security' includes human safety from non-military threats, 'environmental scarcity, overpopulation, disease and poverty'.[2] The realist approach ranks survival as the foundation of security, followed by welfare and protection of the state within the international system. This book largely uses 'security' in its narrow sense – in terms of military capability and protection from external threats.

The discussions of each of the BRICs countries' participation in global security in the previous chapters in Part II show that have been playing significant roles in shaping global security, either through direct influence, or by indirect influence through global and regional organizations of which they are members. Russia and India have been particularly outstanding in this respect, especially because of their veto powers on the UN Security Council. This chapter will supplement these earlier discussions by focusing on the international security role of the BRICs as a group, including that group's relationship with the UN, EU and NATO.

---

1   P.R. Viotti and M.V. Kauppi, *International Relations and World Politics: Security, Economy, Identity*, 3rd edn (2007), p. 23.
2   Ibid., p. 28.

The Joint Role of the BRICs in International Security

Although the BRICs are still far from forming a formal inter-governmental organization that could be termed a true, conventional power bloc owing to the wide diversity among the member countries, their joint influence as a coalition on international security issues cannot be overlooked. The new forums, such as the BRICs leaders' summit meetings, that have been recently devised offer opportunities to voice the BRICs' interests in global affairs and to lobby for joint positions on global security matters. As the BRICs grouping consolidates itself, it is likely to evolve into a new pressure group and supranational body that may challenge the current supremacy of the US and its allies.

Until the end of 2011, the BRICs countries were all members of the UN Security Council (UNSC); both Russia and China remain permanent members, and India is a rotating member, as was Brazil until its term ended on 31 December. Brazil and India are currently lobbying for permanent membership, to reflect their growing international influence.

The BRICs countries have recently shown greater solidarity in approaching world security issues, as illustrated by their common position during the UNSC's deliberations and eventual passing of Resolution 1973 imposing a no-fly zone on Libya, when all the BRICs countries, alongside Germany, abstained.[3] This served as the first litmus test of the solidarity of the BRICs as a pressure group – a test it passed. Another effort to pass a similar resolution against Syria advocated by the US and its traditional allies, the UK, France and Italy, was thwarted by Russia and China's vetoes.[4] In refusing to support the resolution, both countries cited Syria's sovereignty as a nation, the inappropriateness of taking military action in intra-state conflicts while there was still scope for peaceful dispute-resolution, and the possibility of the abuse of such a resolution.[5] The BRICs' role as a counterbalance in global security matters is likely to be enhanced by moves to form a more solid political and economic bloc, entrenching the BRICs' perception of respect for international law and good practices in future approaches to global security issues.

The BRICs nations, particularly those from Asia (Russia, China and India), have sought co-operation on international security issues and other matters of common interest in a variety of international forums, the threats addressed including aggressive nationalism, terrorism, political extremism, drug trafficking and xenophobia. In 2001, China and Russia, alongside Kyrgyzstan, Uzbekistan, Kazakhstan and Tajikistan, formed the Shanghai Cooperation Organization as an initiative to address these concerns. India also expressed an interest in joining the

---

3   United Nations Security Council Resolution 1973, 17 March 2011.

4   'China, Russia Vetoes Thwart U.N. Security Council Resolution on Syria,' CNN, 4 October 2011: http://articles.cnn.com/2011-10-04/middleeast/world_meast_syria-unrest_1_bashar-ja-afari-president-bashar-security-council?_s=PM:MIDDLEEAST (accessed 24 October 2011).

5   Ibid.

SCO,[6] and was eventually granted observer status later that year. Through the SCO, these nations created the Regional Anti-Terrorist Structure, mandated, among other duties, to co-ordinate collective measures to combat terrorism, including the exchange of information and experiences, joint military manoeuvres and financial control.[7] Through these forums, Russia, India and China have been key players in safeguarding global security, particularly in the Asian region, where the most aggressive terrorist groups are believed to have strong bases. Co-operation between Brazil and the other three BRICs countries in these efforts has so far been minimal, but this may change as the BRICs bloc solidifies.

The European Union and the BRICs

The EU has become a major player in Eastern Europe in terms of economic, political and social activities. Its role in this region is particularly evident in Moldova and Belarus, bringing improvements in inter-governmental relations, trade and other economic activities. However, the BRICs also have strong interests in this region. Russia's energy resources mean that it has a lot of influence over Moldova and Belarus, so both nations are determined to build strong relationships within the region in order to retain economic power and promote trade with other countries.

The EU promises many benefits to its members in terms of the facilitation of issuing visas, freedom of trade and immigration control. The EU's Eastern Partnership programme seeks to create economic stability, security and prosperity in Eastern Europe, reaching out to countries like Moldova and Belarus to bring them closer to the EU's principles and practices. This offers a number of advantages to these countries, including integration into the EU economy, easier migration within the EU, more effective border management and enhanced bargaining power.[8] All these factors level the playing field with their international rivals in the EU market. However, the EU's Eastern Partnership does not exist in a vacuum, and its implementation is affected by Russia's strong influence, especially on Moldova and Belarus.

The first policy the European Union will have to instigate towards Moldova and Belarus involves changes in their foreign and security policies to control migration across their borders with other member states. First raised in 1989 by the European Community Council, the policy defines a surveillance system for external frontiers, an information-sharing system to identify those who do not qualify for admission, and general measures to combat illegal immigration.

---

6   See Boris F. Martynov. *'BRICs': Cooperation Perspectives in the International Security Sphere*: http://www.ipea.gov.br/bric/textos/100409_BRICMartynov1.pdf(accessed 21 December 2011).

7   Ibid.

8   Nicu Popescu and Andrew Wilson, *The Limits of Enlargement-Lite: European and Russian Power in the Troubled Neighbourhood*, London: European Council on Foreign Relations (2009).

However, the EU's progress on these fronts has been impeded by the complexities of integrating non-member nations into its system of governance.

A visa facilitation agreement between the EU and Moldova came into force in 2008, providing a greater degree of understanding and co-operation between the parties with reference to migration.[9] As well as helping to combat illegal migration, the agreement has enhanced the mobility of citizens of Moldova and Belarus between their countries and the European Union, enabling them to pursue work and business opportunities outside their own countries.

During 2007–10, Moldova and Belarus received the largest allocation of funds from the EU to boost trade in the international market, improve their economies and implement the visa facilitation process. This was in response to the economic crisis, which has hit Eastern Europe particularly hard, especially Moldova and Belarus and their neighbourhood.

The influence of Russia on the nations of the former USSR is still enormous, and it continues to consider countries like Moldova and Belarus and others it describes as 'states of the Caucasus' as part of its economic and political back yard. Russia's regional policy has for a long time been aimed at perpetuating its influence over Moldova and Belarus, which leads it to enact policies that conflict with those of the EU and seek to restrict the EU's role in this countries.[10] Among the measures Russia has adopted are the use of its energy monopoly to impede the EU's initiatives, exerting influence on the domestic policies of Moldova and Belarus, and attempting to integrate the countries' economies to gain a competitive advantage over the EU.

Russia is the largest producer of natural gas and oil in the world, and Moldova and Belarus rely heavily on it for the supply of fuel and gas at favourable prices. This was illustrated when Russia decided to vary its gas prices on the world market in 2006, charging Belarus US$47 per 1,000 cubic meters while charging other nations like Georgia US$110. This manipulation of prices by Russia is likely to continue as part of its strategy to reward or punish neighbouring countries' behaviour.

During 2004, the EU adopted its European Neighbourhood Policy, which was intended to promote relations with the countries that surround it.[11] Although this policy should be very beneficial for Moldova and Belarus, since it allows signatories free movement of labour, people, goods and services, hence enhancing their trade,

---

9   B. Demirtaş-Coşkun and B. Balamir-Coşkun, *Neighborhood Challenge: The European Union and its Neighbors* (2009), p. 325.

10   UK House of Lords European Union Committee, *The European Union and Russia: Report with Evidence*, 14th Report of Session 2007–2008: http://www.publications. parliament.uk/pa/ld200708/ldselect/ldeucom/98/9802.htm (accessed 19 June 2013), p. 181.

11   Commission of the European Communities, *Communication from the Commission to the European Parliament and the European Council, Eastern Partnership, Brussels, 3.12.2008*, COM(2008) 823 final, p. 8.

prosperity and stability, and offering protection from unfair competition, it has failed to fulfil their high expectations.

The policy's primary weakness is that it does not take adequate account of the differences that exist between the regions that surround it. It first included the Ukraine, then other countries followed, including those in the Mediterranean. However, the southern countries were reacting out of fear that the EU's policies might become more eastward-looking, which could be very detrimental to them in terms of trade and economic stability and prosperity. This has led to up to 70 per cent of Neighbourhood Policy funds being allocated to the Mediterranean nations, compromising the original objectives. Another weakness results from the policy's inflexibility with respect to regional development and other local issues, which has led some countries to withdraw from membership.

Lack of harmonization of between the European Neighbourhood Policy and Russian policy is another problem that is hindering the EU's outreach to Moldova and Belarus.[12] Failure to take account of the diversity of perceptions, interests and actors in the EU has a major effect on the prospects of the policy with regard to the Eastern European neighbourhood. Unless policies are harmonized, there is little chance of integration, but achieving this may not be possible owing to the conflicts of interest between Russia and the EU.

While the EU is a very powerful body in the greater European community, it also has its own challenges. The UK joined its precursor, the European Community, relatively late, and has been at times a reluctant partner. This reflects the fact that the political practices and constitutional attitudes of the founding countries differed from those of the UK, and this problem has persisted. As a result, the UK has maintained a closer relationship with the US. It is important to note that the UK is one of the most powerful nations in the EU despite its lack of commitment to membership, but these tensions continue to pose a threat to the integrity and power of the EU.

The constitutional differences have been a major factor in the UK's reluctance to pursue full integration. For example, the basis of the EU is the separation of the powers of institutions, as well as the formation of political coalitions, in contrast to the UK's emphasis on a centralized state, an adversarial 'winner takes all' style of party politics and its lack of a formal constitution. By the time the UK joined the European Community in 1973, most policies governing crucial sectors in the region had already been developed, and they differed from the country's own policies and practices.[13] This means that the European Community's rules and regulations had already been set before it joined, and those of the EU have often been set against its opposition, including those governing trade as well as other foreign policies that created a common market for the existing members.

---

12   Richard G. Whitman and Stefan Wolff, *The European Neighbourhood Policy in Perspective: Context, Implementation and Impact* (2010), p. 120.

13   J. Buller and A. Gamble, 'Conceptualising Europeanisation', *Public Policy & Administration* 17:2 (2002), pp. 6–15.

The UK has been left behind in a number of important EU policies and initiatives. It remains to be seen whether it will decide to leave the EU, persevere and try to change the course of integration, or allow itself to be changed by the process in order to benefit as the founding states have.[14]

Some political analysts have argued that the UK government suffers from a conflict of interest in its efforts to maintain a close relationship with the US while participating in the EU. The UK has historically been more supportive of US foreign policy than that of the EU. For example, the US invasion of Iraq was a highly controversial issue among the major nations of the West and Europe.[15] While most countries resisted the invasion and distanced themselves from it, the UK was a strong supporter and contributor in terms of resources.

This alliance between the UK and US has created tensions within the EU, and has been detrimental to the UK's relationship with the other European countries.[16] It is clear that the UK has a different perspective on integration compared to the other members. Some argue that the UK remains a close partner of the US because it derives greater benefits from that relationship than it does from EU membership. Indeed, the UK's initial reluctance to join the European community may be partly a result of its special relationship with the US, coupled with its historical commitment to its ex-imperial subjects and the Commonwealth. As a result, the UK's policies towards Europe were influenced by what its government considered would bring the most benefits for the nation. Once it joined the European Community, it proved very difficult to reconcile its foreign policy with existing policies and regulations.[17] It was therefore difficult for the UK to commit itself wholeheartedly to the EU since this would reduce its influence in other spheres. It is therefore important to note that the US has played an important part in influencing the UK's policies and its relationship with Europe.

The existence of tensions such as these may favour the BRICs' emergence as a powerful force, because the EU no longer dominates the region as it has in the past. Russia, China and India have taken strategic positions and have developed good partnerships with certain EU members because of what they have to offer – for example, Russia can provide cheap energy, and India can provide large markets.

The United Nations and the BRICs

The United Nations was initially established with 51 members in 1945, after the Second World War, and currently has 192 member states. Its objective was 'maintaining international peace and security, developing friendly relations among

---

14   Ibid., p. 89.

15   Julia Scheffler, *Towards an Ever Closer Union? The US–UK Special Relationship until the UK's Final Accession to the European Community 1973* (2006), p. 125.

16   Oliver J. Daddow, *Britain and Europe Since 1945: Historiographical Perspectives on Integration* (2004), p. 126.

17   Ibid.

nations and promoting social progress, better living standards and human rights'.[18] The scope of the UN's activities encompasses working on:

> a broad range of fundamental issues, from sustainable development, environment and refugees protection, disaster relief, counter terrorism, disarmament and non-proliferation, to promoting democracy, human rights, gender equality and the advancement of women, governance, economic and social development and international health, clearing landmines, expanding food production, and more, in order to achieve its goals and coordinate efforts for a safer world for this and future generations.[19]

The UN has various organizations and agencies through which it fulfils its mandate, including the General Assembly (which serves as the chief deliberating body on general UN matters) and the Security Council (which is a major subject of discussion here). The UN Security Council has a mandate to maintain and ensure international peace and security. It has wide range of powers that have a bearing on international political relations and global security concerns, including establishing and approving peacekeeping operations, approving military actions (as in the case of humanitarian military intervention programmes), and establishing and enforcing international sanctions regimes.[20] Article 24(1–2) of Chapter V of the UN Charter spells out the roles of UNSC as follows:

> In order to ensure prompt and effective action by the United Nations, its Members confer on the Security Council primary responsibility for the maintenance of international peace and security, and agree that in carrying out its duties under this responsibility the Security Council acts on their behalf.
>
> In discharging these duties the Security Council shall act in accordance with the Purposes and Principles of the United Nations. The specific powers granted to the Security Council for the discharge of these duties are laid down in Chapters VI, VII, VIII, and XII. The Security Council shall submit annual and, when necessary, special reports to the General Assembly for its consideration.

The UNSC may therefore be interpreted as subordinate to the General Assembly, as it reports to the General Assembly, which serves as the UN's highest decision-making body.

Generally, these duties are exercised through UNSC resolutions supported by the majority of UNSC members and not opposed (vetoed) by any of the permanent members. Under the UN Charter, the UNSC consists of 15 members falling into two categories: (1) the permanent members, comprising the UK, the US, China,

---

18   *United Nations at a Glance*: http://www.un.org/en/aboutun/index.shtml (accessed 2 December 2012).

19   Ibid.

20   See Chapter V of the UN Charter.

Russia and France (essentially the winners of the Second World War plus China), and (2) 10 non-permanent members elected every two years on a rotational basis by the General Council from among the other non-permanent UNSC members. The membership and composition of the UNSC is stipulated by Article 24(1–2) of Chapter V of the UN Charter:

> The Security Council shall consist of fifteen Members of the United Nations. The Republic of China, France, the Union of Soviet Socialist Republics, the United Kingdom of Great Britain and Northern Ireland, and the United States of America shall be permanent members of the Security Council.
>
> The General Assembly shall elect ten other Members of the United Nations to be non-permanent members of the Security Council, due regard being specially paid, in the first instance to the contribution of Members of the United Nations to the maintenance of international peace and security and to the other purposes of the Organization, and also to equitable geographical distribution.
>
> The non-permanent members of the Security Council shall be elected for a term of two years. In the first election of the non-permanent members after the increase of the membership of the Security Council from eleven to fifteen, two of the four additional members shall be chosen for a term of one year. A retiring member shall not be eligible for immediate re-election.
>
> Each member of the Security Council shall have one representative.

Of the BRICs countries, as of 1 January 2012, only Brazil no longer has a seat on the UNSC, its term as a rotational member having expired. India is currently serving as a non-permanent member. Since the membership and composition of the UNSC are specified in the UN Charter, these arrangements can only be altered by majority approval in the General Assembly. This legal technicality has been a major barrier to the reform of the UNSC, despite recommendations from a taskforce mandated by former UN Secretary General Kofi Annan that included increasing the number of permanent members to possibly 10. Under the UN Charter, all substantive matters under consideration by the UNSC must be approved by at least nine members through an affirmative vote to that effect. Article 27 of the charter provides as follows:

> Each member of the Security Council shall have one vote.
>
> Decisions of the Security Council on procedural matters shall be made by an affirmative vote of nine members.
>
> Decisions of the Security Council on all other matters shall be made by an affirmative vote of nine members including the concurring votes of the permanent members; provided that, in decisions under Chapter VI, and under paragraph 3 of Article 52, a party to a dispute shall abstain from voting.

However, the UNSC's resolutions are subject to the 'great power unanimity' rule, or power of veto, which provides that a negative vote on a substantive matter by any of the five permanent members (P-5) bars the UNSC from adopting that proposal as a resolution, even though it may have attained the required majority of nine votes or more. Two of the BRICs countries, China and Russia, are permanent members and thus have this veto power. This gives them a key role, along with the other permanent UNSC members, in deciding the course of global security and other vital matters with serious international implications. Although China has traditionally used its veto power sparingly (only six times since it became a permanent member), the USSR, and later Russia, have made the most frequent use of it (a total of 123 times). India's presence on the UNSC, especially as a partner in a growing political-economic bloc, increases the possibility of the BRICs asserting their position in the UN and creating another power alliance similar to that of the Western allies.

India and Brazil, along with Germany and Japan, are currently lobbying for UNSC reforms to accommodate their inclusion as permanent UNSC members under a proposal to expand the number of permanent members to 10 (P-10). It is difficult to predict the outcome of these efforts, but the two countries' strong participation in current UN operations should improve their claims since they are the largest contributors of UN peacekeeping troops, so they play a key role in ensuring that the UNSC fulfils its mandate of maintaining global peace and security.[21] In addition, both Brazil and India currently enjoy good political and diplomatic relations with the current P-5, especially with the US and the UK. With the move towards enhancing co-operation between the BRICs countries by the current leadership, it is also unlikely that China would oppose Brazil or India becoming permanent UNSC members.

However, decisions about changing the structure of the UNSC and which countries would take seats in the expanded structure are not the prerogative of the current P-5, but of the UN General Assembly, and have to be determined through a majority vote. The outcome will therefore depend on how each of the current candidates uses its soft power to influence the global community in its favour. Another barrier is the fact that the current P-5, which also happens to wield a significant amount of influence in the UN General Assembly and global politics in general, have been very reluctant to reform the UNSC.

Regional International Associations and the BRICs

The discussions in earlier chapters highlighted individual BRICs countries' participation in various regional bodies, and by extension their influence in these organizations. Each of the BRICs countries belongs to one or more regional organizations that wield considerable power in shaping international security policy: China, India and Russia are all members of ASEAN+3, Russia is a member of the EU, while Brazil is a member of UNASUR. Since the members of these

---

21 David Hannay, *New World Disorder: The UN after the Cold War – an Insider's View* (2008).

organizations are drawn from across their respective regions, they offer forums through which the BRICs countries may air their security concerns and ideologies. Although Brazil, China and India are not EU members, the EU has shown an interest in working with these countries as development partners, so closer co-operation is likely in future, which will extend their diplomatic influence in the wider European region.

Chapter 9
Summary of Part II

Part II has explored the role of foreign policy and the military in international political relations. A state's foreign policy has been defined as a set of political guidelines, goals and objectives designed to determine, shape or guide that state's relationship and activities with other states or state entities. Foreign policy uses various political, economic and military instruments to safeguard the national security, ideological and economic interests of a nation at the international level and to foster peaceful coexistence and interaction with other entities, including other states, supranational bodies and international organizations. The foreign policy instruments that may be used to achieve these ends include diplomacy, international political alliances, international trade, war or military action, and the granting of foreign and humanitarian aid during and after conflicts and disasters. They also include various economic instruments, such as export and import controls, tariff walls, sanctions and trade embargoes, and control of other barriers to trade.

Part II has shown that the states employing these instruments may secure influence over other states, especially those that stand to gain from these initiatives or those that will suffer the consequences of refusing to submit to their influence. They may also be used to shape public opinion about the nation's position in the global power structure.

In the context of international political relations, military power is often, but not necessarily, exercised as an extension of foreign policy. It plays a vital role in ensuring defence against aggression, subjecting other states to the will of militarily more powerful entities, forging closer relationships with other military powers and influencing public opinion about the state's position in the global power hierarchy.

For these reasons, military power is at the heart of developing a country's hard power, while foreign policy is principally used to develop its soft power, although some of its aspects may also be used to develop a state's hard power (as in cases of financial sanctions). The combination of foreign policy and military power is vital in projecting a nation's influence in international political and diplomatic relations, and they can be used as key power indicators.

Part II then proceeded to assess the BRICs countries' foreign policies and military power, and how these influence their global political and diplomatic positions. Of particular interest was the extent to which the BRICs countries have been taking an active role in matters of global security and other issues of international concern, since such participation defines their public image and influence, and therefore their power ranking. It emerged that in recent times, the BRICs countries have become more involved in geopolitical affairs and have been increasingly wielding their military power. India, China and Brazil have contributed peacekeeping troops to the United Nations, while Brazil and Russia have been core participants in resolving inter-state conflicts in various regions, either by negotiating peace agreements, or in some extreme cases by resorting to humanitarian military intervention.

Each country has unique foreign policy activities, values and objectives. Chinese foreign policy focuses on fostering economic and political development and reform while minimizing the influence of the US. Such policies have allowed China to form links with transnational organizations and to increase its co-operation regionally and globally, stimulating its rapid economic development. China's soft power has contributed to this growth, as it has a lot of economic incentives to offer, especially to developing and under-developed countries. However, it has been accused of a lack of reciprocity, exploiting certain markets, such as those of the European nations, without giving something worthwhile or exhibiting a degree of loyalty in return. A unique feature of China is that it has been able to maintain good business and diplomatic relationships with the West while retaining its political ideology of socialism. The country is said to have the largest military in the world, which is well-equipped, and also possesses a large number of nuclear weapons. It has been an active participant in promoting global peace and security in areas such as arms control, nuclear non-proliferation, peacekeeping and counter-terrorism initiatives. It also engages in joint military exercises and other military-to-military co-operation, peacekeeping training and exchanges with other nations.

India has been keen to develop a strong military, especially its navy. Its foreign policy focuses on ensuring the peace and security of its neighbours and maintaining stable political relations, in addition to maintaining a strong economic base. Key international relations allies of India include the US, the UK and supranational organizations like the EU and the UN. India is therefore strategically positioned to become a major global power. In addition, India has strong democratic ideals and a capitalistic market economy. After a long period of isolationism, India has recently changed course and has shown more interest in world affairs. Its main strengths are its considerable military power, its rapid economic growth, its strong democracy and good international political and diplomatic relations. However, it faces some domestic challenges that could impede its progress as a global power, including ethnic intolerance, population pressure and corruption. It also faces external threats from terrorist groups and other emerging economies that counterbalance its power, including China, Iran and Russia.

Russia, a successor to the defunct USSR, generally tends to pursue self-centred foreign policies, and to wield its influence only when it contributes significantly to its political, economic and territorial interests. It has permanent seats on the G8 and UN Security Council. Its foreign policies have had both positive and negative impacts on global affairs. It has been a major participant in brokering bilateral peace agreements, promoting peace through military intervention in certain cases, while in others vetoing UN resolutions whose effects would authorize military intervention and other measures. It has a strong military, which it is in the process of professionalizing. Its relationship with the West, and particularly the US, has remained quite sceptical, partly a remnant of the Cold War. Some of the challenges it faces include domestic political and ideological tensions, an ageing population and a high prevalence of diseases such as HIV/AIDS. The external threats Russia faces include efforts by the US to check the spread of its powers, terrorism and competition from many other powerful countries in Europe and Asia. Its prime advantages are its strong economy, its large petrochemical reserves, its good network of political relations and diplomatic links, as well as its military power.

Brazil, sometimes described as continent-sized country, has a great deal of natural, economic and human resources and has a well-developed infrastructure. Many developing and developed nations have been keen to court Brazil for trade and diplomatic relationships. It faces few external security threats, and has thus had ample opportunity to concentrate on domestic issues and its international development agenda. Its good relationships with the wider international community and the major world powers coupled with its economic power mean that Brazil has accumulated a lot of soft power that may see it become one of the most diplomatically influential nations in the future. However, it is quite deficient in traditional hard power, and it will take some time for it to create a different public image. It is currently lobbying for a permanent seat on the UN Security Council, a position that would significantly increase its influence in global affairs.

The BRICs countries also seek to bolster their power through relationships and links with international and regional organizations that have key roles in global affairs and security issues, either through membership or as strategic development or business partners. Russia and China are permanent members of the UN Security Council, where they have been asserting themselves, particularly through their veto powers. India is currently a rotating member of the UNSC, while Brazil's term in this role ended in 2011. These forums have enabled the BRICs countries to promote their positions and views among the global community. India and Brazil are currently lobbying for permanent seats on the UNSC, and success in this would boost their power significantly. The BRICs countries also co-operate closely with the EU: Russia is a member, while China, India and Brazil are strategic development partners. All the BRICs countries except Brazil are members of ASEAN+3, and Brazil is a member of UNASUR. The opportunities to further their interests that these memberships bring serve to consolidate the BRICs' political power.

With regard to the BRICs as a collective entity, the grouping has so far had little impact on international relations and global security issues since it is still in its infancy, so its achievements are therefore basically a sum of the individual members' achievements. However, it is worth noting that since the first leaders' summit meeting in 2009, the BRICs countries have tended to show a degree of solidarity in their approach to certain matters of global concern. For instance, all the countries chose to abstain from the UNSC resolution authorizing the Libyan no-fly zone and strongly condemned it, arguing that military intervention was not the best approach.

PART III
Projecting the Future: The BRICs Factor and Future International Power Relations

Chapter 10
Introduction to Part III

Parts I and II provided the background required to assess the likelihood of the BRICs countries attaining the highly coveted status of superpowers. Part III will analyse the likely role of the BRICs nations in shaping future global geopolitics, identify factors that will determine their impact, and examine how the current superpower – the US – and other great powers may be affected, positively or negatively, by shifts in power relations. Drawing on this, each chapter will conclude by summarizing some policy recommendations concerning the possible future role of that country in global geopolitics and international power relations.

Chapter 11
Brazil

Brazil's Prospective Influence on Global Energy Security[1]

Global energy security has become a pressing issue in the twenty-first century, with the available energy sources such as fossil fuels being threatened by exhaustion while their polluting effects remain a global concern. Modern economies rely heavily on oil, which is particularly affected by these considerations. World oil reserves are running out at an alarming rate, while the deposits being discovered in deep water are much more expensive to extract and call for much more advanced technologies than are currently possessed by most countries or oil companies. Although large reserves of coal remain, its use causes much more pollution, thus limiting it as an option. Along with these global energy security factors, energy demand has escalated, especially in the developing countries, and this trend does not seem likely to change soon. This puts the global economy at risk, so any country which can provide solutions will exercise more influence on world affairs, thus gaining an advantage in the race for global power.

Brazil is likely to be well positioned to exert a good deal of influence on future global energy security issues given that it is endowed with abundant resources to face these challenges. The country currently has the cleanest energy mix in the world. In 2008, for instance, renewable sources accounted for 46 per cent of Brazil's total energy supply, compared to the world average of 16 per cent. These renewable energy resources include hydro-electric power and biofuels. Light vehicles in Brazil use more ethanol processed from sugar cane than petrol, while since 2008 it has been mandatory to blend biodiesel with the mineral diesel used for heavy vehicles.[2] Not only has this helped the country to save billions of dollars in mineral diesel imports, it has also reduced pollution while encouraging agriculture to supply vegetable oil for the production of the biodiesel. The country's success in this field gives it a better chance of influencing global energy policies in future, especially in view of the growing necessity to adopt cleaner sources of energy to combat climate change resulting from carbon dioxide emissions.

In addition to the successful use of clean and renewable energy, including biofuels, Brazil's recent discoveries of large natural gas and oil reserves not located in deep water[3] mean that it is headed towards becoming one of the largest oil producers in the world. Given the depletion of oil reserves elsewhere, the

---

1   Wrobel, *Global Security in a Multipolar World*, p. 25.

2   BP, *BP Statistical Review of World Energy* (June 2009).

3   Wrobel, *Global Security in a Multipolar World*, p. 26

country will be able to use this advantage not only to gain economic influence, but also political and social influence. Brazil managed to achieve its current economic development despite energy shortfalls, so this breakthrough will definitely result in increased economic power, and hence more influence in global relationships, which may take the country closer to achieving its ambition of emerging as a superpower.

In view of these factors, Brazil will be much better placed to negotiate future international relationships. Following Nossal's argument that a superpower must enjoy a high degree of independence in international affairs, Brazil's energy security and reduced dependence on energy imports point to its becoming a superpower.[4] As the largest supplier of biofuel in the world, and recently a crucial oil producer, in the future it will play a major role in the supply of the energy to the rest of the world, strengthening its hand in global relationships.

Brazil's Prospective Influence on Global Environmental Security[5]

Various other natural resources are on the verge of depletion in most parts of the world. Some of these are required for vital strategic goods, and scarcities of these would have severe effects on the world economy. Any nation able to provide such goods will wield great influence, and Brazil is again well placed in this regard.

The sheer size of Brazil and its large endowment of natural resources make it likely that it will gain a dominant role in future. For instance, it has very large deposits of minerals, approximately a tenth of the Earth's fresh water and the largest biodiversity in the world. It would only take the development of a reasonable infrastructure and industrial capacity to exploit such resources and make the country a major global supplier of some of these strategic goods. In fact, the country is already the second-largest exporter of agricultural commodities.

Given that Brazil hosts the largest remaining rainforest in the world, the country takes a prominent role in global negotiations concerning environmental issues and climate change. Brazil has led by example by extensively adopting biofuels and renewable sources of energy, and has already developed a number of environmental and energy conservation strategies, including increasing the use of clean fuels, thus reducing the rate at which its resources will be depleted. If this continues, Brazil is likely to gain in global influence on environmental issues, which will inevitably spread to its social and economic international relationships, and finally to the global political arena.

---

4   Nossal, 'Lonely Superpower or Unapologetic Hyperpower?', para. 10.
5   Roberto Mangabeira Unger, *Projeto Amazônia: Esboço de uma Proposta* (2007).

Brazil's Prospective Influence on Global Social Inter-state Relationships

Although Brazil has taken part in restoring peace in other countries, sometimes even managing to find diplomatic solutions to inter-state conflicts, the country has been regarded with a degree of suspicion as an ambitious self-seeking nation, hence impairing its bargaining power on the international scene. However, it seems keen to improve its social influence on global relationships, as shown by its emphasis on diplomacy in global affairs and its efforts to form alliances with countries all over the world.

Brazil has also shown a great deal of commitment to initiating and signing treaties with other nations, not only in South America, but also in other parts of the world, probably as a means of building its social influence. For instance, it has signed up to virtually all the international treaties dealing with non-proliferation of nuclear weapons as well as initiating a number of treaties concerning the use of other weapons of mass destruction, such as biological and chemical weaponry. The country has also been very vocal in pursuing the expansion of the UN Security Council to ensure better and more balanced representation, probably as a way of gaining credibility among the developing countries.

Given that Brazil's policy makers are known to tailor their policies to the country's ambitions of becoming a global power, these moves are all likely to be part of a calculated strategy to help the country gain credibility on the international scene and enhance its soft power. The strategy seems to be succeeding, since the fact that it has managed to peacefully and diplomatically influence other nations to negotiate treaties, alliances and political decisions demonstrates that it is highly esteemed by these states, so it is well positioned to exert greater influence in its international relationships in future.

Brazil's Future Influence on International Peace and Security

Brazil's long-standing self-image as a country with a great destiny has been important in shaping the thinking and actions of the country's decision-makers, especially regarding its foreign policies on defence. The country has long aspired to develop a stronger voice on issues pertaining to global peace and security, and to achieve this it has taken a number of calculated steps, including its efforts to secure a permanent seat on the UNSC, coupled with ensuring that the country attains both energy and economic security and carrying out innovative regional initiatives.

Despite this great ambition and the economic power required to work towards it, one factor still stands in Brazil's way: it lacks traditional hard power. Because the country developed in an environment with hardly any inter-state security threats, Brazil had little incentive to invest in its military, reducing its influence in global peace and security matters. Although the country has recently taken concerted steps to address this by enacting a very elaborate long-term security policy, it may not be easy for it to match its competitors which established their security apparatuses much earlier.

Brazil's soft power is still evolving, and as yet falls far short of the level required of a superpower. Much of the soft power the country does have stems from the quality of the democratic institutions developed since the end of its military regime. Despite Brazil's very active and assertive role in the maintenance of global peace, its ambitions to take a dominant role in global peace and security issues are constrained by a number of factors, including its adherence to the principle of non-intervention coupled with its traditional views concerning sovereignty, both of which prevent it playing a more active role in such matters.

The evidence is that Brazil is better equipped for economic diplomacy rather than the protection and promotion of democracy or the provision of security, which means that the country may never be in a position to accumulate enough influence on global security matters to meet the criteria for being a superpower. Other countries with much more experience on security matters are better placed in this respect. However, Brazil may yet be able to formulate ways to translate its economic power into security influence.

Brazil will undoubtedly be prominent in various spheres of influence in future, mostly as a result of its well-formulated strategies. The country's potential as a future global power was highlighted during the 2008–2009 global economic recession, when its importance was evident at the various meetings held to discuss ways to bring the recession under control, including those held in Washington, DC in November 2008, in London in April 2009 and in Pittsburgh in September 2009.[6] However, Brazil's influence will be limited in certain fields, such as international security, where the country is unlikely to be able to rival its competitors.

The Effects of Brazil's Future Influence on Various Regions

As mentioned above, Brazil's immense natural resources, its vast size and its large economy, coupled with its government's strategies, are likely to enhance its influence in the global arena in the near future. This is likely to have far-reaching consequences in various regions of the world. In fact, the rise of Brazil is likely to change the ways in which the developed world relates to the developing world, and consequently alter the face of world politics. Although some regions are likely to gain from this, others may have to count their losses.

The growing influence of Brazil will affect the developing countries of Africa and the Middle East in a number of ways. This can be seen from the manner in which the country is currently seeking to associate with these countries by forming trade alliances and signing treaties with them. As Brazil gains more and more economic influence, it is likely to offer favourable terms and conditions of trade to the developing countries, hence assisting their progress. Since Brazil has

---

6   Wrobel, *Global Security in a Multipolar World*, pp. 23–4.

characterized the current world powers as acting unfairly towards the developing world with their trade policies, it is likely to use its economic influence to redress the balance.

Brazil is one of the countries advocating for multilateralism, where several regional powers control the world, rather than unilateralism, where control is vested in a single country or bloc. For obvious reasons, this ideology is much more attractive to the developing countries than the developed ones which either aspire to one day achieve superpower status themselves or are already very close to it. In pursuit of this ideology, Brazil needs the full support of the developing countries, so it is very likely to show favour to them. This has been seen in the country's trade policies, where it has lately opted to prioritize the signing of trade agreements with developing countries in Asia, Africa and the Middle East rather than with those of the developed world, like Europe and the US.[7] Although there would be greater immediate economic gains from trading with the developed world, Brazil has opted to diversify its alliances to the developing world. This is also likely to bring benefits for these developing nations, since they will also gain from the increasing global influence of their trading partner.

Brazil's future influence on global issues is likely to enhance co-operation and unity on the international scene, especially among the developing countries, since one of the principles behind Brazilian foreign policy is that of international co-operation. This has led Brazil to set up a variety of regional groups, again mostly with developing countries, helping to foster unity and promoting their development. However, this unity is likely to pose a threat to the developed countries and challenge the current world order.

Brazil's ascension to a position of influence in global issues would help to redefine international democracy and sovereignty, since the country's adherence to the principle of non-intervention and its attitudes to national sovereignty would be likely to lead to new directions for international security and peace initiatives. This was reflected in Brazil's strong opposition to the invasion and occupation of Iraq by the US, where it favoured peaceful diplomatic negotiations rather than military action or economic sanctions.[8] Unfortunately, it is unlikely that the country will ever be influential enough to enforce this.

Nevertheless, the developed world is likely to feel the effects of Brazil's growing influence, since the country's insistence that developed countries are giving the developing countries a raw deal in global affairs is likely to lead to international initiatives to address this. Brazil's term on the UN Security Council, for instance, may give an insight into what might happen if the country has the opportunity to exert more control over international relationships. As a member of the UNSC, Brazil was strongly opposed to reforms that would perpetuate

---

7   J.F. Hornbeck, *Brazilian Trade Policy and the United States*, CRS Report RL33258 (3 February 2006).

8   Information from Hélio Jaguaribe, Dean of the Institute of Political and Social Studies, Rio de Janeiro.

discrimination against the developing nations, such as reserving the permanent seats for the developed countries while allocating only rotating seats to the developing countries.

With greater global influence, Brazil would not feel obliged to maintain cordial relationships with the developed world and would have greater freedom to pursue its own policies. This is illustrated by the fact that under a previous administration, Brazil signed a treaty with Iraq under which the latter would abandon its nuclear weapons, despite the unpopularity of this move among the developed world. However, the current president of Brazil is seen as more closely aligned with the US, so it is unlikely to take such radical steps in the near future. Nevertheless, it serves as an example of the possible consequences of the Brazil's increased influence on global relationships.

Implications of Brazil's Future Influence

As discussed above, Brazil tends to favour developing countries in its trade policies, and since Brazil is expected to be one of the leading oil producers in the future, this will have remarkable implications for the economic development of these countries. Brazil is likely to continue to help the developing countries to accelerate their economic growth, which would lead to an increased economic growth rate in the world as a whole.

This will also have implications for the current world powers, since it is very likely that Brazil's increasing dominance will significantly dilute their influence. Brazil has frequently expressed disagreement with the current powers (as illustrated by its attempted solution to Iraq's nuclear ambitions), so it is likely to use its increased power to overcome their objections.

Brazil's rising influence is also likely to have an impact on the economic growth of the currently industrialized countries, since it is likely to pressure these nations to reduce the amount of pollutants they release into the environment. This will obviously have a negative impact on their economies, since most of them rely heavily on carbon fuels.

Recommendations to Brazil and the Global Community Concerning Brazil's Future Influence

Brazil's elites have always believed that it is a country with a great destiny in influencing global relationships. This is quite likely to be realized, especially in terms of economic, environmental and social relationships. However, the country's influence on global security issues and politics is unlikely to be as great, mainly because of its attitudes towards non-intervention and sovereignty, both of which place severe limits on its active role in matters concerning international peace and security.

It is therefore recommended that the country re-evaluate its policies on international security and position itself strategically to increase its influence. Brazil's security planners should revise their policies to enable them to take a more active role in global security and peacekeeping.

Although Brazil has the potential to achieve a very high level of influence in international relations, it will take effective and stable governance and well-formulated strategies to fulfil this. Brazil's policy-makers should make efforts to identify whatever obstacles it may face in seeking the influence it desires, along with solutions to deal with such issues.

It is virtually inevitable that in the future, Brazil will have a strong influence on global relationships, especially in terms of economic and environmental issues. The global community should therefore prepare for this eventuality. Developed countries in particular should be prepared to accommodate Brazil's growing influence through their behaviour and policies, since Brazil's ascendancy is likely to dilute their own influence on international affairs.

Any increase in Brazil's influence is likely to be a positive development for the developing countries, as long as they position themselves strategically to benefit from it. They should identify the possible gains and plan how to take advantage of them in order to accelerate their economic development.

Chapter 12
Russia

The concept of multipolarity has played a major role in Russia's foreign policy since the mid-1990s, when it became apparent that it was the only way it could integrate with the Western power structure as an equal partner. The idea of a multipolar world was championed by Russian Foreign Minister of the time Yevgeni Primakov as a way to counter the US's unilateral dominance of intercontinental affairs, but he offered no strategy to achieve it. His oratory contributed to the revival of the concept in 2003, when Russia decided to join Germany and France in opposing the Iraq War, although Moscow's primary intent was to bolster its faltering efforts to forge closer relations with the European Union. By the closing stages of the decade, the prospect of multipolarity and the rebuttal of US supremacy were frequent themes in discussions of international affairs. Russia's ambitions in this respect began to evolve into foreign policy strategies to diversify its relationships to include emerging powers such as Iran, China, India and Brazil.

It is indisputable that the twenty-first century saw a great increase in interdependence, which inevitably led to a degree of multipolarity, but the principle of competition as the major impetus in foreign policy still applies, and a major dilemma is how to balance a nation's pursuit of stability and the furtherance of its own interests with embracing globalization.

When a country adopts unilateral approaches in its foreign policies, it can lead to destabilization of the global balance, aggravating disparities between countries and regions, and frequently rebounding on that country. For instance, criteria regarding the use of force began to be modified during the 1990s and early 2000s, when the notion of humanitarian intervention came to the fore with the highly legally questionable 1999 hostilities against Yugoslavia and the US's unilateral moves against Iraq in 2003. These conflicts shook confidence in international law to the core, leading many states to deduce that they could no longer rely on their individual power.[1]

One notable example of the problems that can arise from a unilateral approach was the way the US government departed from the ABM Treaty in 2001. Signed in 1972, the treaty restricted the potential of the superpowers to nullify attacks, in accordance with the concept of nuclear deterrence, and promoted strategic stability. The principle of mutually assured destruction between the US and Russia was compromised even more in the twenty-first century, when the US decision to inform Russia that it was abandoning the principle while offering no

---

1   Fyodor Lukyanov, 'Rethinking Russia: Russian Dilemmas in a Multipolar World', *Journal of International Affairs* 63:2 (2010), pp. 19–32.

negotiations regarding the issues that might arise led to widespread suspicion and misunderstanding. Current arms control initiatives are hindered by the unresolved issue of missile defence, especially since the abrupt decision by the regime of President George W. Bush to mark its departure from the accord by announcing plans for new missile defence installations near the Russian border, in the Czech Republic and Poland. This step has estranged Russia even further, as well as magnifying tensions between the US and its European defence partners, which were not consulted.

Another factor is the increase in the number of significant participants in international relations. The relaxation of the 'bloc discipline' of the Cold War period has increased pluralism strikingly, and the international influence of countries which have recently achieved sovereignty has increased, as has that of non-governmental organizations.

At the close of the Cold War, the theory of a 'new world order' was widely accepted. It was initially brought up in 1988 by Mikhail Gorbachev, and echoed by George H.W. Bush, the US President at the time. On the other hand, between the disintegration of the USSR and the beginning of the new century, it appeared that talks on the subject were irrelevant, since the new world order had already come about.[2] The leader of the West during the Cold War, the US, had assumed the title of global leader – a turn of events which surprised the US itself, as few would have predicted that Soviet supremacy would fade away so rapidly during the final years of the Cold War, and a role for which it was ill prepared.[3]

The US's dominance and military strength meant that it had no credible rival for the role it took on in global governance in the 'new world order', but misgivings about the arrangement soon began to surface because of its conduct following the attacks of 11 September 2001. It responded with a campaign that declared its aim as promoting democracy in the Middle East, but this ultimately boiled down to the Iraq invasion, which eventually showed the limits of US ability to manage post-conflict operations. Since this attempt at unilateral leadership has backfired, doubts have emerged about whether effective global governance can be achieved at all, and efforts to move to collective leadership have yet to come to fruition.

It is common to subject the core international organizations to condemnation, and NATO, the WTO), the UN and the International Monetary Fund (IMF) have attracted their fair share. Each of these organizations was founded in response to circumstances that no longer apply to the current world, and they need to be replaced, or at least reformed. However, the fundamental problem is not these organizations themselves, but rather the pervasive lack of understanding of international relations.

---

2   Nicholas Eberstadt, 'Where Did the CIA Go Wrong?', *National Review* (June 1991): http://findarticles.com/p/articles/mi_m1282/is_n10_v43/ai_10847979 (accessed 26 January 26 2012), pp. 3–10.

3   John H. Wilhelm, 'The Failure of the American Sovietological Economics Profession', *Europe-Asia Studies* 55:1 (1991), p. 5.

The Effects of Russia's Future Influence on Various Regions

The growth in regional powers has attracted global attention, and up-and-coming countries such as Russia, China and India have far-reaching economic effects on their own regions beyond their impact as political heavyweights. This section will examine how far such developments have enhanced the influence of the regional powers on governance, especially in their bordering states.

Since the end of the Cold War, democratization has rapidly become a worldwide trend, even in areas like the Middle East where such moves had been rare during the twentieth century. The process has given rise to a number of stable democracies on a regional level, particularly in the European Union. Nevertheless, the past conduct of Russia as a dominant regional power with regard to its neighbours has been disconcerting, and it has often supported administrations in its bordering states that can be deemed authoritarian.

However, regional powers' influence on the regimes of the countries that border them should not to be overstated, since the creation of stable political regimes is dependent on long-term domestic processes as well as outside influences. Russia has yet to develop autocracy in its region, though its efforts have assisted in promoting moves towards democracy there. Some of the outcomes are examined below.

The Rise of Autocracies

The decade following the end of the Cold War is considered the start of a new era of global multipolarity. Russia is among the 'new' participants that have drawn the most attention, and is also one of the top three territorial nations on the continent of Euro-Asia. Although India features a remarkably stable democratic system despite frequent disputes, Russia has tended towards a dictatorial regime after the provisional democratic openness that was in evidence towards the end of the Soviet era. China has followed a similarly dictatorial path, though despite the hard-nosed nature of its policies there is potential for change.[4]

Direct Political Pressure

A classic example of Russia's direct political pressure is the case of Georgia. After the 2003 Rose Revolution initiated democratic developments sponsored by enormous Western aid, President Saakashvili decided to direct his energy to pursuing NATO membership. Russia promptly started to pressurize its southern neighbour by imposing economic sanctions, providing moral and financial support to the pro-autonomy movements in South Ossetia and Abkhazia, and finally becoming militarily involved in August 2008.

---

4   Julia Bader, Jörn Grävingholt and Antje Kästner, 'Would Autocracies Promote Autocracy? A Political Economy Perspective on Regime-type Export in Regional Neighborhoods', *Contemporary Politics* 16:1 (2010), pp. 81–100.

Economic Incentives

Russia employs economic channels to increase its power over its neighbours, collaboration with dictatorial regimes being its preferred approach. In efforts to stabilize states like Moldova and Belarus, which are intimately economically allied to Russia, it has granted them enhanced labour market access, subsidized prices for natural gas and export privileges.

Conservation or Construction of Structures

In collaboration with China and four other Central Asian states, Russia has formed a regional unit within the Shanghai Cooperation Organization whose official aim is to increase collaboration in order to forestall unrest in the region. As 'unrest' in this context includes the activities of pro-democracy movements, the association serves to legitimize and protect dictatorial regimes within the region.

It is also worth noting that Russia is still pushing for integration with Tajikistan, Kyrgyzstan, Armenia, and recently Belarus. This has led to an increase in institutions such as the Eurasian Economic Community and the Collective Security Treaty Organization. Russia has also taken direct action to safeguard the stability of dictatorial regimes within the region by investing in strategic economic projects, and pursuing military, police and secret service co-operation.

Attraction

The case of Russia illustrates a model of 'managed democracy' pioneered by Putin that serves as a template for the leadership of numerous states. For instance, in recent years, a number of countries have tightened their regulations on the media and non-governmental organizations in similar ways to Russia. Moreover, Kyrgyzstan and Kazakhstan have employed the United Russia Party as a political model.

Russia's moves to promote its brand of democracy are not its only efforts to influence the political regimes of nations within and outside its region. Autocratic regional powers like Russia seek to hamper the processes of democratization and to temper the growth of other autocratic regimes in their regional setting in a variety of ways. For instance, Russia employs a range of means available to a former colonial power, ranging from economic and political pressure to intervention by its armed forces, while China seeks to play down its potential to intervene in international issues, promoting its ambitions instead by countering US efforts to forge coalitions with its neighbours.

Russia's foreign policies imply that dictatorial regional influences can be economically beneficial as well as having a somewhat constructive influence on dictatorial regimes within their regional setting. In this context, those who seek to promote other types of democratization can expect to meet fierce opposition from the ruling elites, especially in Russia's immediate neighbourhood. Moreover, it is unclear whether supporters of Western democratic systems in the field of development will prevail over the various difficulties their co-operative activities are bound to face, since current efforts to establish harmonized and longer-term strategies to support such democratic systems are making little or no progress.

Implications of Russia's Future Influence

The question of Russia's future influence is causing concern among the major world powers, in particular the US. There have been numerous instances where the US, considered to be the world superpower, and Russia, a contender for the slot, have been at loggerheads, and unless the situation changes, tensions are bound to increase in future.

The Significance of Post-Soviet Russia for the United States

Russia may not be as much of a focus of US interest as the USSR was, but collaboration between the two nations is crucial in several areas, especially since Russia remains a major nuclear power. This has significant implications for US security interests in Asia, the Middle East and Europe. Russia has a significant role to play in counter-terrorism, arms control and the non-proliferation of weapons of mass destruction.

Russia is also a potentially significant trade partner. It is the only state in the world with a greater array of natural resources than the US, including enormous gas and oil reserves. Russia is currently the world's second-largest producer and exporter of oil after Saudi Arabia, and the largest producer and exporter of natural gas in the world. Russia also has a massive, well-educated labour force and many high-tech enterprises. In return, the US is well placed to meet the numerous needs of Russia, such as food and food processing, gas and oil extraction technology, communications, computers, investment capital and transportation, though there are still very low levels of bilateral trade.

Russia, Europe and the United States

The dependence of the rest of Europe on Russia's energy varies from state to state. The Baltic states are highly dependent on the supply of gas from Russia, and a number of analysts are of the opinion that Russia is in turn reliant on Western Europe, since revenues from exporting gas and oil are significant to its economy.[5] Europe is currently the largest beneficiary of Russia's oil exports, but efforts to diversify its energy sources and supply lines continue. The EU currently obtains 37 per cent of its energy consumption from oil, 24 per cent from natural gas, 18 per cent from solid fuels, 15 per cent from nuclear power and 6 per cent from

---

5   Andrew Monaghan, 'Russian Oil and EU Energy Security', *Conflict Studies Research Centre* 5:65 (November 2005), pp. 1–18.

renewable sources.[6] The figures for other countries also vary widely: Poland, Slovakia, and Hungary import over 75 per cent of their oil from Russia, whereas Denmark, Germany, Italy and France only import 26 per cent.

The Middle East remains the largest supplier of oil to Europe, but supplies from Africa, Latin America and Russia ensure a degree of diversification. As a result, a number of states perceive Russia's energy policy as a potential threat to their security, while others regard it as a useful addition to their options for diversifying their supplies of resources.

The US has begun to openly encourage the European countries to reduce their dependency on Russian energy. It has supported the idea of constructing numerous pipelines to supply energy from Azerbaijan and Central Asia to Europe, as well as initiatives like the Turkey–Greece–Italy gas pipeline and oil pipeline extensions in Ukraine and Poland.[7] In the meantime, US officials have strongly criticized the Nord Stream project linking Germany to Russia across the Baltic Sea, bypassing the eastern and central states of Europe, since both the US and the Baltic states are worried that the pipeline will give Russia extra leverage in energy-related matters. However, the failure or success of these projects are more dependent on whether the energy companies consider them beneficial than on US diplomatic efforts.

Although the US imports a negligible amount of oil from Russia, it has a keen interest in Russia's business policies. The main bone of contention has been oil, a catalyst for terrorism and a potential weapon in the hands of petro-states, The US is dependent on foreign imports to meet over 60 per cent of its energy needs, and the proportion is anticipated to increase to 70 per cent by 2025.[8]

According to analysts, the world demand for oil will increase by 50 per cent in the next fifteen years, so it follows that rivalry over energy resources will be a growing source of conflict. As a result, US policy makers are promoting integration, diversification and the opening up of energy markets as measures to guarantee global energy security. The US National Security Strategy of 2006 aimed to pursue co-operation with countries that are regarded as being rich in resources to promote the rule of law, transparency and openness, and committed the US to working with Russia to promote its accession to the WTO.

The US government has good reason to be wary of the world's reliance on a small number of suppliers, since this is neither sustainable nor responsible in the long term. To address this, there have been initiatives to investigate alternative energy resources, but none of these are likely to provide an adequate solution in the near future, and the importance of Russia to geopolitics is bound to grow as both the US and most of the countries in Europe continue to rely on it for oil.

---

6   Ibid.

7   Steven Woehrel, *Russian Energy Policy Toward Neighboring Countries*, CRS Report for Congress (2008).

8   Robert L. Hirsch, Roger Bezdek and Robert Wendling, *Peaking of World Oil Production: Impacts, Mitigation, and Risk Management* (February 2005): http://www.netl. doe.gov/publications/others/pdf/oil_peaking_netl.pdf (accessed 19 June 2013), p. 12.

Recommendations to Russia and the Global Community Concerning Russia's Future Influence

Although the European Union and the United States recognize energy independence as a significant aspect of security, their current courses of action seem to be making little headway towards attaining this goal.

History provides many useful lessons in implementing such radical transformations of policy. From the author's perspective, this would an ideal time to apply Scearce and Fulton's tool of scenario thinking to re-examining energy issues: 'Scenarios are designed to stretch our thinking about the opportunities and threats that the future might hold, and to weigh those opportunities and threats carefully when making both short-term and long term strategic decisions.'[9] This book also seeks to contribute to the debate by providing an impetus for foreign policy experts, environmentalists, economists, governmental committees and independent study groups to investigate the issue further and develop strategic plans to address it.

At present, debates over energy issues tend to focus on environmental concerns, whereas the author has focused on analysis from a security point of view in formulating his recommendations. While governments and international organizations will be responsible for putting policies into practice, they will also need to seek support among the general population for any new measures, as well as the willingness to adapt to them.

The author recommends that Russia should maintain its current policies, as it is evident that they are leading to some positive outcomes despite complaints from certain countries, organizations and humanitarian activists. Every country that attains superpower status can be said to have a hidden agenda, and unfortunately most of the countries in the world are bound to have no say in this despite the fact that this agenda may involve global issues. Some matters can only be decided by the major organizations involved in these disputes, such as the WTO, the UN and the EU. These organizations tend to take the blame whenever major crises occur, and the Russian leadership is becoming increasingly powerful through collaboration with autocratic states such as China. The author's overall recommendation is that the constitutions of these global institutions should be amended to bring about a balance of global power by moderating the influence of the current major powers.

---

9   Diana Scearce and Katherine Fulton, 'What If? The Art of Scenario Thinking for Non-profits' (2004): http://www.gbn.com/ArticleDisplayServlet.srv?aid=32655 (accessed 26 January 2012).

Chapter 13

India

The background provided earlier in this book leaves little doubt that in future, India will be an active participant and significant influence in geopolitical power relations, and this chapter will examine which entities will be affected by India's growing power and how a more dominant India will affect the positions of the US, its allies and the EU, all of which currently have close political ties to India. We will begin with an overview of some of India's strengths that are likely to make it a key player in the global power game.

Factors that Will Facilitate India's Influence in International Relations

India, the largest non-Western democracy, has the second-largest population in the world, a rapidly growing economy, ranks tenth in the world in terms of purchasing power parity,[1] and is investing heavily in its military – all of which increase its likelihood of emerging as a powerful force for transformation in future.

India had taken a back seat in international affairs for a very long time before it realized the importance of active participation in the world community. It played a vital role in preventing Japan's advance into Asia during the Second World War, and since then its army has continued to grow, now considered the third-largest in the world after the US and China. The Indian Air Force is the fourth-largest in the world,[2] and its recent programme to modernize its navy, which is expected to be complete by 2015, will make it the best in the world. India also has a nuclear weapons programme, though it is not a signatory of the Nuclear Non-Proliferation Treaty because of security concerns and because it complains that the NPT is discriminatory.[3] However, the rapid growth in military power of other nations in its region, especially China and Russia, means that it may face powerful rivals in any bid to become a superpower.

India is the world's largest arms importer, spending approximately US$16 billion in 2004 alone. The scale of this investment shows that India is making concerted moves to ensure the security of its borders. India has closer trade and political relations than any of its neighbours with the US, Russia and the EU, and it uses these – in particular its relationship with the US – as leverage to achieve

---

1   Llewellyn D. Howell, *The Handbook of Country and Political Risk Analysis* (2001), p. 89.

2   Ibid., p. 104.

3   Ibid., p. 121.

mutual regional objectives. The Indian Army plays a crucial role in combating terrorist activities in its neighbourhood, and its role in enforcing law and order in the disputed Kashmir region has made it even more important to the US. India is also the second-largest participant in UN peacekeeping operations after the US. As outlined earlier, India has continued to support the UN Security Council despite being denied a permanent seat on it. All these factors contribute to India's worldwide influence.

India can be seen as the leader of the world's developing nations. Although it remains one of the poorest nations in the world, its current healthy balance of trade with major Western nations is critical in enabling it to implement its major foreign policies, not only by supporting its military expenditure, but by sustaining this investment. The improvement in India's economy has resulted in many countries seeking to develop better relations with it. Its growth rate is estimated at 7.1 per cent, the world's fourth-largest after Japan, the US and China,[4] and the growth in its GDP is expected to surpass that of Japan in the next few years. This is expected to lead to changes in India's foreign policies and international relations as more countries court it as a business partner and to pursue their other objectives. Together with China, India currently controls much of the business activity around the Indian Ocean, but its manufacturing sector still lags far behind those of its competitors.

Demographic factors and energy requirements are also likely to be important in increasing India's power and influence. Growing industrialization in the developing world has resulted in greater pollution of the environment, so there is a desperate need for cheaper, cleaner renewable energy sources. In the short term, the world is likely to abandon the use of fossil fuels, and in the longer term, nuclear energy.[5] Solar power will be a very important alternative source of energy in future years, and India and its neighbours in the sunny tropical belt will be well placed to exploit it. Also, because of its high birth rate, India will be in a position to provide a large, youthful, well-trained workforce to pursue industrialization, in contrast to the US and most European nations, where high percentages of the population are older and unproductive. This factor is important not only in terms of growing India's economy, but also maintaining its military strength.

Democracy plays a vital role in sustaining stability and growth in a nation, especially one like India where there is a diversity of views, great ethnic diversity and a large population. India is the world's largest democracy, and has managed to maintain its commitment to this ideal while ensuring the peaceful coexistence of its varied ethnic and cultural communities. This is of particular importance in a region where many of its neighbours are often at war or experiencing unrest. India's prioritization of security is illustrated by its efforts to promote peace in its neighbourhood. Its efforts to gain a permanent seat on the UN Security Council

---

4   Peter R. Hartley and Albert S. Kyle, 'Equilibrium Investment in an Industry with Moderate Investment Economies of Scale', *The Economic Journal* 99 (2009), p. 394.

5   Howell, *The Handbook of Country and Political Risk Analysis*, p. 127.

have been supported by Russia, the UK, China and France, but its bids have met opposition from the US, though some political analysts argue that the US is just waiting for the right time to back India.[6] India's strong democracy has enabled it to develop beneficial relationships with the US, Russia, the EU, the African Union and Japan, and along with improvements in its relations with Pakistan and China, this will increase its economic power and influence in future.

India's Role in Shaping International Relations

India's diplomacy and strategic location together with its vibrant diasporas have enabled it to form more allies than enemies in both the developed and the developing world. It is important to note that India is not a formal member of any military alliance, but has a history of forming strategic relationships with other world powers, such as the US, Japan, Israel, France, Russia and the EU, and its regional allies include Afghanistan, Bhutan and Bangladesh. It also has good relations with developing countries such as South Africa, Mexico and Brazil, and its willingness to represent the interests of developing nations at economic forums has won their loyalty, enabling it to expand its trade territory. India emerged as a strong voice for the 30 developing nations during the Doha Round.[7] This enabled it to develop strategic economic collaborations with other nations in South East Asia, like Taiwan, Japan and South Korea, and many members of the African Union are also loyal to India and support its policies. These developments are very important in enabling India to project its influence in other parts of the world and develop as a strategic focus for world governance and power.

India's collaboration with other nations through international organizations also brings advantages, and it has helped to found a number of these, such as the Asian Development Bank, the UN Non-Aligned Movement, the G20, the East Asia Summit, the IBSA Dialogue Forum, the International Monetary Fund, the World Trade Organization and the G8+5. India also participates in regional collaborations, as part of BIMSTEC and SAARC. India has taken part in a number of UN peacekeeping missions around the world, ranking as the largest contributor of troops to these operations in 2007.[8] If it succeeds in gaining a permanent seat on the UN Security Council, it could well be a contender for superpower status.

India was an ally of the USSR during the Cold War, during which period it took a crucial initiative to improve relationships between the African and Asian nations, which had deteriorated severely, and it has also been a key member of the WTO and the Commonwealth, influencing major decisions by both bodies. India's position as a champion of the developing nations has won it much loyalty among

6   Ibid., p. 128.
7   Ibid., p. 130.
8   Chicago Council on Global Affairs, *The United States and the Rise of China and India: Results of a 2006 Multination Survey of Public Opinion* (2006), p. 41.

African and South Asian countries. It is important to note that India's conduct is highly influenced by economic imperatives. India is keen to establish a strong economic base across the world in order to feed its rapidly growing population and support its military. It is slowly but surely rivalling China as an Asian power, and is securing its position by pursuing economic integration with the world economy.

India supports free trade within South Asia, which is likely to lead to the formation of another regional trading alliance that may serve to reduce animosities in the area. As an economically strong and democratic world power, India will be in a position to provide a counterbalance to powerful undemocratic forces and increase world stability by encouraging more democracies to emerge. As an island of peace in its region, India plays an important role in promoting security, particularly in Nepal, Sri Lanka and Bangladesh, and its counter-terrorist activities have made it a vital partner for the EU, the UN, and especially the US. If the relationship between the two countries continues to develop in this way, the US may eventually abandon its opposition to granting India a permanent seat on the UN Security Council, especially given India's possession of nuclear weapons.[9]

India's potential to take on a more prominent political, economic and security role in the world in future is dependent on regional stability, developments in international structures and maintaining its economic growth. India's active participation in international humanitarian programmes has improved the country's standing in international relations, and its tradition of stable internal democracy has smoothed the way for its foreign policy in recent years and enabled it to seek closer collaboration with other nations. After the September 11th attacks, India immediately offered the US overflight and base facilities, which marked a clear departure from its earlier isolationism and showed its desire to improve the difficult relationship between the two countries in the aftermath of the Cold War.

Regions that Will be Subject to India's Growing Influence

India's political influence is likely to spread from its immediate neighbours to the wider international community. Its growing military power has increased its ability to offer humanitarian aid in its region, and its efforts to control its surrounding seas will have an impact on China, Pakistan, Iran, Nepal and Sri Lanka. India's emergence as regional power centre will provide an impetus for improvements in democracy in neighbours like Nepal and Pakistan. India has a strong vested interest in ensuring peace in its region since it will allow it to capitalize on future economic growth in the rest of Asia.

India's nuclear ambitions are an important factor in the far-reaching transformations that are likely to affect its region, along with its partnerships with the US and EU. The political stability and dynamics of Asia are likely to change

---

9 Hartley and Kyle, 'Equilibrium Investment in an Industry with Moderate Investment Economies of Scale', p. 98.

a great deal due to the influence of the US, China and India in the region.[10] India could serve as a regional counterbalance to China, which does not enjoy such a close partnership with the US. This means that Asia is more likely to see India emerge as a unipolar regional power.

The expansion of networks between India and the other Asian countries is very important for the region, promoting economic stability and energy security, and India has ambitions to liberalize trade with a view to forming a regional economic union in the future. Since India has been vocal in championing the interests of developing nations, they are likely to benefit from better trade deals and relationships with the Middle East, the EU and other parts of the world such as Africa and Latin America as it takes a more prominent role.

India's security concerns and its relationships within its region and globally can be viewed from two different perspectives: globalization and hegemony. The US is still the dominant world military and economic force, but this supremacy will be challenged by the emergence of India as a regional power. There is likely to be greater economic interdependence[11] and a move away from US hegemony as a result of globalization, all of which favour the prospects of one of the BRICs countries becoming the next superpower.

Who Stands to Gain from India's Increased Influence?

The US is mainly pursuing a strategic relationship with India, endorsing its position and stature while seeking to exploit its potential in the region and the world as a whole. In this kind of partnership, India expects to benefit from open trade and increased market boundaries. The collaboration is seen as part of the US strategy to develop its influence in the Middle East,[12] where it has had a sour relationship with many nations for a considerable time. However, India has its own agenda, and is using this opportunity to expand its economic empire.[13] Another reason for the partnership between the US and India is linked to India's nuclear ambitions. The signing of the United States-India Nuclear Cooperation Approval and Non-proliferation Enhancement Act in 1998 is clear evidence that the US recognizes India as a nuclear power despite India's refusal to join the NPT. However, what is important in this kind of partnership is whether it will last, or whether it will be abandoned if it no longer benefits the US.

While India and China are both growing much more influential in the world, India is pursuing its agenda through different political and economic models of growth. The great advantages that India enjoys are its proximity to the Western

---

10   Chicago Council on Global Affairs, *The United States and the Rise of China and India*, p. 42.

11   Ibid., p. 43.

12   Martin, *Understanding Terrorism*, p. 217.

13   Ibid., p. 218.

countries and its status as the largest non-Western democracy.[14] This gives India the potential to serve as an example to its neighbours in the region.

The US will benefit greatly in its counter-terrorism efforts if India gains a strategically powerful position in Asia. India has already been assisting the US with the targeting of terrorist groups in most of Afghanistan, Iran, Pakistan and Sri Lanka, and through the provision of information to the US Department of Homeland Security.

The Quadrennial Homeland Security Review of 2010 focused in greater detail than before on dealing with possible attacks using nuclear devices. This has led to greater efforts to identify such threats and introduce more effective cross-border monitoring. The greater integration and collaboration in response to these threats will also help to deal with radiological, chemical or biological agents. The same review also placed a great deal of emphasis on improving the resiliency of the social as well as physical infrastructure, improving response times and speeding up the return to normality. The need for improvements identified by this programme has seen the US increase its spending on both long-term and short-term infrastructural development, which has entailed investment in business technology and education, the involvement of the private sector, and the active participation of governmental and development partners. The US National Strategy for Homeland Security of 2002 and 2007 and the Quadrennial Homeland Security Review of 2010 all focused on enhancing trans-border security to counter security threats from other nations, but the major departure in the 2010 review was that it incorporated partnerships with other nations. This more comprehensive approach has seen the US government work with other governments, non-governmental organizations, local authorities, the private sector and international partnerships in order to enhance border control.[15]

Who Stands to Lose from India's Increased Influence?

The European Union is likely to suffer if India becomes more powerful. The loyalty India has earned from developing nations and some developed nations, both in Africa and other parts of the world, has enhanced its energy security and will enable it to expand its markets. Although the relationship between India and the EU has been very good and continues to improve, the EU is growing weaker and weaker because some of its members, like the UK and smaller countries like Moldova and Belarus, are not committed to integration, partly because other nations have more to offer. For example, Russia can provide access to cheap

---

14   Ibid.

15   Chicago Council on Global Affairs, *The United States and the Rise of China and India*, p. 47.

supplies of energy, and the UK continues its close alliance with the US.[16] This is exacerbated by the fact that political analysts have argued that EU legislation tends to disadvantage members who joined later, like the UK. Distrust of the EU is widespread in the UK, among both the public and politicians, and this historically awkward relationship has hampered moves to promote integration (see Chapter 8 for a more detailed discussion of some of the problems between the UK and EU).[17]

Both India and the US stand to benefit from this discord through their bilateral engagement, which is expected to promote trade and economic growth.

Recommendations to India and the Global Community Concerning India's Future Influence

India is a potentially powerful force for transformation that is likely to take a prominent role in global relations and governance in the future. It is the largest democracy in the world, with strong economic growth, a powerful military, and it enjoys friendly relationships with many other countries. India's foreign policy of collaboration to improve trade and financial relations has seen it emerge as a strong economic power.

However, it is important for India to become more actively involved with other nations outside South East Asia, where it shares dominance with China. There is also a need for a change from its current concentration on economic policy considerations to a greater focus on diplomacy and participation in security initiatives, since its military investments alone cannot guard against threats from the weak democracies in its neighbourhood.

Its continued security depends on gaining US support to obtain a permanent seat on the UN Security Council, and its continued status as the US's main ally in the region means that its relations with its neighbours are likely to grow more strained. It should therefore continue to reach out to its neighbourhood, to countries like China, Pakistan, Nepal, Iran and Bangladesh, in an effort to counter suspicion and overcome animosities.

---

16 Karl Inderfurth and Bruce Riedel, 'Breaking More Naan with Delhi: The Next Stage in U.S.-India Relations', *The National Interest* (November/December 2007), p. 56.

17 Ibid., p. 57.

Chapter 14
China

China has gradually evolved into being a new potential global power after its initiation of economic reforms in 1978. As a result, the rest of world has directed its attention to the country and has been curious about how China's role as a growing power can be incorporated into the operations and activities of the international community. China's economic reforms were not only based on improving its domestic economy, they also embraced a new approach to dealing with the world. This is evident from the sudden turn of its foreign policies from the concept of 'self-reliance' that locked it out from the international community to a multipolar approach that has facilitated China's increased involvement with the international community. Accordingly, it is no wonder that China's greater involvement in global affairs has stirred controversies among experts about its nature and future implications. Some scholars feel that China's rapid integration into the international community is accompanied by an emerging threat from China, as reflected in most realist theories of power transition.

It is notable fact that China's foreign polices do not explicitly differentiate between strategic engagement and strategic ambiguity. This has made it difficult to predict the course of China's ascendancy and its repercussions, which need to be examined in the context of the global economic crisis. Contradictory views have emerged regarding China's steady economic growth during the crisis, in contrast to the struggling US economy, and its increased participation in matters of global interest such as finance, security, diplomacy and trade, with some proposing the formation of a G2 involving China and the US.

It is evident that China's influence has grown due to a rate of economic growth that the rest of the world has been unable to match. This has provided the country with advantages over its rivals in terms of access to a cheap source of skilled labour, a huge domestic market and its financial strength. Although the benefits from the latter are moderated by its excessive holdings of US dollars and the fact that its own currency is non-convertible, China has been able to maintain leverage in the global money markets due to its plentiful foreign reserves and great fiscal capacity, meaning that it enjoys a high degree of autonomy in relation to the global economy and its policy makers have access to a wide variety of economic policy instruments. It is possible that China may use its international influence to bring about currency diversification as well as attempting to change certain UN monetary policies, since there are concerns that they may lead to further economic crises in future.

China's current global outlook is evident from the country's engagement in the international community, with a geostrategic focus in its relations with the

US, the EU, its Asian neighbours, African countries, India and Latin America. The sophistication of China's foreign policies is illustrated by the varying approaches it takes to different countries – for instance, its AIDS diplomacy with Africa and its oil diplomacy with Eurasia, Latin America and Russia – and the challenges it presents to international organizations like the UN with respect to security, trade and environmental issues. Despite the complexity of these relationships, China's main commitment has been to maintain its territorial integrity and sovereignty, as shown by its desire to claim Taiwan as its 23rd province and to retain Xianjang, Macao, Hong Kong and Tibet.

Despite the modernization of China's military and improvements in its capabilities, the US still has far superior forces, and China has also been unable to project its soft power satisfactorily to some of its Asian neighbours and Western countries. It is also obvious that the process of democratization of China will not be rapid, and its economic growth has been accompanied by increased pressure from its upper middle class to be incorporated into the affairs of the government and an increase in protest movements in China's cities and villages. The poor state of civil society in China means that there is a limited likelihood that liberalization will come soon, although the Chinese Communist Party has adopted social, political and economic pluralism.

China's major focus has been to develop a coherent foreign policy rather than addressing domestic issues, but the two are inextricably linked, and its major aim in its international relations is to satisfy its economic needs. For example, its engagement in Sudan has aimed to neutralize security threats to Chinese development workers there, and its programmes in that country and Pakistan seem to be part of its efforts to ensure its long-term energy security. Some experts think that China should continue to concentrate on foreign policies that support its domestic agenda rather than trying to intervene in the general global order.

Although China's involvement in global affairs is significant, its direction in terms of economic, diplomatic and political issues remains unclear. Some see China's pragmatic policies as being geared to ensuring long-term development of the country's economy, incorporating strategic financial management and privatization to speed up its acquisition of high technology. Coupled with this, some feel that China's increased expenditure on social welfare, especially in the field of healthcare, will serve to strengthen its domestic economy due to the increase in income per capita. Proponents of this line of thought therefore believe that China's influence in global international relation will increase as it pursues its economic interests and safeguards its economic development.

However, others think that China's economy and influence are likely to decline in the long term, as the country faces numerous socio-economic challenges, including a wider generation gap between the rich and the poor, a growth in environmental pollution, higher wages, increased corruption at the local level, monopolization of its institutions and regional imbalances.

Although China's participation in global affairs has recently intensified, there is still a lot of scepticism about China's capability and willingness to becoming a global leader because of the extreme caution it has shown in addressing matters such as international financial problems and pollution. During the Doha Round, its low profile in numerous international matters such as enlargement of the UN Security Council, nuclear disarmament, and negotiations on climate change and trade illustrate its lack of commitment to bilateral agreements and its avoidance of key global responsibilities.

In addition, China's approach to other countries in not transformative like the US approach, but is based on adjustment. This has meant that China's involvement in foreign economies and its investment in other countries have met with little opposition. Unlike the US, which has been keen to use its economic might to bring about changes in other countries, China has chosen to abide by the rules of its hosts while maintaining a degree of distance and separation, so its presence in different parts in the world has not been seen as a threat despite the fact that it is more beneficial to China than to the host countries. This makes it likely that China would continue to focus on extracting as many benefits as possible from existing rules rather than engaging in rule-setting were it to ascend to a position of global dominance.

China's modernization of its military, with a specific emphasis on the development of its naval power, has been interpreted as an aspiration to regional hegemony, challenging the US in terms of regional security dominance. However, its increased participation in bilateral relations with the US makes it unclear whether China's strategy involves achieving global dominance, or whether it is content to allow the US to continue as the world superpower.

Despite the widespread suspicions provoked by the modernization and expansion of its military capabilities, China has sought to reassure other countries that it will maintain a peaceful and non-threatening approach in its international policies.[1] The uncertainties over its attitude to the US's status as the sole superpower are exacerbated by its unwavering positions on certain international issues, such as its territorial claims (for instance, the issue of Taiwan), its increased military spending despite calls for arms control, and its reluctance to adopt a more pragmatic human rights regime. Some see this as evidence for the emergence of a bipolar international system run by China and the US, but China's increased participation in and compliance with the UN and other international organizations, its growing emphasis on both global and regional economic integration and its vital role in the North Korean nuclear crisis reflect China's new-found commitment to multilateralism and constructive engagement in global affairs.

To summarize, China's future role in the global international system may be uncertain, but its use of its influence to protect its territorial integrity and pursue economic development are likely to remain constant.

---

1 Bonnie S. Glaser, 'The Changing Ecology of Foreign Policy-making in China: The Ascension and Demise of the Theory of "Peaceful Rise"', *The China Quarterly* 190 (June 2007), pp. 291–310.

The Effects of China's Future Influence on Various Regions

China and Asia

One of China's major objectives is to ensure regional stability in Asia. Most of the countries in the region have autocratic styles of government, and China has frequently provided support to repressive regimes such as North Korea and Burma in the face of interference from the international community. Although this can be seen as part of a strategy to seek regional favour, China's policies towards Asia have made it more difficult to achieve democratization in the area, and their effect has been to promote dictatorial regimes.[2] Although not a universal view, critics believe that China derives a lot of benefits from supporting autocratic governments in its regional neighbourhood, as its own interests would not be served by the rise of democratic societies.

China's influence in Asia has grown significantly in recent years, and the use of its soft power can be illustrated by the growth in popularity of the Chinese language among its regional neighbours and the increasing number of foreign students studying at Chinese universities. Developments such as these are gradually popularizing China's political system beyond its borders. Although it is clear that the US and other Western countries are keen to establish democracy in the region, China has made efforts behind the scenes to counter this trend while seeking to avoid being seen as an interventionary power. By doing so, China has been able to prevent its geographical neighbours from engaging in alliances with the US while maintaining its image and ambitions as a great regional power.

The success of China's foreign policies is evident from the continuous growth of its economy. This progress under China's system of governance is believed to benefit autocratic regimes in the region, since proponents of democracy not only have to oppose the ideologies of the ruling elites, but have a difficult task convincing members of the public that democratic systems would be more successful. For these reasons, it is highly doubtful whether efforts by the US and Western countries to promote democratization in Asia will meet with any more success than they have in recent years.[3]

China's use of economic measures to promote authoritarian regimes in Asia, such as Laos, Burma, Sri Lanka and Cambodia, includes heavy investment, the provision of financial assistance and the favourable trade policies it has instigated in its bid to achieve economic integration. Such support depends on these countries continuing on the path of authoritarianism, and China has so much to offer that its political system of developmental dictatorship is likely to continue to spread to both autocratic and democratic regimes in the region.

---

2   Julia *Bader*, Jörn Grävingholt and Antje Kästner, *The Influence of China, Russia and India on the Future of Democracy in the Euro-Asian Region* (2011), p. 10.

3   Bader, Grävingholt and Kästner, 'Would Autocracies Promote Autocracy?'.

China and Europe

In the past, there has been a healthy relationship between China and Europe, with the EU assisting in Chinese development and being a major trading partner. Recently, the relationship has soured as China has attracted criticism for breaking agreements and blocking access to Chinese markets while continuing to have unlimited access to European markets. In addition, China has been able to transfer most of the costs of environmental measures to the EU despite the continuous decline in the European economy. In brief, it can be said that China's relationship with Europe has been more parasitic than symbiotic, and China's economic strength and its widespread influence in individual EU member states has meant that they have grown increasingly dependent on China despite its failure to honour its obligations.

China has been able to play off the European countries against each other while promoting its economic strategy, rejecting calls to recognize Taiwan as an independent state, resisting interference in its domestic political system and continuing with its military development despite the existence of the EU arms embargo.

China's refusal to meet its obligations to the EU has engendered increasing caution, leading to the possibility that the terms of their relationship will be revised to limit China's access to Europe and make China more accountable for the environmental effects of its activities. However, if the EU continues to allow China access to its markets while disregarding its non-compliance with bilateral agreements, increased competition between Chinese products and European goods may lead to a reduction of profits in their domestic industries, increased dependency on China and further economic hardship.

China and the US

During the Clinton and George W. Bush presidencies, limited attention was paid to China's continuous economic growth and military development since the focus shifted to the war on terrorism and the invasion of Iraq. China took the opportunity to further its political and economic interests by adhering to US international monetary policies and supporting the counter-terrorism campaign. Until recently, the US considered the emergence of a new economic powerhouse in Asia as a threat, since Asia is currently its largest economic partner. In light of this, it is puzzling that the US has not imposed more restrictive policies on China. In addition, China's and Japan's military spending and defence budgets have increased beyond those of most of the European countries after they complied with the treaty proposing a reduction in military expenditure after the Cold War. Unless the US and the international community as a whole apply certain checks and balances to China's increasing power, they may see the five hundred years of Western global dominance come to an end.

China, Latin America and the Caribbean

In recent years, China has shown increasing interest in the Latin American and Caribbean countries. China's major aim in the region is to gain access to its rich mineral resources, such as iron and copper, and agricultural products such as soya beans through increased investment and trade. Although China's influence and economic links in the region have increased, full access to its markets has been thwarted by US investment and trade due to the competitive advantage conferred by its close geographical proximity.

Chinese investment in Latin America has been welcomed by some countries, but others see its entry into their markets as a threat to their existing domestic industries as a result of competition from cheap Chinese goods. Despite the various checks and balances imposed on China by the US and Latin American countries, the prospect of an increase in China's role in the region has long-term implications for US interests and influence there.[4]

China and Africa

China plays a significant role in African countries, especially those of Sub-Saharan Africa, involving major industrial investment and the provision of financial assistance to help in the development of the region. In addition, China has also offered loans on far more favourable terms than Western countries.

China's foreign policy in Africa has been characterized by non-interference in the sovereignty and internal affairs of the African states and allowing them a high degree of autonomy in their internal affairs and governance. It is believed that China's major aim is to secure African support and votes in international forums such as the UN, along with discouraging criticism of its policies towards Taiwan. Analysts feel that China's increasing influence in Africa will have both positive and negative effects. On the negative side, they argue that China's foreign policy and influence in Africa is a competitive threat to investment in the region by developed countries. However, others believe that China's influence in Africa will lead to increased development of the African countries' economies due to their access to Chinese markets and enable them to be more autonomous in their international affairs due to their decreased dependency on Western countries. China's influence is also likely to provide African countries with an alternative global power to align with when faced with political demands from Western countries in exchange for political co-operation, financial aid and loans.

China's increased participation in peacekeeping operations in Africa is an essential aspect of its foreign policy. Although China has yet to request a permanent

---

4   Congressional Research Service, Library of Congress, *China's Foreign Policy and 'Soft Power' in South America, Asia, and Africa: A Study Prepared for the Committee on Foreign Relations United States Senate Committee on Foreign Relations United States Senate* (April 2008), p. 16.

military base in the region, it is believed that in future its peacekeeping operations may present a challenge to the US and the West. Meanwhile, anti-piracy operations in the Gulf of Aden provide an opportunity an expansion of China's influence in the Indian Ocean, which may in future give it control over access to certain African countries.

Implications of China's Future Influence

China had made remarkable achievements over the past three decades in economic terms. However, it unlikely that China will become a dominant force in the global economy unless it makes significant changes to its mercantilist policies. Although, China has used its economic progress to establish itself as a global power, the methods it has adopted in recent times can be seen as a waste of capital, as they are directed towards the protection of financial institutions with poor balance sheets. Furthermore, China's capacity to achieve economic transformation is hindered by its cultural features. In addition since the US and EU are China's largest export markets, China's potential to become a global or regional economic powerhouse depends on the health of their economies, which China's current policies threaten.

If China does succeed in becoming a global leader and spearheading international economic and monetary policies, its approach to these issues is likely to be significantly different from and incompatible with the approaches adopted by the US and the powerful countries of the West. China's policies are likely to promote autocracy, not democracy, and to favour communism over individualism. Other areas where its approaches are likely to differ include the rule of law, equal rights, the co-ordination of economic activities, and the perception of economic growth as being based on improving the welfare of citizens and developing market economies.[5]

China's aspirations to be a global power face numerous challenges, including increased environmental degradation, an ageing population due to its one child policy, the strength of its geopolitical neighbours, the unstable political environment, its dependence on foreign markets rather than its domestic market, and over-reliance on an economic model that is state-driven.

Finally, China's current economic model is unsuited to coping with the current global financial crisis since it has exhausted most of its options and lacks a market-oriented way to continue increasing its influence and power. Unless China adopts a market economy, it is possible that it may resort to assertive nationalism as its economic model as it takes on a more dominant role in world affairs.

---

5   Centre for Policy and Development Systems, 'China's Development: Assessing the Implications' (November 2007): http://cpds.apana.org.au/Teams/Articles/china_as_economic_engine.htm (accessed 26 January 2012).

Recommendations to China and the Global Community Concerning China's Future Influence

Owing to the failure of numerous summits between EU presidents and Chinese representatives to overcome the difficulties that have been identified, EU member states have reached a consensus that there needs to be a new forum to resolve the issues that gives priority to those states that have the most pressing problems with China.

The problems identified include China's lack of commitment in honouring its obligations and its blocking of foreign access to its markets. In light of this, it is recommended that the EU adopt an effective framework focusing on reciprocity, comparable to the US policy towards China, which emphasizes co-operation and a case-by-case strategy rather than trying to attribute blame in a bilateral relationship.

In order to avoid the rise of autocracy in Asia, it is recommended that the US and other countries mount a concerted effort to increase US involvement and influence in the region. Although the US still maintains a considerable amount of influence in East Asia and China is unlikely to supersede it in the near future, the US and the rest of the world cannot afford to ignore China's steadily increasing influence in Asia as a whole.

Chapter 15

The BRICs as a Bloc: Their Collective Role in Shaping Future Geopolitics

Generally speaking, the BRICs countries share very little in terms of political and economic backgrounds, political and economic ideologies, foreign policies and strategies, and even their diplomatic alliances and geopolitical inclinations. This diversity makes the BRICs a very amorphous entity, with few bonds to hold the group together. As shown in Chapter 1, the categorization of the BRICs group was a creation of economists who noted similarities in the countries' rates of economic development. The economists then projected that the combined economy of the BRICs countries would be capable of overtaking that of the G7 in the next four decades or so, when they would account for about a fifth of the global population. From this projection, a number of scholars inferred the possible emergence of another powerful bloc and the diversification of the global poles of power. However, although this study concludes that the BRICs countries are likely to have an extensive influence on future global politics, the future of the BRICs as a unified bloc is still subject to many uncertainties.

On one hand, it is arguable that should the BRICs group develop into a sustainable long-term political and economic alliance, it would pose many challenges to the current hegemony enjoyed by the US as the sole superpower. The BRICs alliance's growing economic strength is likely to enable it to pursue its international and diplomatic agenda, with each of the nations contributing its own circle of influence, leading to an intricate global web. On the other hand, achieving the solidarity required to bring this about will present the greatest challenge, in view of the many political, diplomatic and economic hurdles the BRICs, individually and collectively, would have to clear.

To begin with, there are so many factors that affect or influence economic growth, quite a number of which are not easy to predict. Factors such as technological transformation, strategic information and communication flows and scientific innovations have significant influence on economic and development trends, as they affect the nature, cost and rate of production and transactions. They also influence investment choices and opportunities. On the complex nature of economic growth, Paulo Roberto de Almeida explains:

> When we look at the overall picture for the global economy, we reach an inevitable conclusion: the same forces that have transformed the world since the 16th century are still shaping the contemporary world. These forces include not only the flow of goods and services, but forms of economic organization

and above all, the production of ideas and concepts to support those physical flows. Therefore, it is inconceivable to consider that developing or emerging nations could be independent from the core of the global economy. The path and economic destination of the Brics and other emerging economies cannot be different from those followed by developed nations. The latter set the basic parameters on which the economy is based. However, this dynamic process is not exclusive to a specific centre, but shared by several centres producing and spreading ideas and practical knowledge.[1]

It is obvious that scientific and technological inventions and innovations have not yet reached their peak, and it is difficult to predict what new technologies countries will embrace in the near future. The complex relationships between such developments may well work in favour of the BRICs' competitors, including the US and other great powers. But a counter-argument to this would be that the scientists, technologists and scholars of the twenty-first century have shown a high degree of willingness to share information, and any development in one country or region is soon disseminated to other countries or regions (whether at a cost – as in the case of selling or licensing of patents – or simply through the drive to share scientific discoveries).

Assuming the BRICs overcome these problems, they would still face political and diplomatic hurdles. For instance, each of the BRICs countries currently has its own political and diplomatic agendas, which in some cases are at odds with those of the other BRICs. For instance, India has traditionally been a close ally of the US and UK, whereas Russia has been very cautious in its relationships with the US and the West in general, preferring to court the nations of the East. The US has been equally cautious in its relationship with Russia, and would be keen to ensure that its political power does not rise to the level of its predecessor, the USSR. A political alliance whose impact would probably dilute US power in global politics is likely to provoke diplomatic turmoil between the US and India. It is unlikely that India would be willing to sacrifice its well-established diplomatic relations for new political ties from which it might gain very little.

It should be remembered that each of the BRICs countries has other economic partners, and the rise of the BRICs as a bloc is likely to pose a threat to these interdependencies. Political relationships are shaped by factors beyond the economics of GDP and export or import volumes. There are delicate diplomatic and political balances that would have to be ensured – including diplomatic and political reciprocation. In light of the diverse diplomatic ties of the BRICs countries, which have been highlighted by their diversity in foreign policy objectives and ideals, navigating these issues is likely to be very difficult.

In addition to the foregoing arguments, as emerging economies, the BRICs still depend on other developed nations and the G7, which they hope to compete with or even displace in the global power game. In view of the scientific and

---

1   Almeida, 'The BRICs' Role in the Global Economy', pp. 153–4.

intellectual dominance of these other international entities, the BRICs countries need to pursue intellectual, scientific and technological exchanges to promote their development to a higher level. They also need the G7 and other developed economies as trade and business partners with which to exchange goods and services. The market share attributed to the G7 and the developed economies, with their large populations and great purchasing power, cannot be ignored. Thus, if the BRICs countries were to sever international ties with these developed and powerful nations, which is the implication of creating a credible new global pole of power, it would risk diminishing the very rapid economic and technological developments the BRICs countries rely on to rise up the ladder of power.

Finally, the BRICs have diverse ideological backgrounds and values. Russia and China have socialist and totalitarian backgrounds, and to a large extent have authoritarian ideologies and values (although Russia is gradually and reluctantly adopting democratic structures and practices). India and Brazil have democratic backgrounds, India being a parliamentary and Brazil a presidential democracy, and both have capitalist-oriented market structures. In fact, as shown in the previous chapters, Brazil has more advanced capitalistic practices than the other BRICs countries and most of the world's other economies. The literature reviewed in Chapter 2 indicated that the urge to spread a particular ideology globally is a key factor in determining the emergence of a global power. In fact, it is principally the diverse ideologies pursued by the USSR on one hand and the US on the other that defined and distinguished the two as world powers. The questions are whether the BRICs should form a joint front in a bid to develop a new pole of power, what ideologies they should advocate, and what would distinguish this new pole. It is highly unlikely that the BRICs will be able to achieve either a political or economic ideological compromise, despite their current close co-operation. But even if this unlikely compromise could be reached, adopting and implementing it might entail a fundamental change in structures that would risk provoking domestic opposition. The whole transformation process would be likely to result in a slowdown in political and economic growth.

To summarize, while the BRICs countries may continue to co-operate to promote their mutual economic and political development and gain more power and influence, it is unlikely that they will form a collective pole of power that will shake up the existing world order. They may co-exist as influential economic development partners, but they are hardly likely to form a powerful political bloc. As Paulo Roberto de Almeida rightly asserts:

> Whatever the future of global geopolitics in the 21st century – be it a new Cold War of a 'Cold Peace' – it has nothing to do with being a member of a group invented by an economist, even though there might be conflicts generated by some of these members' candidacy as emerging global powers. The Brics' situation is accidental and fortuitous, whereas being a global emerging economy is a structural condition that was acquired by a long and slow process

of productive and technological qualifications that will naturally convert into military and political power.[2]

The role of the BRICs countries in global politics and power games is likely to depend more on the influence of the individual members rather than the BRICs as a united front. There are many political, economic and ideological obstacles that the BRICs would need to navigate in order to command any worthwhile worldwide power, and this would not be an easy task. The BRICs countries will need the developed economies as partners, not opponents, to optimize their growth – economic, political and diplomatic.

---

2   Ibid., p. 154.

Chapter 16

Are there Prospects of the BRICs Being the Next Superpower?

Introduction

Part II presented detailed findings about the circumstances of the BRICs nations which have a bearing on their international relations and global power positioning, while the earlier chapters in Part III have analysed the future role of the BRICs countries in political and diplomatic relations. This chapter draws together the findings of these previous chapters in order to assess the BRICs' chances of becoming the next superpower. It will analyse the capabilities and prospects of each BRICs country in terms of military, economic and political power, followed by a summary at the end of the chapter.

The Prospect of Superpower Status

As discussed in the previous chapters, many scholars have viewed the BRICs countries – Brazil, Russia, India and China – as potential superpowers, chiefly because they are believed to be the most rapidly developing economies in the world. However, as was shown in Chapter 2, becoming a superpower calls for more than merely gaining global economic strength – there are other factors that are essential to enable a country or bloc to project its hard and soft power globally. Lyman Miller sets out four axes of power in which a country must excel in order to achieve superpower status, and his model will form the basis of the evaluation, supported by the views of other acknowledged scholars on the concept of superpower.[1] Miller identifies the critical axes as political, economic, military and cultural power. The analysis in this chapter combines Miller's cultural power axis with the political axis, terming it 'political and diplomatic power'. This is because the social aspect of power in international relations has more to do with diplomatic relations and inter-country assistance pursued under the general foreign policy framework, which is a political tool, so we will avoid repetition by consolidating and discussing the two axes in this way.

It should be acknowledged that other than the common factors of having promising economies and rapid economic growth, the BRICs countries tend to be unique in terms of their military, economic and political strengths, so what might

---

1   Miller, 'China an Emerging Superpower?', para. 4.

help one country to stand out as a world power might not help the others to achieve this status. For this reason, the analysis in this chapter will not focus on comparing the similarities between the countries on in terms of the power axes, but will assess each country's unique strengths or weaknesses on a particular power axis to examine its potential for attaining world superpower status.

Military Power

Brazil

Although Brazil has experienced some internal security threats, including a coup d'état, the country has been through a period of peace in the international arena ever since it gained independence from the Portuguese. In fact, the country won its independence and defined its borders without the need for armed conflict. While this peaceful background has favoured economic development, it has meant that Brazil has tended to neglect its national defence and security policies, and it was not until 2008 that the country developed a long-term security strategy.

The National Defence Strategy developed in 2008 clearly defines the operating environment of the country's security forces, and outlines the priorities and targets of each branch of the armed forces, as well as their major tasks. The strategy is very elaborate, outlining various specific goals and how they are to be achieved. It emphasizes the importance of channelling more investment into developing an indigenous arms manufacturing industry,[2] and defines the role of the armed forces in ensuring national integrity and their civil duties towards Brazilian society.

Although the adoption of such an elaborate strategy marks a break from the long history of lack of focus on national security issues, the document reveals many elements of continuity in views that have dominated the country's defence system for decades. For instance, it prioritizes the development of a nuclear-powered submarine programme, possibly because the navy lobbied for it, given that this branch of the forces is highly esteemed in the country.[3] This reveals that the National Defence Strategy could serve to further some of the arguably unrealistic ambitions of Brazilian defence planners.

The history of Brazil's national security has been characterized by a lack of incentives to justify large-scale investment in the military, given that the country has thrived in an environment with scarcely any inter-state security threats. In fact, apart from the War of the Triple Alliance of 1864–70, the country has had hardly any experience of war, since most other conflicts involving Brazil have been resolved diplomatically. This has made it quite difficult for the country's defence planners to sell their military ambitions by referring to past experiences.

---

2   Ibid.

3   Wrobel, *Global Security in a Multipolar World*, p. 17.

The lack of a history of warfare coupled with the long period of neglect of external security policies mean that Brazil has a long way to go if it is to accumulate sufficient military power to emerge as a global superpower. This inexperience is reflected in the fact that Brazil did not form a defence ministry operating under civilian control until 1999, which means it still lacks civilian expertise to deal with defence and security issues. This may explain why it took close to a decade to develop the National Defence Strategy after the setting up of the Ministry of Defence. It therefore goes without saying that it would be very difficult, if not impossible, for Brazil to develop its military power rapidly enough to overtake its competitors, which have already amassed a great deal of experience in this field.

Russia

Russia is a nuclear weapons state, with the capacity to deploy them to any region in the world. This gives it a great tactical advantage, but some critics point to the theory that the more hazardous or powerful a weapon is, the less chance of it being used, considering the fact that the Cold War came to a close without any of the missiles being launched.

Russia is currently receiving a great deal of revenue from petrochemicals, and many countries rely on it for the supply of oil and gas. The general assumption is that this income could be used to upgrade its armed forces, which are known to be suffering from a shortage of funds along with other problems.

India

Activities within India's Defence Ministry have revealed overwhelming developments which many nations have ignored, but are very important for this discussion. While previously China had dominated the region in terms of military power, India's role is becoming increasingly important, and it is currently investing heavily in its military compared to the past.[4] These huge allocations are mainly geared to providing India with the capacity to dominate the entire region of Southern Asia through the acquisition of weaponry, posing a challenge to Pakistan and China. Political analysts feel that these kinds of developments mainly serve to escalate the perceived threat to Pakistan and other nations to the north.

This increase in India's military power is mainly aimed at countering that of the Chinese, and vice versa. It should be noted that India's efforts to counterbalance Chinese military power are bolstered by the backing of the US, whose partnership with India is likely to be the most significant factor in India's future foreign policy. However, despite the support of powerful Western nations, it is important for India to review its relations with its neighbours such as Pakistan if it is to achieve its ambitions for regional leadership, since most of them have a sour relationship with the US. The backing by the US government became clear in the Pentagon's 2010

---

4   Madrigal, 'Nuclear Power to Explode in India, but China Prefers Coal'.

Quadrennial Defense Review, which welcomed India's focus on 'more influential roles in global affairs', including the Indian Ocean region.[5]

India is capable of creating a new security regime within the region and in wider international relations as a result of its soft power and impressive military capabilities, and it is expected to take an even more active role in future. Other areas of strength include its nuclear programme, where it will enjoy certain advantages in the non-proliferation arena since it is currently not a signatory of the NPT, its intelligence-sharing with major world powers and its high level of military training. Despite its multi-ethnic communities with a wide range of religious diversity, India has a high standard of democracy, and coupled with its economic strength and improving trade relations with the West, this is expected to make it a strong force for transformation in the future.

India has the largest armed forces in the world after the US, and is still developing them, which raises the question of why India is concentrating on military strength despite the fact it is the most peaceful nation in its region. With a greater focus on Asia in future world affairs, India will play an important part in influencing the direction of developments, because its interests are not limited to its region, but include engagement with international organizations and Western nations, European countries and Japan, among others.[6] As the Asian continent moves from its current geopolitical configuration to take a more co-operative stance, India is well placed to extend its influence to other parts of the globe for its own benefit. India has therefore projected itself as one of the dynamic countries in Asia that is ready and confident to play an important and growing role in ensuring that there is security, peace and stability in the world.[7]

China

China's large military and its possession and continued development of nuclear weapons provide it with the military power to enable strategic coercion and denial. Although China has embraced the principle of no first use of its nuclear weapons, it is continuing to deploy survivable missiles that are capable of targeting the US, Australia, New Zealand, the Asia-Pacific region, Russia and India. Because of this, China has been able to maintain its territorial sovereignty and prevent foreign military intervention in areas of strategic interest such as the Taiwan Strait.

China's has a very versatile military, and increasing modernization and investment mean that the PLA's capabilities will continue to grow, though its potential is limited due to the lack of proper co-ordination between its command, support, supply and planning functions. China has the largest military in the world in terms of staff, with a total complement of about 3.2 million in the PLA along

---

5   Katherine L. Lynch, *The Forces of Economic Globalization: Changes to the Regime of International Commercial Arbitration* (2003), p. 213.

6   Mohan, 'Nine Ways to Look West'.

7   Ibid.

with a police force of around 800,000. It is one of the five global nuclear powers, and its naval forces have improved to the point where it is the dominant power in its region. Since the end of the Cold War, China is the only country whose military budget has continued to rise. However the total amount invested in the military cannot be determined since the PLA has it own sources of finance apart from the national budget. The PLA's history of producing civilian products dates back to its guerrilla days, and it is still involved in activities such as motor vehicle manufacturing, running hotels and the production of pianos and motorcycles. Not only is the PLA engaged in the production of civilian goods, it is also a major participant in the export and import of arms. Since the PLA operates autonomously, its operations cannot be limited by the Foreign Ministry. Nevertheless, despite this huge investment in its armed forces, the US military budget is still double that of China, so China's military power is unlikely to surpass that of the US in the foreseeable future.

It is believed that the increase in China's military expenditure was fuelled by the realization that its weapons were far inferior to those of the US during the Gulf War. In response, China began to purchase 1970s-technology weapons from Russia to replace its existing 1950s-technology weaponry that was several decades behind that of the US. Russia still refuses to sell more up-to-date weaponry to China, so this large technology gap continues to exist.

Economic Power

Brazil

For a long time, the belief that Brazil has the potential to become a world power has dominated the minds of the Brazilian elites and policy-makers, and this ambition has influenced the country's economic policies, which have been geared strategically towards helping the country to gain international influence.[8] Currently, Brazil's success in trade and economic issues has greatly enhanced its international profile, giving it even better hopes of becoming a superpower. The country has successfully developed quite a stable macroeconomic environment, and has established a stable currency. Brazil is not only a powerful exporter of commodities, but it has also managed to diversify its economy, hence encouraging a great deal of direct foreign as well as portfolio capital investment. The Brazilian stock market has also risen to become one of the largest in the world in recent years.[9]

Brazilian exports have greatly benefited from its diversification of trading partners. The US's position as Brazil's foremost trading partner was taken over

---

8   Alexandre Q. Guimarães, 'Historical Institutionalism and Economic Policymaking: Determinants of the Pattern of Economic Policy in Brazil, 1930–1960', *Bulletin of Latin American Research* 24:4 (2005), p. 530.

9   Wrobel, *Global Security in a Multipolar World*, p. 23.

by China in 2009, and it is also seeking to increase its trade with countries in Africa and the Middle East. Brazil's trade and economic diplomacy has been very active over the years, including participation in World Trade Organization negotiations.[10] In fact, Brazil has been among the most vocal WTO members complaining about trade measures that are seen as unfair to certain nations, especially developing states.

Brazil also currently enjoys a very positive international image, given that it has had hardly any armed conflicts with other states in the recent past. These factors contribute to giving the country an upper hand in the arena of global trade.[11] Brazil's economic advancement can be attributed to the long periods of freedom from external security threats that the country enjoyed, giving it an opportunity to concentrate on its economic policies. In addition, the country's large population of close to 20 million provides not only a large workforce to develop the economy, but also a vast domestic market for its goods. Brazil also has a large amount of diverse natural resources, which give it a competitive advantage.

If economic success is any guide, then Brazil has the capacity to rise above the status of a mere regional power and achieve superpower status. This is supported by the fact that the country is still undergoing rapid economic development, compared to most of its competitors, which are either approaching or have already reached the peak of their development. If economic power was all that it took to become a global superpower, then Brazil would definitely be on its way to becoming one, but it needs to address the other three axes of power if it is to succeed.

Russia

Among the BRICs countries, Russia has a unique position in terms of economic power. Unlike the other BRICs countries, which principally rely on trade and manufactured products, and to some extent agriculture, as the backbone of their economies, Russia is endowed with massive natural resources, including virtually all types of hydrocarbons and various mineral resources, including metals. It is viewed as a nation that is set to become an energy superpower because of its high oil and gas exports and its market leadership in gas and oil production. With its large reserves of high-quality petroleum products and the steady rise in demand and the cost of fuel, Russia is a strategic economic power not just in Eurasia, but globally.

Secondly, while the rest of the BRICs countries tend to exhibit a rapid population growth rate with a higher proportion of young people, Russia has a significantly low population growth rate and population density with a higher proportion of older people – a trend that is projected to continue in the near future. Thirdly, while the rest of the BRICs countries could be categorized as developing countries that are making progress towards actualization of their development, Russia is a

---

10   Ibid.
11   Ibid.

one-time superpower (through its predecessor, the USSR). It is a country that was at one time significantly developed, but was brought down by the disintegration of the USSR, which brought to an end its dream of being a superpower. During the existence of the USSR, the government of the day invested significantly in education, research and technology, as well as concluding significant bilateral and multilateral trade and economic agreements. Upon the fall of the USSR, Russia inherited its predecessor's rights and liabilities, including these connections. The excellent educational standards among its citizens position Russia as a nation that is well equipped to meet its needs in terms of communications, technology, scientific research, the dissemination of information and so on. These are key prerequisites for effective economic transactions, and could be harnessed to project Russia's economic power even further on a global scale. Russia therefore remains a beneficiary of the USSR's legacy, including its economic and trade ties – factors that give it a head start over its competitors.

However, Russia still needs to strive to come to terms with some major constraints on its aspirations to global economic dominance. First, it needs to address its demographic decline, a factor that threatens its existing and future labour force. Secondly, it needs to address the limited transparency of its economic and financial institutions, particularly in the energy sector that forms the backbone of the nation's economy. Nevertheless, Russia is a significant economic force owing to its copious natural resources, its globally competitive supply of human resources, its healthy national economic and financial base, its network of international trade and economic partnerships, and the legacy of goodwill from the USSR.

India

As the previous chapters have illustrated, although India is not yet as economically developed and sophisticated as the other BRICs members, it is rapidly emerging as a major modern trading nation. It is gradually reaching out other parts of the world in a bid to expand its economic base, driven mainly by its export of services (especially in the fields of education and medicine) and manufactured commodities such as jewellery, clothing and chemicals. The current government's emphasis in building trade and economic partnerships for mutual gain, India's economic growth rate is expected to continue to increase. According to Goldman Sachs, India will be among the leading economies in the world in terms of GDP within the next four decades, ranking third behind China and the US, and hence will achieve significant economic dominance. India also takes pride in having a large supply of highly educated, trained and talented labour drawn from its numerous renowned universities. This puts India in the position of being a global supplier of human resources to various private and public organizations that are seeking to expand their businesses globally.

However, India still needs to address some challenges that may mar its economic power. First, many Indians still live below the poverty line, although the majority are middle-income earners. It needs to make serious efforts to minimize the economic gap so that it may command a demographic advantage, particularly by developing a large population with increased purchasing power. This would empower its domestic market and avoid over-reliance on foreign markets, increasing its degree of independence.

China

China is perceived as a potential superpower because of the rapid growth of its economy, which has doubled since 1979, and has seen it move from being a demoralized, isolated and impoverished country to a confident, prosperous and dependable global trading power. In addition, China's ability to engage in bilateral and multilateral agreements with other countries through organizations such the East Asia Summit, the Shanghai Cooperation Organization and the China–Africa Cooperation Forum while excluding the US shows how much influence and power it has accumulated.

China's large population gives it a competitive advantage over most countries in the world since it provides a cheap source of labour, meaning that it does not need to rely on outsourced foreign manpower. The size of its population also ensures the survivability of the PLA, as there would be a ready supply of replacement personnel if a war broke out.

Despite China's evident success in many fields, it would be premature to consider it the next superpower. Its emergence as a great power is in no doubt, given its ability to protect its sovereignty and its influence in security and economic issues, but being a great power does not necessarily lead to superpower status, and at present it is in no position to challenge the US, which satisfies all the criteria of a world superpower: a flourishing, technologically advanced economy; a modernized, high-tech and formidable military; overwhelming economic advantages compared to its rivals; the ability to appeal to the whole word ideologically; a global capacity to supply public goods, and a fully integrated national political system. Although the USSR was considered a superpower in its heyday, it was only capable of competing with the US in one dimension: military strength.

Although China had a GDP of over US$5 trillion in 2010, it still faces daunting challenges in its bid to become a superpower since its average annual income per capita is approximately US$4,000, a tenth that of other economic powerhouses such as the US and Japan. Due to China's huge population, most of its populace still lives in villages that suffer from water shortages, lack of access to safe drinking water, lack of basic health care facilities, and inadequate education. At its current urbanization growth rate of 1 per cent a year, it would take more than thirty years for China to reduce the size of its peasantry to less than half its total population. Given these circumstances, China, is highly unlikely to ascend to superpower status with hundreds of millions of its population still struggling to survive on the margins of modernity.

The belief that China may become the next superpower is based on the assumption that there will be constant growth in its economy at the same rate that has prevailed since 1979, but there is no certainty that this will be the case. On the contrary there is a high probability that its growth rate will reduce substantially over the next few decades, since its current unlimited access to global markets, subsidized costs of environmental protection and the demographic advantages as a result of its youthful population will slowly cease to exist. In fact, it is feared that China may become an ageing society because of the government's strict one child policy, so that the country's urban demographics may come to resemble Japan's. If this policy continues, by 2020, approximately 17 per cent of China's population will be aged 60 years or above, leading to increased expenditure on healthcare and pensions and a reduction in the amounts saved and invested. Although there is still uncertainty about the scale of these problems, their combined effects are likely to have a substantial adverse impact on China's economic growth.

Since 1979, China has relied heavily on exports to build its economy, and it is currently the largest exporter in the world, having superseded Germany in 2009. Although this strategy has been largely successful in East Asia, it is highly doubtful that it will continue to be viable in future, not least because the US and the EU countries have begun to pursue more protectionist policies.

As outlined earlier, some claim that China is keen to develop itself in a selfish fashion, as is evident from its blatant derogation of its bilateral agreements with the EU. There have been complaints that although China enjoys unlimited access to the EU market, it has placed significant restrictions on US and EU penetration of its domestic market, leading to charges that China is not participating in dealing with the global economic crisis. In addition, some of its trading partners complain that China's under-valued currency could be a major factor behind escalating global imbalances and the weakening of their economies.

Since other countries in East Asia are less powerful in terms of trade, China finds it easy to impose its will and initiate economic disruption among its rivals and trading partners. Therefore, unless the Chinese government moves away from its mercantilist strategy in the near future, there is likely to be a global backlash against China's export policies. Since 2 per cent of China's economic growth over the last five years has been linked to its exports, a general reduction in exports will reduce China's economic growth rate. Although China can compensate for the lost export markets by catering to its domestic demand, this would mean a complete departure from its current export and growth strategy – a step the Chinese Communist Party has long been reluctant to take.

China's potential for becoming a superpower is also limited by the substantial environmental degradation as a result of its ineffective regulatory policies and the blatant disregard of the need to conserve the environment that underlies most of its foreign policies. The environmental consequences China has already suffered include loss of agricultural land due to water shortages, contamination and increased salinity. Furthermore, China is dependent on coal and oil as its major sources of energy, so it is a major contributor to world carbon dioxide emissions.

Approximately 750,000 Chinese people die from air and water pollution per year, and it is believed that the costs of pollution amount to approximately 8 per cent of its GDP. China has realized that this is a growing global concern and it needs to address these issues, but Chinese experts estimate that to do so would require an additional investment of 1.5 per cent of its GDP annually, which would reduce its growth rate. The adverse climate change caused by the production of greenhouse gases by China's heavy industries is likely to worsen the decline in China's water supplies and exacerbate the drought in northern China. This all means that China's energy policy, based on access to cheap energy sources with limited expenditure on addressing pollution, will be unsustainable.

China is the second-largest energy consumer in the world, consuming more than it can produce, so it has to rely on imports. The increase in China's population means there is a likelihood of energy shortages, which would be a serious setback for China's growing economy. Among the developed countries, China has made the least progress in seeking alternative sources of energy, and this will inevitably have to change in future, calling for the diversion of some of its resources to address these issues, reducing its potential to emerge as a world superpower.

Political Power

Brazil

Political power is an essential prerequisite for commanding global respect as superpower, and Brazil scores quite highly on this axis. The country's political success is attributed to the fact that it is located in a fairly peaceful region where it experiences few international conflicts. As a result, the country has made very few political enemies, if any, enhancing its international political influence, which has been manifested in a number of ways. The most impressive is the country's success in initiating a large number of treaties, such as those covering the manufacture, trade and possession of various types of weapons of mass destruction, and convincing other nations to sign up to them.

The country registered a landmark success when it convinced Iraq to enter into a treaty committing it to abandon its nuclear weapons programme,[12] an achievement that had eluded even the acknowledged superpower, the US. However, this agreement was condemned by the US as a delaying tactic by Iraq to avoid economic sanctions the UN was planning to impose on it, giving it more time to build up its weaponry.[13]

Another clear manifestation of Brazil's political power is its active participation in a wide range of international organizations. Brazil was one of the founder members of the UN, and has regularly held a seat on the UN Security Council,

---

12   Ibid.
13   Isacson, 'Brazil's Foreign Policy Awakens'.

where it has been quite vocal, often opposing policies that it sees as working against the interests of developing nations. Brazil also plays a leading role in a number of regional organizations, and has recently taken to forming alliances with developing countries outside Latin America, expanding its influence to other regions such as Africa and the Middle East.

Brazil has also managed to promote diplomatic solutions to state and inter-state conflicts such as that in Haiti in 2004, again demonstrating the country's international influence. It is currently working strategically to amass more political influence, not least through advocating for the rights of the developing countries in international forums, including the UN Security Council. The country's emphasis on diplomacy in conflict-resolution can also be seen as an effort to gain international recognition, and hence political influence.

Brazil's degree of social influence over other nations is indicated by the readiness of many countries to form alliances with it, though others still treat it with a degree of suspicion. For instance, when Brazil intervened during the conflict in Haiti in 2004, it had to send its football team to play against Haiti as a demonstration that it was seeking peace, and not acting from any other motive.[14] Isacson also argues that this suspicion even extends to Brazil's own neighbours, among some of whom it is seen as self-seeking, and therefore untrustworthy. This limits Brazil's prospects of rising to the status of a superpower, as has been its ambition for decades, though it is continuing work to enhance its soft power, for instance by pursuing an alliance with all the Portuguese-speaking nations.

Russia

Russia's position as one of the five permanent UN Security Council members gives it a great deal of political power in negotiations on various issues of global concern. Of particular interest is the way Russia has used its veto powers as a permanent member of UNSC to counter initiatives by the US and its Western allies, such as its recent rejection, along with China, of a resolution to impose sanctions and possible military intervention against Syria.

Russia also benefits from the diplomatic legacy of the USSR, and maintains close ties with most of the states in the North and South Caucasus and Eastern Europe which were once key Soviet allies. In addition, it enjoys good political relations with other major world powers like Germany, China, India and, more recently, Brazil. Such relationships are vital in building a bloc capable of countering the current unipolar hegemony of the US. Russia's energy resources and military strength also puts it in a position to wield much soft power over other nations, as they clearly stand to gain from the relationship. This has been a major factor in Russia's links with China, as China needs a large supply of oil for its rapidly developing industries and armaments for its massive armed forces.

---

14   Ibid.

However, Russia still faces various political challenges in projecting its political power globally. For instance, it currently has no clear, distinct political ideology that would be attractive to the global community. It appears to be relying on a combination of autocracy and democracy – two conflicting political ideals which have given rise to domestic political conflict. It has yet to fully embrace democracy, and its political institutions have been widely condemned for corruption. It will need to improve this image if it is to command a significant political following. It is also rivalled by many other emerging powers in Eurasia, including China, South Korea, India, and established powers elsewhere in the world, like the UK and France. It therefore needs to improve its foreign policy in order to enhance its projection of soft power.

Finally, the mounting pressure to change the structure of the UN Security Council poses a threat to the advantages currently enjoyed by the five permanent members, including Russia and China, and if successful, may enhance the status of a number of countries which have so far been disadvantaged in projecting their political power globally, but may as a result come to rival Russia.

India

India's efforts to attain what it sees as its 'rightful position' in the world have led its government to focus mainly on building its leadership and strategic stature.[15] India's youthful population is advantageous in developing its economy and supporting its large military, and its soft power continues to grow, along with its diplomatic outreach. India's success in accommodating a wide range of religious groupings and ethnic communities – including Hindus and the largest Muslim population in the world – has been attributed to its high standards of democracy.[16] These are some of the factors that contribute to the likelihood of India becoming a superpower, as they have enabled it to cope well in the volatile region of the Middle East, where strong democracies are scarce. India's status as a leader of the developing nations is growing, and is being recognized by the developed nations.

India's faces opposition from two major rivals in the quest for leadership in its region – Japan, and especially China, which reacted to efforts to exclude it from participation in Middle Eastern affairs by promoting the formation of the East Asia Summit.[17] Many political analysts criticized this move as it was seen as a bid to lessen the influence of India, Australia and New Zealand.

India's participation in international affairs is not confined to its immediate borders, but extends to the region as a whole, as well as engagement in important activities affecting the major world economies. For example, its involvement in relief efforts after the Indian Ocean tsunami in 2004 and its position as the second-largest contributor of humanitarian aid after the US clearly demonstrate

---

15   Thomas R. Mockaitis, *The 'New' Terrorism: Myths and Reality* (2008), p. 27.
16   Ibid., p. 28.
17   Ibid.

that India should not be ignored when discussing candidates for future superpower status. Unlike most its neighbours, India has been an enthusiastic participant in a number of important international organizations, such as APEC and ASEAN,[18] and it has also been very active in the UN, for instance by responding to calls for international aid.

Despite India's unsuccessful attempts to become a permanent member of the UN Security Council, not least because of Chinese opposition, UN membership has benefited India in a number of ways.[19] It has helped India to develop a closer relationship with Japan, which has assisted India in terms of commerce and the achievement of its objectives. Its relationship with the UN Security Council as a rotating member has also increased India's profile as a major advocate for UN reform. India also continues to lead the G77 and the Non-Aligned Movement, and in this capacity has negotiated on behalf of other developing nations in high-profile meetings such as the WTO Doha Round and the UN General Assembly.[20]

The impact of India's foreign policy is largely dependent on the activities of its neighbours and trade partners. Despite its political and economic impact on world governance and international issues, its influence is countered by nations like China. India's developing partnership with the US is important in this political landscape, as India would benefit in terms of better trade relations, while the US would benefit in terms of exerting control over the Middle East through India. India's status as a strong and stable democracy puts it at a strategic advantage in influencing major issues across the region. However, it is uncertain whether the relationship between the US and India will continue to flourish as each nation pursues its own agenda.

India continues to influence Sri Lanka and Bangladesh, promoting the benefits of democracy to both nations as well as providing military and material support to ensure stability.[21] During the terrorist attacks in Sri Lanka, described by many political analysts as nationalist terrorism, India has been in the forefront of peacekeeping operations and efforts to promote stability. Afghanistan is also another nation in which India has vested interests. It has developed a long-lasting relationship with the Northern Alliance in Afghanistan to support growth and stability, providing US$750 million to boost its economy.[22]

Discussion of India's involvement with the international community cannot ignore its very active participation in the UN, in which it plays a major peace-building role, not only in the Middle East, but also in the other parts of the world. In 2007, India was reported to be the largest supplier of peacekeeping troops to

---

18   Bjørgo, *Root Causes of Terrorism*, p. 167.

19   Mockaitis, *The 'New' Terrorism*, p. 27.

20   Bjørgo, *Root Causes of Terrorism*, p. 169.

21   'Indian Retailing: Mall Rats – Reliance Moves into Low Fashion', *The Economist* (20 October 2007), p. 86.

22   Ibid., p. 86.

the UN,[23] and its standard of training for these operations is unsurpassed. This is part of India's strategy to maintain good relations and strong democracy within and outside the Middle East. India has been prominent in offering humanitarian assistance to many nations affected by disasters. For example, it was part of the Asian Tsunami Core Group formed within four hours of the occurrence of Indian Ocean tsunami in December 2004, and despite being struck by the tsunami itself, India gave more assistance than any country except the US.[24] This illustrates that India is a highly capable military power, but it also shows its potential an emerging superpower. However, it is unclear whether India is likely to follow this route or whether it will continue to support the status quo. Other nations in the region like China are also emerging as significant forces, and their involvement in international affairs cannot be ignored.

China

As covered earlier, China has recently been extending its international network of diplomatic relationships. It has been intensifying its trade with various African, Asian and European countries while extending commercial incentives to them, especially the developing nations. It is also a strategic partner of the EU and a permanent member of the UN Security Council – factors that give China forums for the exposition of its ideologies and positions on matters of global concern. Its rapidly expanding GDP and economic strength also give China an advantage in funding its foreign policies and reaching out to other countries while granting incentives to them – measures that boost its soft and hard power. With its high population that wields ever-increasing purchasing power, China is likely to become less reliant on foreign markets. This would increase its independence, and therefore give it greater immunity from international and diplomatic dynamics that would otherwise weaken its institutions and impede the implementation of its foreign policy.

Achieving superpower status depends on a nation's mission and visions being embraced by the rest of the world. This would limit China's prospects of emerging as a superpower, since it would require that Chinese leaders develop a global mission and vision that are universally acceptable. The example of the US illustrates this: even though the US had already risen to the level of a superpower long before Pearl Harbor, it had to participate in the Second World War to win world recognition as a true superpower. At present, however, China's ideologies lack a vision, despite its flourishing economy. Although China has started to acquire soft power through offering unconditional loans to many countries and increasing its investment in others, it has not integrated its citizens into its leadership – a fact that will limit its international power in the near term.

---

23   Sahni, 'India and the Asian Security Architecture', p. 187.
24   Madrigal, 'Nuclear Power to Explode in India, but China Prefers Coal'.

The Chinese Communist Party has survived to the current day despite calls for its abolition, but this may not continue. Although the party has been able to survive through political repression of its opponents and by ensuring continuous economic growth, Chinese society is becoming more complex, with most individuals embracing the ideology of autonomy in their activities. Accordingly, the Chinese Communist Party will find it more difficult to repress the activities of the urban middle-class population, who are likely to demand to exercise their rights of political participation. In addition to the lack of democracy in China's political environment, corruption is emerging as a serious issue. With these problems persisting in the RPC, there is a possibility of a future revolution in China in a bid to establish a multi-party political system that could lead to disruption of trade, and might even prove disastrous.[25]

To protect India from Chinese pressure, Japan and the US have more than once extended economic aid to the country. While facilitating China's rapid military development, Russia has refused to supply it with top-line weaponry, and has even reduced the amount of energy it is supplying. Wary of China's future plans, South Korea has leaned on the US for security and economic development, whereas Indonesia and Vietnam have avoided openly declaring any alliances for fear of provoking China, while occasionally relying on China's arch-rivals, Japan and the US, for support. In order to become a superpower, it is essential for China to have the capacity to dominate its regional rivals, and the current resistance makes this highly unlikely, as any such move would be met with hostility.

China's ascent to become a global superpower will also be obstructed by geopolitical factors. Unlike the US, which is surrounded by relatively weak neighbours, China is surrounded by formidable rivals such as Russia, Japan and India. In addition, the opposition of other countries such as Vietnam, South Korea, North Korea and Indonesia cannot be ignored. In a bid to resist China's rise to power and deter it from achieving certain ambitions and goals, there has been increased geopolitical realignment in the region. A political democratic revolution is not the only fear faced by the Chinese government, since ethnic secessionism is also a growing threat. According to some scholars, China is simply a multinational empire inhabited by different groups of people with different schools of thought, the ethnic secessionists being in the minority. In addition to the historical problem of Taiwan, the threat of internal fragmentation may suddenly erupt, and this has prompted China to tighten its defences and devote more resources to enforcing its security in a bid to protect its territorial sovereignty. This may limit the country's capacity to expand its power and influence abroad, since its adversaries could initiate political turmoil in China in an effort to bring it to its knees.

---

25 Minxin Pei, 'China's Not a Superpower', *The Diplomat* (2010): http://apac2020. the-diplomat.com/feature/China%E2%80%99s-not-a-superpower/3/ (accessed 21 January 2012).

Overall Assessment

The BRICs countries seem to be conscious of their potential superpower status, and have been seeking to build up their political, military and economic strength in a bid to realize these dreams. All the BRICs countries will be capable of wielding greater soft and hard power in the near future, although to varying degrees and subject to unique factors.

Brazil

Despite its great population, continent-sized land mass, immense natural resources and great economic power, Brazil still stands a very slender chance of becoming a superpower, especially in comparison to its competitors. Although the elites in the country have long dreamt of piloting the country to the coveted status of a superpower, this is likely to remain just a dream, at least for most of the twenty-first century. Brazil is not likely to meet the criteria for a superpower in the near future since does it lacks sufficient soft and hard power to command global influence. In terms of hard power, the country scores highly in terms of economic considerations, but falls far short when it comes to military power in comparison to its competitors. On the other hand, Brazil has greater soft power than most of its competitors, and has commanded respect in the international arena through its efforts to foster peace through diplomacy, not least by engaging other countries in. Although this has won Brazil a lot of political influence in the international arena, gaining sufficient social influence has proved more of a challenge. Some other countries tend to view it with suspicion as a self-seeking nation, which indicates that it lacks sufficient social power to attain superpower status.

Brazil has relatively high soft and hard power, giving it some potential as a prospective superpower. The country's elites share this ambition, and the country's policies are formulated strategically to achieve it. A superficial view of the country would therefore suggest that it could be the next superpower, given the diminishing influence of the US. However, it is unlikely to fulfil this dream, since analysing the situation of Brazil in terms of the four power axes discussed earlier reveals many shortfalls.

Russia

Russia remains a unique member of the BRICs: it benefits from the legacy of the traditional hard and soft power commanded by its predecessor, the USSR, and it has been able take advantage of this in consolidating its own soft and hard power, unlike the other BRICs countries, which are still developing theirs and have yet to reach their peak. Russia benefits economically from the high income from its oil and natural resource exports, a number of bilateral and multilateral trade partnerships and significant independence from the West. It has established diplomatic relations with various countries, and has also used its status as the USSR's successor to rekindle relationships with other states of the former USSR in a bid to achieve global dominance. It also has a good deal of military power by virtue of its status as a nuclear weapons state, its high investment in military equipment and training, and its permanent membership of the UN Security Council.

Nevertheless, Russia is hampered by domestic problems, including allegations of institutionalized corruption, political extremism and an ageing population. It also needs to address external threats, such as competition from other emerging powers in its region, changes to the UN Security Council, and its deteriorating relationship with China.

India

In future, India stands a higher chance of becoming a dominant transformatory regional power in Eastern Asia than a superpower, bearing in mind the increasing military and soft power it commands in the region. It has the largest military in the region, and is also increasing the strength of its navy with the aim of gaining control over the Indian Ocean. This would give it powerful political and economic influence in the region, strengthening its military and economic power even further.

India's massive investment in its military is a result of its historical focus on ensuring security among its neighbours and in the wider region.[26] These efforts have included peacekeeping initiatives as well as offering financial assistance for infrastructure development in Sri Lanka, Bangladesh, Nepal and Afghanistan – a clear indication that India has changed its military policies from those of the past and is now interested in international issues like peacekeeping. It has also increased its participation in international forums through its involvement with the UN. Despite lacking a permanent seat on the UN Security Council, India has always been co-operative in providing humanitarian aid when called upon, for example in response to the 2004 Indian Ocean tsunami, when its humanitarian and financial contributions ranked second only to those of the US.[27]

China

China is a global economic powerhouse, and thus can be dubbed an 'economic superpower'. However, this is as far as this title goes, as there are numerous areas where China needs to improve in order to meet the requirements for becoming a superpower. Chinese leaders are aware of their country's capabilities and limitations, and their approach to global issues treats their newly acquired position with great caution to ensure that China maintains sovereignty and protects its territorial integrity. This is why at this stage, China still conforms to international rules and policies created and dominated by the US with respect to the global economy and security. China may also fail to achieve regional dominance in

---

26   Holslag, *Europe's Normative Disconnect with the Emerging Powers*, p. 3.
27   Ibid.

future, as its military strength will always be constrained by its domestic problems and external checks on its power.

Chapter Summary

Power in the context of international relations and in relation to the attainment of the status of superpower, great power, middle power or regional power is all about influence and might. This influence or might needs to be assessed in comparison with other states and non-state actors in international relations, and especially those other states that are also candidates for dominance.

Since power, might and influence are quite abstract and not easy to observe or quantify, analysis of a state's power will tend to focus on easily observable or identifiable features. Some of these features which the analysis in this chapter took into consideration include: foreign, domestic, economic and defence policies; military, economic and demographic capacities, and the record of political, economic, diplomatic and military relations with other states and entities. Attaining global power is not a direct combat where one state seeks to test its might against another, but a product of a complex blend of these and other factors. As Nye notes, it is these indirect factors that lead other actors to submit to the influence of the state possessing or exercising these attributes.

This chapter has established that all the BRICs countries are keen to develop their soft and hard power by optimizing the international relations and military instruments and resources at their disposal. Each country is seeking to widen and strengthen its diplomatic ties with other developed and developing powers, supranational institutions and organizations. They have also formed a wide range of alliances, co-operations, agreements and coalitions, either formal or informal, to advance their military and international relations objectives and ideologies. China and Russia in particular have used their permanent seats on the UN Security Council to assert their positions on matters of global security concern, especially in opposition to positions taken by the dominant US and its Western allies. Unlike Russia, Brazil, China and India have always been cautious of the US tendency to resort to military intervention in response to foreign or global security issues.

Other than the measures employed by the BRICs countries to boost their power profiles, this chapter has also established that they generally enjoy the advantages of favourable economic, demographic and geographical factors which have the effect of increasing their hard and soft power. These factors include good economic performance, vast geographical territory and a high population with a good deal of purchasing power.

The economic performance and high GDPs of the BRICs countries have served to give them a significantly positive image in the global arena. While international relations do not depend solely on these factors, they are essential in assessing a country's global competitiveness, its ability to achieve its long- and short-term international relations and diplomatic goals, and therefore its ascent up the global power ladder. In fact, the initial identification of the BRICs countries as potential major powers or superpowers of the future was prompted by their rapidly growing economic performance.

All the BRICs countries have the advantage of large geographical territories. Although territorial extent in itself has no direct influence on international relations, it plays strategic roles which serve to boost a state's security or economic base, and by extension its military and economic power. The sheer size of Brazil, Russia, China and India contribute to their military security, since it makes rapid aggressive penetration of the country's mainland very difficult. In addition, where climatic conditions are favourable, a vast territory implies a large potential for agricultural production, thus bestowing food security and boosting the potential for exports which can help to build a stronger economy. This advantage has been best exploited by Brazil, and to some extent India, so the value of a large territory in boosting the power profile of the BRICs countries cannot be overlooked.

The BRICs countries also benefit from population/demographic strength. Again, although having a large population does not have a direct impact on international and diplomatic relations, it plays facilitative roles. Having a population with high or average purchasing power enhances a nation's market capacity, attracting both domestic and foreign investors, boosting its economic power, which may then be used to facilitate implementation of the nation's military and foreign policy goals. Inflow of foreign investment fosters diplomatic relations with the investors' home countries and also promotes the host country's image, thereby boosting its soft power profile. Both India and China have grown to be Asia's regional economic and political giants partly due to the size of their middle-class populations, which have made the countries attractive to investors by offering a large market base and suitable business and investment opportunities. The same factors apply to Brazil, but Russia seems to be lagging behind the other BRICs countries, since it has a large number of old people among its population and may need to implement policy measures to address this.

However, all the BRICs countries are subject to some internal or external constraints on their quest for power. Brazil, China and India have yet to revitalize their global military images, as they have traditionally been reluctant to resort to military action beyond territorial defence. Only recently have they begun to be actively involved in international military operations in the context of peacekeeping. They will need to make strenuous efforts to overcome the common perception that they lack notable hard power that can be projected on a global scale. China, Russia and India are surrounded by many other rapidly developing and militarily powerful nations such as North and South Korea, Malaysia and Iran, and supranational entities like the EU. China, Russia and India also happen to be neighbours. This presents a chain of complex competition for supremacy among them, and diminishes the chances of any of them attaining the status of a superpower, or at least regional dominance. In addition, these three nations have numerous domestic challenges in common, including religious and political extremism, internal political discontent and opposition, and threats from terrorist groups. They also face external security threats: India, by the virtue of its close ties with the US and West European countries, remains a major target for terrorist groups that often perceive the US as its core enemy and may retaliate against US allies. India has also been facing diplomatic turmoil with its neighbour Afghanistan. Russia's emergence as a world power is likely to be countered by the US, since it would be too reminiscent of the Cold War period. It will not be easy for other great powers aligned to the US to establish long-term, sustainable alliances or co-operation with Russia if their impact would be to injure the US's international image, influence or ideologies.

PART IV
Conclusions

Chapter 17

Conclusions

The rapid rise in the economic and geopolitical influence of Brazil, Russia, India and China have prompted speculation that these countries are headed towards attaining a dominant global power position, possibly even attaining superpower status in the future. The core question for the research in this book was whether the BRICs countries, individually or as a bloc, had any prospects of becoming the next superpower, considering their past, current and likely future diplomatic and international relations and military capabilities.

Chapter 2 examined the notion of superpower and the general global power architecture with a view to establishing what it takes to be a superpower, assessing different perspectives. It established that determination of a state's position in the international power hierarchy calls for numerous observations of its role in global politics and international relations. A vital consideration is to take into account how the state utilizes its foreign policy instruments to form alliances, coalitions, unions and diplomatic ties with other states and international organizations. Other factors that need to be considered include the size of the state's population, its GDP, its territorial range, and the size and capacity of its armed forces and weaponry, particularly if it possesses nuclear weapons. The conclusion was that there is more to attaining superpower status than merely achieving a high rate of economic growth, and many other aspects of power need to be considered – economic, military, political, cultural and diplomatic. Foreign policy and military power are two instruments that are crucial in developing foreign relations, and by extension enhancing the state's projection of its soft and hard power. As a result, a superpower was defined as: 'a leading nation in the international power system that is able to project its soft and hard power globally'.[1]

Part II examined each of the BRICs countries in turn, and Part III drew on this to conduct an analysis of the future prospects of each of them. The findings from this revealed that the BRICs countries have generally shown a rapid rise up the global power ladder, although none them have yet advanced their soft and hard power to the extent of attaining anything near superpower status. Brazil and China were found to be heavily reliant on soft power, but still need to improve this aspect. Brazil, India and China lack traditional hard power profiles, and it may take them some time to address this. Russia, on the other hand, has well-developed and sophisticated hard power capacities, and benefits from the legacy of its predecessor and superpower of its time, the USSR. Its soft power is also well developed, though there is still room for improvement.

---

1   Dreyer. 'Chinese Foreign Policy'.

The analysis carried out after the deep investigations of each country points towards the conclusion that none of the BRICs countries except Russia are likely to become the world's next superpower. They may qualify, at best, as great powers or regional powers, but certainly not superpowers. Below is a summary of the conclusions for each country:

Brazil

Brazil's prominence in geopolitics and international relations, particularly since the dawn of the twenty-first century, cannot be doubted. It is a country of promising and exponential socio-economic growth which appears to enjoy much better diplomatic and international relations with its neighbours than the other BRICs nations. Owing to its close political ties with other world powers, its demographic advantages, its rapid pace of technological and economic development, its stable internal political environment and leadership, its sizeable markets and its more recent active participation in matters of global concern and peace-making efforts, it is viewed as a country with great potential to rise much higher in the global power ranking.

Brazil has utilized various foreign policy tools to enhance its international image and to improve diplomatic relations with other nations. It has participated in international peacekeeping operations and has also undertaken proactive efforts that have seen regional integration of states of South America, where it easily commands regional power. Brazil's membership of the UN Security Council has put it in a position to be a key balancing force in the determination of crucial global affairs. Its aspirations for further global power may be promoted if it acquires a permanent seat on the UN Security Council – a move that it has been zealously pressing for. Brazil therefore scores well in terms of soft power.

Despite Brazil's economic might and its good regional and global diplomatic relations, it is highly unlikely to become a superpower in the near future. First, it lacks hard power, and neither has it traditionally invested in developing it. The country has been known for its non-interventionist foreign policy and strong advocacy of respect for the doctrine of sovereignty, although it has recently begun to contribute to regional peacekeeping efforts. Its military power is therefore still in its infancy in relation to the scale of military strength and participation expected of a superpower, and has mainly been exercised at a regional level. Brazil therefore banks heavily on its soft power, mainly through its global economic participation and diplomatic initiatives. This is still developing, and its soft power is not yet at its peak, so although Brazil may not attain superpower status, it may well emerge as a major global power and a regional power in South America.

Russia

Russia enjoys a number of advantages over the rest of the BRICs nations in seeking superpower status. First, the legacy of goodwill from the former USSR means that it does not face the same struggle to set up new diplomatic ties as the other BRICs countries. The same legacy gives it a good international image through its association with a former superpower. Its heavy investment in military power and the scale of its armed forces boost its hard power. Russia also has a permanent seat on the G8 and UN Security Council – positions that give it a great deal of influence over decisions concerning other states and global affairs. Russia's foreign policies have also encouraged greater regional and global integration, and have seen it join a number of major international organizations, including the EU and ASEAN+3, which again gives it an opportunity to access the global community and sell its ideologies. It has typically been vocal on global affairs, and has traditionally remained openly critical of US dominance. As its economy grows and other major powers emerge, Russia may find powerful political allies and create another power bloc, thereby diluting the US's global dominance and setting the stage for a multipolar world. It is the only country among the BRICs that commands notable hard and soft power globally.

However, achieving superpower status will depend on resolving a number of issues that might render its prospects an elusive dream. In particular, it needs to address its internal security concerns, including the suppression of extremist groups and combating terrorism.

India

After many years of perceived global dormancy, India has in recent decades emerged as an active, vocal member of the international community. It enjoys very close and cordial diplomatic ties with the US, the European Union, ASEAN and most African states. It has taken an increasingly prominent role in global peace and security issues, is a rotating member of the UN Security Council, and has been seeking a permanent seat on that body. Its membership of the UNSC and UN Peacebuilding Commission gives it an opportunity to serve as a major balance of power and be party to crucial international security decisions by the UN. It also has a rapidly developing economy and may soon be able to decrease the deficit that it experiences today.

Despite these strengths, India has very limited prospects of attaining superpower status. First, it has traditionally been viewed as a weak, irresolute nation that has been reluctant to court controversy. Although India has changed tack in its international relations, it will have to work hard to change this perception, which significantly impairs its soft power. India's regional location also presents another challenge: it neighbours China, which is also pursuing global dominance and will be keen to contain India's growing influence. While India may still employ its soft power, including foreign policy instruments, it may find it more difficult to employ hard power tactics like military measures to advance its influence, especially within Asia, since such efforts are likely to be countered by China, which is more militarily, economically and technologically advanced.

China

Like Brazil, China wields significant soft power and has used various foreign policy tools to advance its global power. Its rapidly growing economy has led other nations to court China for economic and political diplomatic relationships, as they view it as a potential investment partner. Its leaders have also been reaching out to other parts of the world through bilateral and multilateral agreements, and using economic, humanitarian and military incentives to woo various countries, particularly the developing nations, into good diplomatic relations. China enjoys a significant degree of financial stability, and some economists have projected that its economy will be the world's largest in the next four decades. This gives it strong economic power that it can use to advance other aspects of its power and pursue its foreign policies.

Nevertheless, it is unlikely that China will emerge a superpower in the near future since it faces a number of challenges that may not be quick to resolve. First, like Brazil, China has always been cautious in exerting the hard power that is a criterion for gaining superpower status. Even as a permanent member of the UN Security Council, it has been wary of voting in favour of resolutions whose effect would be to create room for military action against other states' sovereignty. Its internal stability also remains questionable given the secession of Taiwan and in light of the recent increase in political extremism in the country, and it faces strong competition for power from other developing neighbouring states, including India and Russia, which also happen to be BRICs members.

The BRICs as a Bloc

As a group, the BRICs still have a very long way to go since they have yet to establish a formal bloc or co-operation. Indeed, their ideological diversity, their different and sometimes contrasting foreign and military policies and their limited common ground on other issues mean that there may be few incentives for forming such a formal political bloc. Thus, the BRICs are likely to remain an informal grouping for quite some time. Nevertheless, evidence of a more unified approach to global security issues means that the BRICs may yet constitute a new pole of power among the many predicted by various commentators, which may reduce the US's current hegemony. However, although such a development may portend a shift in international relations, it is unlikely that the BRICs will develop as another power bloc, owing to the group's current amorphous nature and the early stage of its development. It is equally unlikely that all the BRICs countries will rally behind one of their members as a superpower since each of them has its own ambitions. The implication is that the US's position as a superpower will be difficult to challenge.

Overview

To sum up, this book has argued that each of the BRICs countries is destined to increase its power in the future, and this is bound to have an impact on global power politics, and to a large extent dilute the hegemony of the US, currently unchallenged in the geopolitical power games. The future of global power politics is likely to be multipolar, with several centres of power that interact in complex ways with one another and with the countries and other entities under their influence. The future is not likely to bring obvious political dominance with the US leading its Western allies or backed by the G7, as more states will have grown and developed, and will have their own interests to pursue and their own influences to exert. The individual BRICs countries are more likely to expand their military power and diplomatic links in their own regions, leading to a significant improvement in their hard and soft power.

However, forming a joint power bloc, where an entity named 'the BRICs' acts as the global superpower, is quite unlikely. The BRICs countries are a world apart, and have only been brought together by chance, by virtue of their current economic and developmental similarities, and their resemblances essentially end there. The BRICs face major dilemmas that are unlikely to be resolved in any bid to form a solid power bloc, including the diversity and sometimes conflict between their political and economic ideologies, their diverse and sometimes conflicting diplomatic inclinations, the differences in their foreign policies and values, and the variety of internal and external threats they face.

Overcoming these challenges in order to form a unified power bloc might come at the expense of each nation's core diplomatic, economic, ideological or political interests, so the BRICs may prefer to maintain a loose economic co-operation that will not end up conflicting with each nation's long-term interests.

Further Recommendations and Policy Implications

To rise higher in the global power ranking and maintain their current status, let alone attain superpower status, each of the BRICs countries will have to overcome a number of challenges that lie ahead. Most of the recommendations and policy implications as a result of this study have been discussed in Part III, but there are further recommendations and policies that have not yet been addressed.

Both Brazil and India will have to invest more on their security profiles, probably by improving their military capacities, forming military alliances with more advanced and militarily high-profile great powers and pressing harder to be granted permanent seats on the UN Security Council. These measures will boost their global security images and enable them have greater say in vital contemporary global issues. If Brazil or India, or both, are given permanent seats on the UNSC, then a global power shift is very likely, as the four BRICs countries would all have veto powers and could form a political alliance. Recent voting trends regarding UNSC resolutions have shown that the BRICs countries already tend to adopt a common position and voting pattern, and permanent membership would present a totally new power paradigm.

China, India and Russia need to increase efforts to address their domestic problems, including political extremism, the threats of terrorism, corruption and the gap between the rich and the poor. This will call for thorough policy auditing and the development of short-term and long-term strategic plans to meet these challenges. It would be against the public interest for these states to pursue implementation of their foreign policies at the expense of their domestic problems and needs.

Russia should also temper its aggressive and uncooperative tendencies towards the West, particularly towards the US, since its strong opposition to the US on crucial global matters risks impairing its relationships with the US's allies, most of which are also major powers. Russia needs them to promote its global agenda, and cannot take close diplomatic ties with them for granted. Russia also needs to take initiatives to increase its birth rate, to provide good generational security and to replenish its ageing population.

The strong financial and economic capabilities of the BRICs countries imply that they will not be particularly reliant on loans from other economically powerful states or international financial institutions. If the BRICs opt to form an economic bloc with its own financial institutions as the EU has, then their reliance on other traditional lenders such as the IMF and World Bank will be significantly diminished. The Western great powers (including the UK, Germany, Italy and France) that may be threatened by the growing prominence of the BRICs are dominant in the current multinational financial institutions and could easily use them to curtail the BRICs' influence. Maintaining their economic strength will therefore be a key factor in safeguarding the sovereignty of the BRICs in general. Furthermore, forming a solid, well-structured, well-equipped and well-financed economic bloc and financial institutions – remote as this prospect currently seems – would make a significant contribution to securing the BRICs' sovereignty and international freedom.

Bibliography

Books

Agnew, John. *Globalization and Sovereignty*. New York: Rowman & Littlefield, 2009.

Almeida, Paulo Roberto de. *O Estudo das Relações Internacionais do Brasil*. São Paulo: Unimarco Editora, 1999.

Almeida, Paulo Roberto de. 'The BRICs' Role in the Global Economy', in Cebri-Icone-British Embassy in Brasília, *Trade and International Negotiations for Journalists*, Rio de Janeiro, 2009.

Aubrey, Stefan M. *The New Dimension of International Terrorism*. Zurich: Hochschulverlag, 2004.

Bjørgo, Tore. *Root Causes of Terrorism: Myths, Reality and Ways Forward*. Abingdon: Routledge, 2005.

Blasko, Dennis J. *The Chinese Army Today: Tradition and Transformation for the 21st Century*. New York: Routledge, 2006.

Bull, Hedley. *The Anarchical Society: A Study of Order in World Politics*. New York: Columbia University Press, 1977.

Buzan, Barry. *The US and the Great Powers: World Politics in the Twenty-first Century*. Cambridge: Polity Press, 2004.

Buzan, Barry and Foot, Rosemary (eds). *Does China Matter? A Reassessment: Essays in Memory of Gerald Segal*. London: Routledge, 2004.

Codato, Adriano Nervo (ed.). *Political Transition and Democratic Consolidation: Studies on Contemporary Brazil*. New York: Nova Science Publishers, 2006.

Collins, John M. *U.S. Defense Planning: A Critique*. Boulder, CO: Westview Press, 1982.

Combs, Jerald A. *American Diplomatic History: Two Centuries of Changing Interpretations*. Berkeley, CA: University of California Press, 1983.

Cox, Robert W. *Production, Power and World Order: Social Forces in the Making of History*. New York: Columbia University Press, 1987.

Crane, Keith, Cliff, Roger, Medeiros, Evan, Mulvenon, James and Overholt, William. *Modernizing China's Military: Opportunities and Constraints*. Santa Monica, CA: Rand, 2005.

Daddow, Oliver J. *Britain and Europe Since 1945: Historiographical Perspectives on Integration*. New York: Manchester University Press, 2004.

Demirtaş-Coşkun, B. and Balamir-Coşkun, B. *Neighborhood Challenge: The European Union and its Neighbors*. London: Universal Publishers, 2009.

Dukes, Paul. *The Superpowers: A Short History*. London: Routledge, 2000.

Dunne, Timothy. *International Relations Theories: Discipline and Diversity.* Oxford: Oxford University Press, 2007.

Fox, William T.R. *The Superpowers: The United States, Britain and the Soviet Union – Their Responsibility for Peace.* New York: Harcourt Brace, 1944.

Fraser, Matthew. *Weapons of Mass Distraction: Soft Power and American Empire.* New York: St. Martin's Press, 2005.

Garcia, Eugênio Vargas. *Cronologia das Relações Internacionais do Brasil*, 2nd edn. Rio de Janeiro: Contraponto Editora, 2005.

Gill, Bates. 'European Union–China Cooperation on Security Issues', in Shambaugh, D. and Wacker, G. (eds), *American and European Relations with China: Advancing Common Agendas.* Berlin: German Institute for International and Security Affairs, 2008.

Gill, Bates. *Rising Star: China's New Security Diplomacy.* Washington, DC: Brookings Institution Press, 2007.

Goldman Sachs, *BRICs and Beyond.* London: Goldman Sachs, 2007.

Graebner, Norman A. *Ideas and Diplomacy.* New York: Oxford University Press, 1964.

Hannay, David. *New World Disorder: The UN after the Cold War – an Insider's View.* London: I.B. Tauris, 2008.

Hogan, Michael J. and Paterson, Thomas G. *Explaining the History of American Foreign Relations.* New York: Cambridge University Press, 1991.

Hurrell, Andrew. 'Brazil as a Regional Great Power: A Study in Ambivalence', in Neuman, Iver B. (ed.), *Regional Great Powers in International Politics.* London: Macmillan, 1992.

Jain, Subhash C. (ed.). *Emerging Economies and the Transformation of International Business.* Cheltenham: Edward Elgar, 2006.

Joffe, Josef, 'The Secret of US World Domination', *The Globe and Mail* (Toronto), 27 September 1997.

Katzman, Martin T. 'Translating Brazil's Economic Potential into International Influence', in Selcher, Wayne A. (ed.), *Brazil in the International System: The Rise of a Middle Power.* Boulder, CO: Westview Press, 1981.

Lafer, Celso. *A Indentidade Internacional do Brasil e a Política Externa Brasileira: Passado, Presente e Futuro.* São Paulo: Editora Perspectiva, 2001.

Landau, Georges D. *The Decision-making Process in Foreign Policy: The Case of Brazil.* Washington, DC: Center for Strategic and International Studies, 2003.

Lemke, Douglas. 'Dimensions of Hard Power: Regional Leadership and Material Capabilities', in Flemes, Daniel (ed.), *Regional Leadership in the Global System: Ideas, Interests and Strategies of Regional Powers.* Aldershot: Ashgate, 2010.

Lohbauer, Christian. 'Die Beziehungen zwischen Brasilien und seinen Nachbarländern II', in Calcagnotto, Gilberto and Nolte, Detlef (eds), *Südamerika zwischen US-Amerikanischer Hegemonie und Brasilianischem Führungsanspruch: Konkurrenz und Kongruenz der integrationsprozesse in den Amerikas.* Frankfurt am Main: Vervuert Verlagsges., 2002.

Lynch, Katherine L. *The Forces of Economic Globalization: Changes to the Regime of International Commercial Arbitration*. Alphen aan den Rijn: Kluwer Law International, 2003.

Magnoli, Demétrio. *O Corpo da Pátria: Imaginação Geográfica e política Externa no Brasil, 1808–1912*. São Paulo: Moderna, 1997.

Martin, Gus. *Understanding Terrorism: Challenges, Perspectives, and Issues*, 3rd edn. Thousand Oaks, CA: Sage Publications, 2009.

Mattlin, Mikael. 'Thinking Clearly on Political Strategy: The Formulation of a Common EU Policy Toward China', in Gaens, Bart, Jokela, Juha and Limnell, Eija (eds), *The Role of the European Union in Asia: China and India as Strategic Partners*. Farnham: Ashgate, 2009.

McCann, Frank D. 'Brazilian Foreign Relations in the Twentieth Century', in Selcher, Wayne A. (ed.), *Brazil in the International System: The Rise of a Middle Power*. Boulder, CO: Westview Press, 1981.

McCormick, John. *The European Superpower*. New York: Palgrave Macmillan, 2007.

Mockaitis, Thomas R. *The 'New' Terrorism: Myths and Reality*. Stanford, CA: Stanford University Press, 2008.

Montgomery, John D. and Glazer, Nathan (eds). *Sovereignty Under Challenge: How Governments Respond*. Piscataway, NJ: Transaction Publishers, 2002.

Nye, Joseph S. *Soft Power: The Means to Success in World Politics*. London: Public Affairs, 2004.

Nye, Joseph S. *The Paradox of American Power*. Oxford: Oxford University Press, 2002.

O'Rourke, Ronald. *China Naval Modernization: Implications for U.S. Navy Capabilities – Background and Issues for Congress*, CRS Report to Congress, 18 November 2005.

Overholt, William H. *Asia, America, and the Transformation of Geopolitics*. Cambridge: Cambridge University Press, 2008.

Pastor, Robert. A. (ed.). *A Century's Journey: How the Great Powers Shape the World*. New York: Basic Books, 1999.

Popescu, Nicu and Wilson, Andrew. *The Limits of Enlargement-Lite: European and Russian Power in the Troubled Neighbourhood*. London: European Council on Foreign Relations, 2009.

Ricupero, Rubens. 'O Brasil, a América Latina e os EUA desde 1930: 60 Anos de uma Relação Triangular', in Albuquerque, José A.G. (ed.), *Sessenta Anos de Política Externa Brasileira 1930–1990: Crescimento, Modernização e Política Externa*. São Paulo: Cultura Editores, 1996.

Rosefielde, Steven, *Russia in the 21st Century: The Prodigal Superpower*. Cambridge: Cambridge University Press, 2005.

Scheffler, Julia. *Towards an Ever Closer Union? The US–UK Special Relationship until the UK's Final Accession to the European Community 1973*. Norderstedt: GRIN Verlag, 2006.

Shiping, Tang and Yunling, Zhang. 'China's Regional Strategy', in Shambaugh, David (ed.), *Power Shift*. Berkeley, CA: University of California Press, 2005.

Smith, David A., Solinger, Dorothy J. and Topik, Steven C. *States and Sovereignty in the Global Economy.* New York: Routledge, 1999.

Sutter, Robert. *Chinese Foreign Relations*. Lanham, MD: Rowman & Littlefield, 2008.

Vaidya, Ashish K. *Globalization: Encyclopedia of Trade, Labour and Politics* (2 vols). Santa Barbara, CA: ABC-CLIO, 2006.

Viotti, P.R. and Kauppi, M.V. *International Relations and World Politics: Security, Economy, Identity*, 3rd edn. New Delhi: Dorling Kindersley, 2007.

Whitman, Richard G. and Wolff, Stefan. *The European Neighbourhood Policy in Perspective: Context, Implementation and Impact*, Palgrave Studies in European Union Politics. Basingstoke: Palgrave Macmillan, 2010.

Wilson, Andrew. *Virtual Politics: Faking Democracy in the Post-Soviet World.* New Haven, CT: Yale University Press, 2005.

Wood, James. *History of International Broadcasting*, vol. 2. New York: IET, 2000.

World Bank. *The Little Data Book*. Washington, DC: The World Bank, 2007.

Articles from Journals and Reviews

Alden, Chris and Vieira, Antonio M. 'The New Diplomacy of the South: South Africa, Brazil, India and Trilateralism', *Third World Quarterly* 26:7 (2005): 1,077–95.

Bader, Julia, Grävingholt, Jörn and Kästner, Antje. 'Would Autocracies Promote Autocracy? A Political Economy Perspective on Regime-type Export in Regional Neighborhoods', *Contemporary Politics* 16:1 (2010): 81–100.

Barany, Zoltan. 'Resurgent Russia? A Still-faltering Military', *Policy Review* 43:147 (2008): 4–6.

Barnett, Michael and Duvall, Raymond. 'Power in International Politics', *International Organization* 59:1 (2005): 39–75.

Codato, Adriano Nervo. 'A Political History of the Brazilian Transition from Military Dictatorship to Democracy', transl. Miriam Adelman, *Revista de Sociologia e Política* 2, Selected Edition (November 2005): 83–106.

Baldwin, David A. 'Power and International Relations', in Carlsnaes, Walter, Risse, Thomas and Simmons, Beth A. (eds), *Handbook of International Relations*, London: Sage, 2002, 177–91.

'Defence Ministry Touts Deepened China–ASEAN Security Cooperation', Xinhua Domestic Service, Beijing, 30 March 2009.

Dupas, Gilberto. 'South Africa, Brazil and India: Divergence, Convergence and Alliance Perspectives', in Villares, Fábio (ed.), *India, Brazil and South Africa: Perspectives and Alliances*. Sao Paulo: Editora UNESP & IEEI, 2006.

Fan, Y. 'Soft Power: Power of Attraction or Confusion?', *Place Branding and Public Diplomacy* 4 (May 2008): 147–58.

Felgenhauer, Pavel. 'A Radical Military Reform Plan', *Eurasia Daily Monitor* 198:5 (2008): 13.

Gardner, Richard N. 'The Comeback of Liberal Internationalism', *Washington Quarterly* 13 (Summer 1990): 23–39.

Glazebrook, G. 'The Middle Powers in the United Nations System', *International Organization* 1:2 (1947): 307–15.

Goh, Evelyn. 'Great Powers and Hierarchical Order in Southeast Asia', *International Security* 32 (2007/2008): 113–57

Guimarães, Alexandre Q. 'Historical Institutionalism and Economic Policymaking: Determinants of the Pattern of Economic Policy in Brazil, 1930–1960', *Bulletin of Latin American Research* 24:4 (2005): 527–42.

Hartley, Peter R. and Kyle, Albert S. 'Equilibrium Investment in an Industry with Moderate Investment Economies of Scale', *The Economic Journal* 99 (2009): 394.

Holslag, J. *Europe's Normative Disconnect with the Emerging Powers*, BICCS Asia Paper 5:4. Brussels: Brussels Institute of Contemporary China Studies, 2010.

Howard, Michael. 'Military Power and International Order', *International Affairs* 40:3 (July 1964): 397–408.

Howell, Llewellyn D. *The Handbook of Country and Political Risk Analysis*. East Syracuse, NY: PRS Group, 2001.

Hurrell, Andrew. 'Hegemony, Liberalism and Global Order: What Space for Would-be Great Powers?', *International Affairs* 82:1 (2006): 1–19.

Ikenberry, John G. 'The Rise of China and the Future of the West', *Foreign Affairs* 87:1 (2008): 23–7.

Inderfurth, Karl and Riedel, Bruce. 'Breaking More Naan with Delhi: The Next Stage in U.S.-India Relations', *The National Interest* (November/December 2007).

Johnston, Alastair Iain. 'Learning Versus Adapting: Explaining Change in China's Arms Control Policy in the 1980s and 1990s', *China Journal* 35 (January 1996): 27–61.

Keohane, Robert O. 'Lilliputians' Dilemmas: Small States in International Politics', *International Organizations* 23:2 (1969): 296.

Ladurie, Emmanuel Le Roy and Greengrass, Mark. *The Ancient Regime*. New York: Wiley-Blackwell, 1998.

Lafer, Celso. 'Brazilian International Identity and Foreign Policy: Past, Present, and Future', *Daedalus* 129:2 (2000): 207–38.

Lake, David. 'Escape from the State of Nature: Authority and Hierarchy in World Politics', *International Security* 32:1 (2007): 47–79.

Lake, David. 'Regional Hierarchy: Authority and Local International Order', *Review of International Studies* 35:S1 (2009): 35–58.

Lima, Maria R. Soares de. 'Aspiração Internacional e Política Externa', *Revista Brasileira de Comércio Exterior* 82 (2005): 4–19.

Lima, Maria R. Soares de and Hirst, Mônica. 'Brazil as an Intermediate State and Regional Power: Action, Choice and Responsibilities', *International Affairs* 82:1 (2006): 21–40.

Lucarelli, Stephen. 'The European Union in the Eyes of Others: Towards Filling a Gap in the Literature', *European Foreign Affairs Review* 12:3 (2007): 249–271.

Medeiros, Evan S. and Fravel, M. Taylor. 'China's New Diplomacy', *Foreign Affairs* 86:2 (2003), p. 6.

'New-generation Warships for the PLA Navy', *Military Technology* 28:2 (February 2004), pp. 90–91.

Nolte, Detlef. 'How to Compare Regional Powers: Analytical Concepts and Research Topics', *Review of International Studies* 36 (2010): 881–901.

Norris, Robert S. and Kristensen, Hans M. 'Nuclear Notebook: Russian Nuclear Forces 2008', *Bulletin of the Atomic Scientists* 64:2 (2008): 54–7.

Norris, Robert S. and Kristensen, Hans M. 'Nuclear Notebook: Russian Nuclear Forces 2009', *Bulletin of the Atomic Scientists* 65:3 (2009): 55–64.

Onis, Juan de. 'Brazil's New Capitalism', *Foreign Affairs* 79:3 (2000): 107–19.

Perry, William. 'Has the Future Arrived for Brazil?', *Orbis* (2000): 399–415.

Ringmar, Erik. 'The Recognition Game: Soviet Russia Against the West', *Cooperation & Conflict* 37:2 (2002): 115–36.

Rodrigues, José H. 'The Foundations of Brazil's Foreign Policy', *International Affairs* 38:3 (1962): 324–38.

Sotero, Paulo and Leslie, Elliott Armijo. 'Brazil: To Be or Not to Be a Bric?', *Asian Perspective* 31:4 (2007): 43–70.

Veiga, Pedro da Motta. 'A Política Comercial do Governo Lula: Continuidade e Inflexão', *Revista Brasileira de Comércio Exterior* 83 (2005): 2–9.

Wortzel, Larry M. 'China Pursues Great Power Status', *Orbis* (Spring 1994): 157–76.

Xiaofon, Li. 'Environmental Concerns in China: Problems, Policies and Global Implications', *International Social Review* (Spring/Summer 2006), pp. 1–10.

Articles from an Online Data Base and Websites

Barabanov, Mikhail. 'Russian Tank Production Sets a New Record', *Moscow Defence Brief* 16 (2009): 10–11: http://mdb.cast.ru/mdb/2-2009/item4/article1/ (accessed 22 January 2012).

Bussert, James C. 'China Builds Destroyers around Imported Technology', *Signal* (August 2004): http://www.afcea.org/signal/articles/anmviewer.asp?a=252 (accessed 20 January 2012).

Centre for Policy and Development Systems (CPDS). 'China's Development: Assessing the Implications (November 2007): http://cpds.apana.org.au/Teams/Articles/china_as_economic_engine.htm (accessed 26 January 2012).

CIA. 'World Facts: South America, Brazil': https://www.cia.gov/library/ publications/the-world-factbook/fields/2055.html#br (accessed 4 January 2011).

Dreyer, June T. 'Chinese Foreign Policy'. *The Newsletter of FPRI's Wachman Center* 12:5 (February 2007): http://www.fpri.org/footnotes/125.200702. dreyer.chineseforeignpolicy.html (accessed 19 January 2012).

Eberstadt, Nicholas. 'Where Did the CIA Go Wrong?', *National Review* (June 1991): http://findarticles.com/p/articles/mi_m1282/is_n10_v43/ai_10847979 (accessed 26 January 2012).

Embassy of Brazil. 'Foreign Policy Overview': http://www.brasilemb.org/foreign-policy/overview (accessed 20 January 2011).

Evans, Gareth. 'NATO and Russia, the International Crisis Group', statement to the Shadow Globalsecurity.org: http://www.globalsecurity.org/military/world/ brazil/intro.htm (accessed 29 November 2011).

Guang, Pan. 'China's Anti-terror Strategy and China's Role in Global Anti-terror Cooperation', *Asia Europe Journal* 2 (2004): http://www.irChina.org/en/news/ view.asp?id=357 (accessed 21 January 2012).

Hornbeck, J.F. *Trade Policy and the United States*, CRS Report RL33258: http:// www.nationalaglawcenter.org/assets/crs/RL33258.pdf (accessed 14 January 2011).

International Crisis Group. 'The Great Debate: NATO and Russia' (2 April 2009): http://blogs.reuters.com/great-debate/2009/04/02/nato-and-russia/ (accessed 22 January 2012).

Johnson, Toni. 'Backgrounder: G8's Gradual Move toward Post-Kyoto Climate Change Policy', Council on Foreign Relations (25 January 2008): http://www. cfr.org/europerussia/g8s-gradual-move-toward-post-kyoto-climate-change-policy/p13640 (accessed 22 January 2012).

Konovalov, Ivan. 'Towards the Restoration of Russian Air Power', *Moscow Defense Brief* 11 (2008): http://mdb.cast.ru/mdb/1-2008/item2/article3/ (accessed 22 January 2012).

Kramnik, Ilya. 'Restoring the Tradition: Russian Navy on Long-distance Tours on Duty', RIA Novosti (December 2008): http://en.rian.ru/ analysis/20081215/118867561.html (accessed 22 January 2012).

Kramnik, Ilya. 'Tank Force Reductions or Statistical Juggling', RIA Novosti (July 2009): http://en.rian.ru/analysis/20090703/155424380-print.html (accessed 22 January 2012).

Lampreia, Luiz Felipe. *Brazilian Foreign Policy: Continuity and Renewal*: http:// www.un.int/brazil/brasil/brazil-un.htm (accessed 16 January 2012).

Martynov, Boris F. *'BRICs': Cooperation Perspectives in the International Security Sphere*: http://www.ipea.gov.br/bric/textos/100409_BRICMartynov1. pdf (accessed 21 December 2011).

'Military Corruption Costs Russia Almost $80 Million in 2008', RIA Novosti (December 2008): http://en.rian.ru/russia/20081202/118637765.html (accessed 22 January 2012).

Miller, Lyman. 'China an Emerging Superpower?', *Stanford Journal of International Relations*: http://www.stanford.edu/group/sjir/6.1.03_miller. html (accessed 12 January 2012).

Mission of Brazil to the United Nations: http://www.un.int/brazil/brasil/brazil-un. htm (accessed 6 January 2012).

Mission of Brazil to the United Nations. 'Security Council Reform: Brazil's Position': http://www.un.int/brazil/brasil/brazil-scnu-reform.htm (accessed 2 January 2012).

Norris, Robert and Kristensen, Hans. 'Russian Nuclear Forces, 2008', *Bulletin of the Atomic Scientists* (May/June 2008): http://thebulletin.metapress.com/ content/t2j78437407v3qv1/fulltext.pdf (accessed 22 January 2012).

Nossal, Kim R. 'Lonely Superpower or Unapologetic Hyperpower? Analyzing American Power in the Post-Cold War Era', paper presented at the biennial meeting of the South African Political Studies Association, Saldanha, Western Cape, 29 June–2 July 1999: http://post.queensu.ca/~nossalk/papers/ hyperpower.htm (accessed 12 January 2012).

Petrov, Nikita. 'Russia to Start Training Professional Sergeants Soon', RIA Novosti (20 January 2009): http://en.rian.ru/analysis/20090130/119894538. html (accessed 19 June 2013).

'Press Conference with Presidential Economic Adviser Andrei Illarionov', Moscow World Climate Change Conference, October 2003: http://www.sysecol.ethz. ch/Articles_Reports/Illarionov_Press_Conf.pdf (accessed 22 January 2012).

Putin, Vladimir. 'Address to the Federal Assembly of the Russian Federation', official website of the Kremlin (May 2006): http://www.kremlin.ru/ appears/2006/05/10/1357_type63372type63374type82634_105546.shtml (accessed 22 January 2012).

Russian Federation, Ministry of Defence. 'News Details – Stability' (22 September 2008): http://www.mil.ru/eng/1866/12078/details/index.shtml?id=51595 (accessed 22 January 2012).

Scearce, Diana and Fulton, Katherine. 'What If? The Art of Scenario Thinking for Non-profits' (2004): http://www.gbn.com/ArticleDisplay Servlet. srv?aid=32655 (accessed 26 January 2012).

'Stenographic Protocol of the Enlarged Session of the Defense Ministry Collegium', official website of the Kremlin (February 2009): http://www.kremlin.ru/ appears/2009/03/17/1450_type63376type63378type63381_214076.shtml (accessed 22 January 2012).

Tel'manov, Deniz. 'Participants in Non-Commissioned Officers' Training Courses are No Comrades', GZT.RU (March 2009): http://gzt.ru/ politics/2009/03/25/223011.html (accessed 22 January 2012).

'The State Armament Program for the Period 2007–2015 Envisages the Equipment of 18 Regiments with the New S-400 Systems: Second S-400 Air Defense Regiment Put into Service in Russia', RIA Novosti (March 2009): http:// en.rian.ru/russia/20090317/120604177.html (accessed 22 January 2012).

Official Reports and Publications

Albuquerque, Augusto G. (ed.). *Sessenta Anos de Política Externa Brasileira 1930–1990 – Crecimento, Modernização e Política Externa.* São Paulo: Cultura Editores 1 & 2, 1996.

Bader, Julia, Grävingholt, Jörn and Kästner, Antje. *The Influence of China, Russia and India on the Future of Democracy in the Euro-Asian Region,* Briefing Paper 2/2011, 10. Bonn: DIE.

BP. *BP Statistical Review of World Energy.* London: BP, June 2009.

Chicago Council on Global Affairs. *The United States and the Rise of China and India: Results of a 2006 Multinational Survey of Public Opinion.* Chicago, IL: Chicago Council on Global Affairs, 2006.

Christie, Ryerson and Dewitt, David. 'Middle Powers and Regional Security', paper prepared for the conference 'Emergent Powers and Regional Security: The Experience of IBSA (India, Brazil, South Africa)', Universidad de San Andrés, Buenos Aires, May 2006.

Commission of the European Communities, *Communication from the Commission to the European Parliament and the European Council, Eastern Partnership, Brussels, 3.12.2008,* COM(2008) 823. Brussels: European Commission, 2008.

Conference on 'U.S.-China Strategic Nuclear Dynamics' co-organized by the Center for Strategic and International Studies, Institute for Defense Analyses, the Rand Corporation, and the China Foundation for International and Strategic Studies, 8–10 June 2008: http://www.csis.org/media/csis/pubs/081015_intro_ and_key_findings.pdf (accessed 20 January 2012).

Congressional Research Service, Library of Congress. *China's Foreign Policy and 'Soft Power' in South America, Asia, and Africa: A Study Prepared for the Committee on Foreign Relations United States Senate Committee on Foreign Relations United States Senate.* Washington, DC: US Government Printing Office, April 2008.

Dethlefsen, Knut. *China's Foreign Policy in Transition,* FES Briefing Paper, May 2004.

Deutsche Bank, 'Globale Wachstumszentren 2020. Formel-G für 34 Volkswirtschaften', *Aktuelle Themen* 313 (2005).

Derluguian, Georgi. *The Fourth Russian Empire?.* PONARS Policy Memo 114. Washington, DC: Center for Strategic and International Studies, 2006.

Dumbaugh, Kerry. *China's Foreign Policy: What Does it Mean for U.S. Global Interests?,* CRS Report to Congress, 18 July 2008.

European Commission. *The EU, Africa and China: Towards Trilateral Dialogue and Cooperation: Communication from the Commission to the European Parliament, the Council, the European Economic and Social Committee and the Committee of the Regions on Trilateral Dialogue and Cooperation between the EU, Africa and China,* COM(2008) 654 final, 17 October 2008.

European Union. 'Joint Statement of the 8th EU–China Summit', Press Release no. IP/05/1091, Brussels, 5 September 2005: http://europa.eu/rapid/pressReleasesAction.do?reference=IP/05/1091 (accessed 21 January 2012).

Fox, John and Godement, François. *A Power Audit of EU–China Relations*. London: European Council on Foreign Relations, April 2009.

Gill, Bates and Huang, Chin-Hao. *China's Expanding Role in Peace Keeping: Prospects and Policy Implications*, SIPRI Policy Paper no. 25. Stockholm: SIPRI, November 2009.

Glaser, Bonnie S. 'The Changing Ecology of Foreign Policy-making in China: The Ascension and Demise of the Theory of "Peaceful Rise"', *The China Quarterly* 190 (June 2007): 291–310.

Goldman Sachs. *Building Better Global Economic BRICs*, Global Economics Paper. London: Goldman Sachs, 30 November 2001.

Hirsch, Robert L., Bezdek, Roger and Wendling, Robert. *Peaking of World Oil Production: Impacts, Mitigation, and Risk Management*. Washington, DC: US Department of Energy, February 2005: http://www.netl.doe.gov/publications/others/pdf/oil_peaking_netl.pdf (accessed 19 June 2013).

Hornbeck, J.F. *Brazilian Trade Policy and the United States*, CRS Report for Congress RL33258. Washington, DC: Congressional Research Service, Library of Congress, 3 February 2006.

Information Office of China's State Council. *China's National Defense in 2008*, 20 January 2009: http://www.gov.cn/english/official/2009-01/20/content_1210227_16.htm (accessed 20 January 2012).

International Institute for Strategic Studies (ISS). *Military Balance 2009: Annual Assessment of Global Military Capabilities and Defense Economics*. London: ISS, 2009.

Lamond, Claudine. *Tactical Nuclear Weapons in Russian Foreign Policy*, International Security Report, June 2009.

Lukyanov, Fyodor. 'Rethinking Russia: Russian Dilemmas in a Multipolar World', *Journal of International Affairs* 63:2 (2010): 19–32.

Monaghan, Andrew. 'Russia and the Security of Europe's Energy Supplies: Security in Diversity?', *Conflict Studies Research Centre* 7:2 (January 2007): 1–18.

Monaghan, Andrew. 'Russian Oil and EU Energy Security', *Conflict Studies Research Centre* 5:65 (November 2005): 1–18.

National Institute of Defensive Studies. *NIDS China Security Report*. Tokyo: National Institute of Defensive Studies, 2011.

Office of the Secretary of Defense. 'The Military Power of the People's Republic of China 2005', *Annual Report to Congress*. Washington, DC: US Government Printing Office, 19 July 2005.

Office of the Secretary of Defense. 'The Military Power of the People's Republic of China', *Annual Report to Congress*. Washington, DC: US Government Printing Office, 2007.

Office of the Secretary of Defense. 'Military Power of the People's Republic of China', *Annual Report to Congress*, 2008: http://www.defenselink.mil/pubs/pdfs/China_Military_Report_08.pdf9 (accessed 20 January 2012)

Riddell, R.G. 'The Role of Middle Powers in the United Nations', *Statements and Speeches* 48:40. Ottawa: Department of External Affairs, 1948.

'Securing Borders: China's Doctrine and Force Structure for Frontier Defense', *Journal of Strategic Studies* 30:4–5 (2007), pp. 705–37.

Sleivyte, Janina. *Intellectual Excellence in Defense: Russia's European Agenda and the Baltic States*, The Shrivenham Papers no. 7. Shrivenham: Defence Academy of the United Kingdom, February 2008.

UK House of Lords European Union Committee. *The European Union and Russia: Report with Evidence*, 14th Report of Session 2007–2008: http://www.publications.parliament.uk/pa/ld200708/ldselect/ldeucom/98/9802.htm (accessed 19 June 2013).

UN, Department of Public Information. 'Security Council Underscores Importance of Supporting African Union's efforts to Improve Regional Peacekeeping Capacity', Press Release no. SC/9615, March 2009: http://www.un.org/News/Press/docs/2009/sc9615.doc.htm (accessed 21 January 2012).

Unger, Roberto Mangabeira. *Projeto Amazônia: Esboço de uma Proposta*. Brasília: Secretaria de Assuntos Estratégicos da Presidência da República, 2007.

Wilhelm, John H. 'The Failure of the American Sovietological Economics Profession', *Europe-Asia Studies* 55:1 (1991): 5.

Wilson, Dominic and Purushothaman, Roopa. *Dreaming with BRICs: The Path to 2050*, Goldman Sachs Global Economics Paper no. 99 (2003). London: Goldman Sachs.

Woehrel, Steven. *Russian Energy Policy Toward Neighboring Countries*, CRS Report for Congress. Washington, DC: Congressional Research Service, Library of Congress, 2008.

Wrobel, Paulo (ed.). *Global Security in a Multipolar World*, Chaillot Paper no. 118. Paris: Institute for Security Studies, October 2009.

Zebichi, Raúl. *Brazil and the Difficult Path to Multilateralism*. Silver City, NM: International Relations Center, Americas Program, 8 March 2006.

Magazine and Newspaper Articles

Acharya, Amitav. 'The Emerging Regional Architecture of World Politics', *World Politics* 59:4 (July 2007): 629–52.

Barma, Nazneen, Ratner, Ely and Weber, Steven. 'A World Without the West', *The National Interest* 90 (July–August 2007): 23–30.

Bryanski, Gleb and Faulconbridge, Guy. 'BRIC Demands More Clout, Steers Clear of Dollar Talk', Reuters, 26 June 2009: http://www.reuters.com/article/marketsNews/idUSLG67435120090616 (accessed 21 January 2012).

Buller, J. and Gamble, A. 'Conceptualising Europeanisation', *Public Policy & Administration* 17:2 (2002): 6–15.

Gittings, Danny. 'General Zhu Goes Ballistic', *Wall Street Journal*, 18 July 2005, p. 18.

Huntington, Samuel P. 'The Lonely Superpower', *Foreign Affairs* 78:2 (March/April 1999): 35–49.

'Indian Retailing: Mall Rats – Reliance Moves into Low Fashion', *The Economist*, 18 October 2007: http://www.economist.com/node/9998869 (accessed 19 June 2013).

Isacson, Adam. 'Brazil's Foreign Policy Awakens: Is the United States Ready? Is Brazil Ready?', *Foreign Policy Digest* (1 January 2011): http://www.foreignpolicydigest.org/2011/01/01/brazil%E2%80%99s-foreign-policy-awakens-is-the-united-states-ready-is-brazil-ready/ (accessed 9 January 2011).

Ivanov, Sergey. 'The Armaments Order is Reliably Protected from the Crisis', *Rossijkaja Gazeta*, 26 February 2009.

Johnson, Reuben. 'Sukhoi's T-50 PAK-FA Fighter Enters First Stage of Assembly', *Jane's Defence Weekly*, 14 January 2009.

Khramchikhin, Alexander. 'Liquidation is Considered to Constitute Reform', *Nezavisimoe voennoe obozrenie*, 13 February 2009.

Madan, Tanvi. *The Brookings Foreign Policy Studies Energy Security Series: India*. Washington, DC: Brookings Institution, 2006.

Madrigal, Alexis. 'Nuclear Power to Explode in India, but China Prefers Coal', *Wired*, 25 October 2007: http://www.wired.com/science/planetearth/news/2007/10/nuclear_report (accessed 27 July 2013).

Mohan, C. Raja. 'Nine Ways to Look West', *The Indian Express*, 8 January 2007: http://www.indianexpress.com/story/20387.html (accessed 27 July 2013).

Pei, Minxin. 'China's Not a Superpower', *The Diplomat*, 2010: http://apac2020.the-diplomat.com/feature/China%E2%80%99s-not-a-superpower/3/ (accessed 21 January 2012).

Roberts, Paul Craig. 'The Coming End of the American Superpower', *Counterpunch*, 1 March 2005: http://www.counterpunch.org/2005/03/01/the-coming-end-of-the-american-superpower/ (accessed 19 June 2013).

Rohter, Larry. 'Brazil is Leading a Largely South American Mission to Haiti', *New York Times*, 1 August 2004: http://www.nytimes.com/2004/08/01/world/brazil-is-leading-a-largely-south-american-mission-to-haiti.html (accessed 19 June 2013).

Sahni, Varun. 'India and the Asian Security Architecture', *Current History* (April 2006): 161–6.

Steel, Ronald. 'A Superpower is Reborn', *New York Times*, 24 August 2008: http://georgiandaily.com/index.php?option=com_content&task=view&id=6527&Itemid=68&lang=ka (accessed 19 June 2013).

Socor, Vladimir. 'Shortfalls in Russian Oil Deliveries to Germany', *Eurasia Daily Monitor*, 5 September 2007.

'The Russian Army Revealed Itself Not to be Ready for the Wars of the Future', *Izvestiia*, 16 December 2008.

Wang, Shanhe. 'The Air Force Vigorously Promotes the Improvement of Aviation Field Station Supply System', *PLA Daily*, 8 December 2008.

Zubov, Mikhail. 'The Officers are Being Retrained for Duty in Administration', *Moskovskii Komsomolets*, 18 December 2008.

Interviews

ECFR interview with Feng Zhongping, European Studies Analyst at the Chinese Institutes of Contemporary International Relations, Beijing, 6 June 2008.

ECFR interview with Shi Yinyong, Chinese international relations expert, Beijing, 3 June 2008.

Medvedev, Dimitri. 'Russia, First Channel, and NTV TV Channels Interview'. Official website of the Kremlin, 31 August 2008: http://www.kremlin.ru/appears/2008/08/31/1917_type63374type63379_205991.shtml (accessed 22 January 2012).

News

'China, Russia Vetoes Thwart U.N. Security Council Resolution on Syria', CNN, 4 October 2011: http://articles.cnn.com/2011-10-04/middleeast/world_meast_syria-unrest_1_bashar-ja-afari-president-bashar-security-council?_s=PM:MIDDLEEAST (accessed 24 October 2011).

'First Summit for Emerging Giants', BBC News, 16 June 2009: http://news.bbc.co.uk/1/hi/business/8102216.stm (accessed 21 January 2012).

'Russia CGS Says No Plans to Give Up Conscripts', BBC Monitoring Global Newsline, Former Soviet Union Political File, 17 December 2008.

'Russian Air Force to Develop "General-purpose Forces" Commander', BBC Monitoring Global Newsline, Former Soviet Union Political File, 11 February 2009.

'Russian CGS Meets Military Attaches, Discusses Army Reform, Other Issues', BBC Monitoring Global Newsline, Former Soviet Union Political File, 12 December 2008.

'Russian Fighter Jets Become Obsolete', *Kommersant*, 16 March 2009.

'Russia's Latest Fighter Jet Carries out 100th Test Flight', BBC Monitoring Global Newsline, Former Soviet Union Political File, 25 March 2009.

Smith, Keith C. 'Russian Energy Pressure Fails to Unite Europe'. Washington, DC: Center for Strategic and International Studies, January 2007.

'Top Russian General Reaffirms Key Role of Ground Troops in Year-end Interview', BBC Monitoring Global Newsline – Former Soviet Union Political File, 1 January 2009.

Index